DATE DUE

JUL 07 2009	
OCT 2 9 2013	
DEC 0 1 2013	

BEYOND REDEMPTION

NUMBER 1
Red River Valley Books, sponsored by
Texas A&M University–Texarkana

Series Editor
Doris Davis

Beyond Redemption

Texas Democrats
after Reconstruction

PATRICK G. WILLIAMS

TEXAS A&M UNIVERSITY PRESS   COLLEGE STATION

Library of Congress Cataloging-in-Publication Data

Williams, Patrick G., 1957–
Beyond redemption : Texas Democrats after Reconstruction /
Patrick G. Williams. — 1st ed.
p. cm. — (Red River Valley Books ; no. 1)
Includes bibliographical references and index.
ISBN-13: 978-1-58544-573-8 (cloth : alk. paper)
ISBN-10: 1-58544-573-8 (cloth : alk. paper)
1. Democratic Party (U.S.)—History—19th century.   2. Political
parties—Texas—History—19th century.   3. Texas—History—19th century.
4. Reconstruction (U.S. history, 1865–1877)—Texas.   I. Title.
JK2318.T4W55   2007
324.2773'0609—dc22
2006024955

Frontispiece: Composite portrait, 1875 Texas Constitutional Convention.
Courtesy Texas State Library and Archives Commission

FOR BETH

Red River runs rusty
The Wichita clear
Down by the Brazos
I courted my dear

CONTENTS

ACKNOWLEDGMENTS

I suspect (and earnestly hope) that I am not the only author who begins plotting out the acknowledgments before writing a word of the book. Now that the time of thanksgiving has arrived, though, it seems too daunting a task to do justice to all those who midwifed this woefully protracted gestation. This study began at Columbia University as a dissertation sponsored by Eric Foner. The discerning will surely glimpse Professor Foner's fingerprints all over this book, but neither he nor anyone else named here should be charged with its crimes. Through the whole of my graduate career, I was privileged to work for John A. Garraty. He provided a livelihood but, more importantly, set a standard to be aspired to—with his catholicity of interest, clarity of prose, and historical common sense. Mark Carnes, Barbara J. Fields, and James P. Shenton also offered aid and inspiration of various and vital sorts. As for my fellow graduate students, they are comfortably distinguished professors by now. I am especially grateful to Tyler Anbinder and David Stebenne for their sharp eyes and warm friendship.

The history faculty at the University of Arkansas has afforded me every opportunity, courtesy, and privilege, even when a crowded job market would have allowed them to do otherwise. Each one of them deserves a cheer and a slap on the back, but I will single out Jeannie Whayne, Randall Woods, Elliott West, Daniel Sutherland, David Sloan, and Willard Gatewood for their example, encouragement, material aid, and corrective measures.

My editorial work on the *Arkansas Historical Quarterly* has slowed completion of this book, but I would not trade it in for the opportunity to write ten more. Thanks to Michael Pierce for holding down the fort when I scrawled "GTT" on the office door, and thanks to the Arkansas Historical Association for reposing faith in a native Texan. The AHA's older sister, the Texas State Historical Association, funded crucial early research for this study through a Coral Horton Tullis Fellowship.

I am profoundly grateful to Mary Lenn Dixon at Texas A&M University Press for her very *patient* interest in this project. Tom Paradise, my favorite "anthropologist with skills," skillfully made the map. Certain of this book's arguments and ideas were earlier offered in an article, "Of Rutabagas and Redeemers: Understanding the Texas Constitution of 1876" (*Southwestern Historical Quarterly* 106 [October 2002]: 231–53). Some of the material in chapter three initially appeared in "Suffrage Restriction in Post-Reconstruction Texas: Urban Politics and the Specter of the Commune" (*Journal of Southern History* 68 [February 2002]: 31–64). I appreciate both journals' kind consideration.

Anyone who writes about postbellum Texas piggybacks on the work of scholars who left conventional wisdom so bruised and battered that it was no longer presentable in polite company. Among them, Robert Calvert, Carl Moneyhon, James Smallwood, Dale Baum, and John Mauer, in particular, have helped this book along its way. Anybody in this field will know what a boon it was to have Barry Crouch on my side.

Most all of my scholarly life since earning the B.A. degree has been spent beyond the boundaries of my beloved Texas. But many Texans gave me a place to stay and, more importantly, made sure I never forgot that Texas is more than a problem in political economy. I am proud to count among these friends Paul Cullum, Andrew Lee, Dell Edwards, Michael Saenz, Cathy Crane, Michael Hall, and Teri Tynes.

All scholars pile up a debt they will never pay out to librarians and archivists. Mine are owed to the reference and interlibrary loan departments at both Butler Library, Columbia University, and Mullins Library, University of Arkansas, as well as to the Center for American History at the University of Texas and the New York Public Library. Some of the greatest pleasures of this project came in working in the archives at the Texas State Library, and I especially thank Donaly Brice for his help and good fellowship.

One librarian in particular has seen this project through many dangers, toils, and snares—my wife, Beth Juhl. Any attempt to express what I owe her would quickly degenerate into embarrassing mush. But she knows what song I would sing for her if I could be Levi Stubbs for just three minutes and three seconds.

This book has its deepest roots in a curiosity and love of learning that my parents, Josephine and Donald Williams, instilled early on.

INTRODUCTION

South by Southwest

On the morning of September 28, 1874, federal troops under the command of Col. Ranald Mackenzie overran a sprawling encampment of Comanches, Kiowas, and Cheyennes in Palo Duro canyon, where a fork of the Red River cuts into Texas' high plains. Although only a few Indians died in the engagement, the rout doomed any prospect that these native peoples might yet enjoy of an independent existence beyond the confines of Indian Territory. Mackenzie's men put the Indians' villages to the torch, seized a winter's worth of food and fodder, and slaughtered over one thousand of their horses.

The Indians of the southern plains had in 1867 agreed to base themselves in Indian Territory but had insisted on their right to hunt buffalo elsewhere. Enraged by white hunters' decimation of the bison, the federal government's failure to provide adequate alternate sustenance at their agencies, and depredations of their own stock, bands of Comanches, Kiowas, and Southern Cheyennes had in 1874 gone to war in western Texas and Kansas. Palo Duro represents the most decisive moment in the army's counterinsurgency campaign—a campaign that represented the deathblow to native resistance on the southern plains. Sporadic raiding continued through the end of the decade, but the danger of any comprehensive threat from Plains Indians to Euro-American expansion in Texas had certainly ended.[1]

A mere eight months before Palo Duro, Texas had passed another milestone. With a bristling of arms though not actual bloodshed, Democrats had forced the Republican governor, Edmund J. Davis, from the Capitol in Austin—a moment usually taken to mark Reconstruction's end in the state. In the language of the day, Texas had been "redeemed," its deliverance the work of "Redeemer Democrats."[2] Those Democrats assembled the following year to write their party's triumph over Reconstruction into the organic law of the state. Their constitutional convention followed closely on the heels of the final surrender of Quanah's holdout band of Quahadi Comanches. That very same summer of 1875, the Rio Grande borderlands passed a milestone of their own. Mexican authorities arrested Juan Cortina, the Tamaulipas caudillo, alleged rustler of American cattle, and would-be tribune of oppressed Tejanos, who had roiled South Texas since 1859. The transnational rapine and reprisal that Texans associated with Cortina had grown endemic in the early 1870s. But with the ascension after 1875 of Porfirio Diaz as Mexico's leader, raiding along the border diminished.[3] Within these same two years of 1874–75, then, Texas had reached turning points in its history as a western, southern, and borderlands state.

Yet these regional histories have often been studied in isolation from one another. The western dimensions of postbellum Texas loom large in the popular imagination, what with decade upon decade of myth-making about cattle drives and gunfights. But its southern aspects—the experience Texas shared with other slaveholding states that joined the Confederacy—have, along with the South Texas borderlands, probably garnered more scholarly attention in recent decades. In all but a few of these works, the world of African American slavery, emancipation, and Reconstruction could seem very distant indeed from the worlds of Palo Duro or Juan Cortina.[4]

That the scholarship of southern, western, and borderlands Texas seem often to exist independently of one another should by no means suggest their respective inadequacy. The distance between "southern" and "western" Texas was literally quite vast in the 1870s, as indicated by the fact that the first comprehensive report about the battle at Palo Duro to appear in the state's most widely circulated newspaper had to be reprinted from the *New York Herald*. An earlier brief report also came via New York (interestingly, the *Galveston Daily News* of that date gives considerably more attention to the prospect of a border war sparked by Cortina).[5] Being so far flung, Texas' component parts can, therefore, be reasonably studied as entities unto themselves. Each possessed distinctive histories of settlement, sustained distinctive populations, and supported distinctive ways of life. The piney woods (and in places red dirt) of East Texas would have seemed familiar to many migrants from the Southeast. Slave-based plantation agriculture there had concentrated in those areas most accessible to Red River trade routes but also thrived along the lower Brazos, Colorado, and Trinity rivers near the Gulf Coast. Some of these plantation counties also sustained large commercial stockraising operations on the flat coastal prairie laying back of the bottomland favored by planters.[6] West of the coastal prairie and piney woods lay a broad swath of fertile blacklands stretching up from near San Antonio to the state's northern border. Unlike comparably rich land in the Southeast, however, the Black and

Grand prairies had not, before the Civil War, seen intensive cultivation of southern staples like cotton. Distance and difficulties of transport had left the region rather isolated from national markets.[7] Biting into these prairies from the north were wedges of more marginal land known as the "Cross Timbers," whose sandy soil sustained hardscrabble cultivators and stockmen—as did the broken and rocky "Hill Country" west of Austin, beyond the Balcones Escarpment.[8] The southern reaches of the state were marked only by scattered pockets of permanent settlement, pioneered for the most part not by Anglo and African Americans headed west and south, but by an earlier migration of Hispanics north and east. Not even open-range stockraising of the sort practiced in South Texas had, by the end of Reconstruction, much penetrated the Llano Estacado, lately the hunting grounds of Kiowas and Comanches.

Such wild diversity prompted one of the state's most talented writers to pronounce Texas "so wrongfully muddled and various that it is difficult to conceive of it as all of a piece."[9] Yet this expansive hodgepodge was, in fact, all of a piece—in the sense that it operated as a single political unit. The same federal and state officials and codes of law that piloted Texas through Reconstruction and Redemption had also to address issues raised as Anglo and African American farming populations spread into territory formerly the province chiefly of Indians or Tejanos. Given this, the fight at Palo Duro, the scrapping of Democrats and Reconstruction Republicans at the state capitol, and the simultaneous spasms of rustling and violence along the Rio Grande border could not exist as entirely unrelated phenomena. The state's southern politics inevitably intertwined with its frontier and borderland dimensions.

The Radicals who led Texas from 1870 through 1873, for example, like other southern Republicans, had to bear the burdens associated with their party's support for universal education, the more thoroughgoing commercial development of the South, and black citizenship. But they also had to formulate an Indian policy. In the years before Palo Duro, groups based in Indian Territory continued to raid into Texas, as had Indians from Mexico. As late as 1873, depredations were being reported not far west of San Antonio and Fort Worth.[10] Accordingly, one of the biggest state budget items during the term of Radical governor Davis was an expense that no other Reconstruction regime had to bear—frontier defense. The same legislature that spent huge sums establishing a school system and state constabulary, and promised generous subsidies to railroads, also created ranger forces and minute companies for service against Indian raiders, ultimately running up a bill of over half a million dollars for them.[11]

The costs of these units—piled on top of more familiar Reconstruction spending on education and law enforcement—made Texas Republicans all the more vulnerable to a key Democratic strategy in attacking Reconstruction, which was to emphasize the Republican administration's fiscal sins as much as its sins against white supremacy. Vast stretches of Texas were overwhelmingly white and thus less susceptible to being panicked by the prospect of "negro rule." But even citizens in the whitest counties had faced a sharp rise in state and local taxes. Reconstruction, Democrats repeatedly emphasized, handed taxpayers' wealth over to corrupt and incompetent officials and their ragged followers. ("The supporters of the Radical party," the *Galveston News* declared, "are those who have scarcely any taxes to pay.")[12] Democrats never attacked the principle of frontier defense, but they seem neither to have subtracted out its expenses in offering various calculations purporting to prove that the Davis administration taxed and spent extravagantly.[13]

If frontier defense showed how intertwined the state's southern history could be with things that set Texas apart from the South, this book charts larger intersections of regional histories. Part One examines in unusual detail how Democrats, between 1872 and 1876, established the power their party would exercise in Texas for over a century. Part Two offers not a conventional political narrative as much as a study of what Democrats did with power—in terms of shaping Texas government's authority to tax and spend, cultivate economic growth, and promote social well being. In doing so it will show how Texas' distinctly southwestern situation fundamentally affected the ways Democrats engineered Reconstruction's collapse and how it influenced the regime they constructed in its stead. Like their erstwhile partners in rebellion, Lone Star Democrats had to work though the political, economic, and social consequences of the emancipation and enfranchisement of the state's black population and the maturation of a more thoroughly commercial cotton economy. But qualities that distinguished Texas from other former Confederate states very much influenced how such questions were answered.

For example, Texas' rate of population increase between 1860 and 1890—270 percent—far outstripped those of other southern states. Only Arkansas and Florida, similarly positioned on Dixie's periphery, even exceeded 100 percent growth. Texas' demographic surge more closely resembled the growth of western states during these decades, its vast expanses of thinly settled land and agricultural and commercial opportunities drawing a steady stream of migrants. This frontier population boom had specifically political results, for a disproportionate number of migrants to Texas were white southerners, the great bulk of whom appear to have been Democrats. A Republican party with a chiefly African American constituency would have been from the outset at a greater disadvantage in Texas than in places like Louisiana, Mississippi, or South Carolina since less than a third of Texas' population had been enslaved in 1860. But in contrast to most other southern states, as white migration surged after the war, the percentage of African Americans to total population in Texas dropped sharply, declining by 1890 to 22 percent, the smallest in the former Confederacy.[14]

Yet the state's frontier demography would be something of a double-edged sword for Redeemer Democrats. The demographic advantage they enjoyed made the establishment and maintenance of party control at the statewide level all the more easily accomplished. But, as will be explored in Part One, this very situation complicated crucial dimensions of Redemption—the reestablishment of conservative authority in the judiciary and in local government—and probably slowed disfranchisement. Because their hold on the state government quickly became so secure—and because the westerly regions growing ever more thickly settled were overwhelmingly white and, in the mid-1870s, Democratic—many party members proved decidedly reluctant to take extraordinary measures to strengthen the position of peers in those often distant communities where a significant political threat did remain, most particularly in old plantation counties.

Texas' unparalleled growth and the expansion of white settlement in frontier areas affected the situation of its Redeemer Democrats in other ways. Their party's leadership was, through the 1870s and 1880s, composed largely of men who had risen to prominence in political, military, or legal circles before the Civil War and had sided with the Confederacy. Four of the first five post-Reconstruction governors, for example, took an active role in the state's secession: one as president of the secession convention, two as delegates supporting disunion, and one by voting for the legislative resolution establishing the convention.[15] Studies suggest that at the local level, many of those who dominated individual counties and towns before secession remained on the top of the heap after Reconstruction collapsed.[16] But it would be more difficult in the case of Texas than with other southern states to see such persistence among elites as evidence for a fundamental "continuity" between the antebellum and postbellum eras or for Redemption as representing merely the restoration of an old order. The tremendous numerical growth and spatial expansion of the Euro-American population through the latter 1860s and 1870s reconfigured the state to an extent unmatched elsewhere in Dixie, placing once-peripheral regions at the very center of political and economic life. The Texas over which conservative elites reestablished their authority between 1872 and 1875 was a very different place than the Texas that had left the Union in 1861.

The booming growth and frontier settlement of these years also meant that Texas possessed a political geography doubtlessly more complex than that of any other southern state. If, as Michael Perman has suggested, the classic schema of black belt versus upcountry (or white county) is inadequate for understanding *any* southern state's progress toward disfranchisement, it will certainly not do for describing Texas politics at any point in its postbellum history.[17] The extensive blackland prairie offers the most conspicuous example of a region that does not fit this model. Although generally level, this predominantly white area resembled upcountry sections of the Southeast in adopting extensive cotton cultivation only after the Civil War, at which point it developed a large tenant class. But the blacklands were never as hardscrabble a district as Georgia's wiregrass or upper piedmont regions, which became focal points for anti-Redeemer political dissent. (Populism in Texas centered in far-more-marginal counties on the prairie's peripheries.) Instead, it represented some of the best agricultural land in the state and, by 1880, also the most thickly settled.[18] At the same time, unlike fertile areas in the Mississippi and Arkansas deltas that similarly engaged in intensive cotton agriculture only after the Civil War ended, the prairie never became part of any recognizable "black belt" (though in some areas black sharecroppers were increasingly employed). This region always remained distinct in history and situation from Texas' antebellum plantation districts, and its many Democrats did not necessarily see eye-to-eye with brethren in black-majority counties on such matters as suffrage restriction. The explosive population growth of the blacklands and areas to their west, in fact, ensured that the old plantation regions of northeastern and southeastern Texas in the 1870s and 1880s would be rapidly shrinking parts of the whole. Plantation elites could not hope to exercise the sort of clout within state politics that planters elsewhere in the South might aspire to via skewed legislative apportionment or manipulation of the African American vote.[19]

But something else made Texas' political geography very different from that of other reconstructed states. Democrats—unlike Redeemers elsewhere in the South—governed a state with an international boundary and a population that was not neatly "biracial." South Texas included a large Latino population whose racial identity was still not entirely fixed, at least in the minds of "Anglo" Democrats.[20] While politicians there might assume the familiar party labels, in this very different setting (characterized by only a very small black population and an economy not based on the cultivation of crops), the

6

issues they grappled with and the factionalism they engaged in were often only tangentially related to those dividing Democrats and Republicans elsewhere in Texas. Indeed, while both Republicans and Democrats fought bitter internal battles in this part of the state, they seemed to connive more frequently and openly with members of the opposing party. Erstwhile Radical governor Davis, formerly of Brownsville, carried on a friendly correspondence with Stephen Powers, one of the pioneers of Democratic machine politics along the Rio Grande, concerning their mutual political interests. Noting that allegiances in South Texas seemed to correspond more closely to antebellum than more recent partisan alignments, Davis remarked, "Wars and rumors of war haven't changed Rio Grande politics *much,* whatever might be said of the rest of the nation."[21]

If redeeming Texas meant extending their control over the whole of the state, Democrats had to come to terms with this non-southern portion of it. They could not simply wish away Latino majorities in South Texas—often larger in proportion than the African American majorities in old plantation counties.[22] By the time Redeemers took power, Latino voting, officeholding, and jury service had become well-established traditions. In El Paso County in 1873, for instance, three of the five justices of the peace spoke Spanish exclusively, and court proceedings were routinely translated for Latino jurors.[23] Unless they wished to write the borderlands off, Democrats had to make their peace, at least in the short term, with Tejano citizenship.

This would not necessarily be an easy thing for members of a party that championed white supremacy. As Neil Foley has shown, Latinos—particularly those of the laboring classes—were often understood to be members of a nonwhite "mongrel" race.[24] Many Anglos despised and exploited them. Yet Democrats' definitions of whiteness proved responsive to political imperative. During Reconstruction, San Antonio Democrats bid for Latino support against Republicans in the name of white supremacy. A Democratic daily later described Tejano Democratic leaders in San Antonio as "men with the blue blood of old Castile and her chivalrous cavaliers—the brother heroes of 'The Heroic Cid'—in their veins—men representing the most distinguished families from old Spain."[25]

But even when Latinos were construed as nonwhite, Redeemers did not seem to entertain the same sort of ambitions toward their comprehensive disfranchisement as many possessed when it came to former slaves. Latinos did not have as compelling reason to vote for the other side—the party of Lincoln and Reconstruction—as African Americans had, though Republicans did remain far more competitive in some border counties than in the state at large. Instead, as organized by political bosses, powerful ranchers, or other members of local elites, the Hispanic vote in South Texas could serve the interests of whichever party was the better organized and funded in the region. Local Democrats, accordingly, sought to make this vote work for them. Shortly after Redeemers took control of the legislature in 1873, for instance, a bill was passed to make it easier for immigrants to gain the right of suffrage by declaring their intention to become citizens. Republican governor Davis vetoed it, saying it would facilitate the wholesale enfranchisement of Mexican nationals along the Rio Grande for the express purpose of determining the outcome of elections.[26] In the decades that followed, South Texas Democrats continued to cultivate the Tejano and noncitizen vote along the border; Jim Wells, the leading light of Rio Grande machine politics, considered Mexican ballots essential to party victory.[27]

Democrats had to work to secure this support, though. Although sometimes voting in blocs, South Texas Latinos were not merely a mute and manipulated mass. Like immigrant voters in northern cities, they seemed to demand some quid pro quo, such as political leaders who could speak their language, public employment, and occasional relief.[28] Democrats made places on their county and city tickets and in their local party organizations for members of the Tejano elite, even in San Antonio, which by the 1870s no longer had a Hispanic majority. They accommodated themselves to the fact that along the Rio Grande much politicking and litigating continued to be conducted in Spanish. Democrats welcomed Santos Benavides of Laredo to the Texas House of Representatives in 1879, though he could not participate in deliberations without an interpreter. Tejanos held county and municipal office in assorted border counties throughout the 1870s, 1880s, and 1890s.[29]

A striking recognition of Latino citizenship occurred in 1875 at the height of the border troubles preceding Cortina's arrest. U.S. soldiers patrolling the Rio Grande had had deadly run-ins with local Latinos. Some had been arrested by local authorities.[30] When military men and the Grant administration complained that soldiers were being "placed at the mercy of civil authorities selected by a population almost entirely composed of Mexican cattle thieves and their allies," Texas' first Redeemer governor, Richard Coke, rushed to the defense of people he termed "citizens of Texas of Mexican origin." He wrote the general commanding the Department of Texas: "The Mexican population on this side of the Rio Grande are usually a tractable, docile people, perfectly submissive to lawful authority, whether civil or military—that has always been their history. There are a great many most excellent citizens among them, indeed the great majority of them are of that character."[31]

One must not overstate Redeemers' broadmindedness when it came to South Texas, though. James Leiker's study of the military along the Rio Grande clearly suggests that Coke's 1875 defense of Latinos was driven by a wish to portray border trouble as the work of Mexican nationals rather than resident Tejanos (thus making its suppression the responsibility of federal and not state authorities) as well as by the simultaneous, almost instinctive, hostility of southern Democrats to the army as an instrument of federal power and to the African American soldiers who made up much of the border force.[32] Four years later, with other fish to fry, Coke, now a U.S. senator, spoke very differently. In seeking federal support for the building of a railroad to the Rio Grande, he saw fit to portray South Texas in terms that echoed the military men's earlier complaints: "The great desideratum in the country between the Nueces and the Rio Grande Rivers is a white or American population. Ninety per cent of the people inhabiting that country are Mexican, and from that fact flows the ills and woes by which it is afflicted.... The lawless and vagrant element of the population of Mexico ... dominate the Mexican population on the Texas side of the Rio Grande, and find many confederates and abettors among the vagrant or floating class, which is very considerable."[33]

Yet even in vacillating between this emphasis on racial difference and a defense of Tejano citizenship, Texas Redeemers showed how distinctive their position was. Social relations between "Anglos" and Tejanos continued to show considerably more fluidity and local variation in the mercantile towns and on the farms and ranches of South Texas than did those between landlords and their black laborers in cotton lands elsewhere in Texas—or in Dixie generally. David Montejano has noted the "Mexicanization" of many early Anglo settlers in South Texas and the *patronismo* that developed between white ranchowners and their Mexican workforce.[34] To exercise the sort of power other Redeemers did, Texas Democrats had to negotiate social worlds very different than those their fellow white southerners dwelt in.

Even outside the borderlands, Texas politics distinguished itself by an ethnic complexity that only Louisiana, among former Confederate states, could match. In 1870 and 1880, the U.S. Census reported, over 7 percent of the state's population was foreign born. Of the other Confederate states, only Louisiana's and Florida's immigrant populations topped 2 percent.[35] In addition to natives of Mexico, Texas possessed a politically significant population of European immigrants. The number of Texans of German descent more than tripled between 1870 and 1890, coming to exceed Latinos. The Hill Country, as well as the cities of Galveston, Houston, and San Antonio, sported numerous culturally distinct communities of these first- and second-generation German

Americans, many of whom demanded representation in party councils as a distinct interest group.[36] Texas Redeemers would, accordingly, have to occasionally practice ethnic politics of a sort more associated with northern than southern Democrats.

Given this more complex geographic and ethnic setting, it should come as no surprise that the tools of political taxonomy developed to describe postbellum southern Democrats prove most unwieldy when it comes to Texas. Historians' increasing tendency to characterize southern Democratic parties as sprawling and intricately divided bodies, rather than modular structures built from a few interchangeable factional parts, suggests the declining utility of those tools generally.[37] Certainly when it comes to Texas, it is difficult in any very coherent way to sort Democrats into the planter-Bourbon and entrepreneurial "New South" factions familiar to historians.

In the abstract one can detect a prevailing "agrarian" influence among Texas Democrats. The special role that the issue of tax reduction played both in Redeemers' crusades against Reconstruction and in the fiscal policy they implemented once in power suggests this, for Democrats seemed always to focus on ad valorem taxation—as opposed to occupation or capitation taxes. This emphasis served the landed, for in this era rural real estate and livestock together accounted for the largest part of the state's taxable property.[38] When it came to landlord-tenant legislation, usury laws, and convict lease, Texas Democrats did just the sorts of things that have led historians to conclude that an agrarian bloc—or planters in particular—dominated Democratic parties in other southern states.[39] Yet, even more so than in other southern states, Texas' sprawling diversity and frontier growth meant that there was no single agricultural interest. The farm population, and the politicians who supported its interests, could be extraordinarily varied. While landowners might share a common interest in property-tax relief and low interest rates, their priorities when it came to other matters could easily diverge. In the case of suffrage restriction, for example, the interests of the elite of plantation counties were defeated in large part by those representing a second landed interest—rural cultivators in whiter and more politically secure counties. Accordingly, the term "agrarian" turns out to be of decidedly limited analytic use. In post-Reconstruction Texas the divisions between politicians who might enjoy a roughly equal claim to being labeled agrarian would be among the most politically consequential of the era.

Furthermore, these fractious "agrarian" interests did not together represent one end of a Democratic spectrum whose other extremity was occupied by a group of commercially minded "New South" Democrats with a distinct socioeconomic base. Texas' frontier aspects may well have discouraged any clean division of the party into such factions. Some scholars have seen in the South of the 1870s and 1880s fundamental conflicts between planters and industrial and railroad interests, such as in competition for labor.[40] But during this era, economic growth in Texas—as in much of the West—was primarily a matter of expanding settlement, commercial agriculture, and extractive enterprise, along with improving access to national and global markets, rather than the creation of a new industrial sector. Planters as commercial farmers and absentee landowners could well support this goal. In the 1870s, residents of plantation counties like Brazoria, Harrison, and Matagorda were assessed for tens of thousands of acres of land lying outside their home counties.[41] Harris County planter, physician, and former diplomat Ashbel Smith, for example, could expect to benefit materially as railroad expansion and population growth raised low land values.[42] Other of the state's most prominent politicians, entrepreneurs, and attorneys—including Richard Coke, Richard Hubbard, Benjamin Epperson, T. W. House, and William P. Ballinger—at least at some point in their postbellum careers both operated plantations and actively involved themselves with railroad development.[43]

Elite landowners had special reason to believe that the state government's promotion of railroads and economic growth need not come at their expense, for it would not necessarily require the impressment of their wealth through taxation. Here was another, crucial way that Texas' specifically southwestern heritage—in this case its history as a frontier of the Spanish empire, and Mexico, and subsequent existence as an independent republic—made its experience of Redemption distinct. Upon surrendering its nationhood and entering the Union, Texas, unlike all but the first states, retained control of its public domain. As will be explored in Part Two, this vast landed wealth allowed many Texas Democrats to believe that they could sidestep many of the unpleasant choices faced by Redeemers elsewhere. They hoped that through public land and the revenue it generated, they might keep the promises made in their campaigns against Reconstruction to reduce taxation while meeting their frontier state's need for basic civil and economic infrastructure. State land, not tax revenues or bond issues, would supply the requisite public investment.

If the prospect of utilizing the public domain persuaded Texans of varied interests to support government activism in promoting economic development, it by no means created consensus on matters of political economy. Redeemers who agreed that the state should foster economic growth could well differ, for example, over the role it should play in financing and managing public education. In debating such issues they often hurled epithets at one another that might suggest some bipartite or tripartite division within their party—such as when urban editors sneered at "fossils," "fogies," and "backwoods" Democrats in contrast to "progressive" or "liberal" ones.[44] But such rhetoric can be deceptive in suggesting a stable factionalism. And the sides Texans took in one debate did not necessarily carry over to the next. Instead, Democrats proved fairly promiscuous in the ways they mixed and matched with respect to individual issues. In legislatures and conventions they built shifting coalitions rather than the sort of enduring alliances that might allow one to declare an agrarian-Bourbon or Whiggish New South faction in control. Instead, at least four basic orientations toward government and the public interest can be detected among Texas Redeemers.

The fact that differences over policy during these years typically did not yield a stable factionalism does not mean that there were not identifiable sources of division and allegiance within the Democratic party. Democrats, for instance, distinguished among themselves by antebellum affiliation and wartime allegiance. Former Whigs, erstwhile opponents of secession, and wartime Unionists often seemed to feel that, however much they might have embraced the doctrines of postbellum Democracy, party colleagues, forgetting nothing, conspired against their success.[45] Not surprisingly, Texas Democrats were also party to a pronounced sectionalism. Often this manifested itself as little more than communities preferring favorite-son candidates for state office. A general sense seemed to exist that U.S. Senate seats should be fairly distributed among East Texans, North Texans, and West Texans (at that time meaning all those hailing from south or west of the Colorado River).[46] But, as will be discussed, sectionalism might also involve far more serious competition for limited state resources.

With multiple sources of division within—but lacking even the internal coherence strong and stable factional affinities might have lent—the Democratic party of Texas had as its fundamental organizing principles little more than a visceral dislike of the Reconstruction regime and all its works, particularly the higher taxation and "centralization" that had been enforced. This meant that, even with all of the state's western and borderlands elements, what united the party was its southern politics. Through the postbellum decades, and indeed through the twentieth century, Texas remained oddly situated—ahead of and beyond but very much within the South. While the western dynamism of its economy and its natural wealth continued to make it more prosperous than the rest of Dixie, like much of Dixie, Texas would clothe many of its citizens in rags.

PART 1

~

Making Texas Safe for the Democracy

1

Redeeming
State Government,
1872–74

T he winter before the battle at Palo Duro—on January 15, 1874—
Democratic legislators installed Texas' first Redeemer governor.
Like the cold, wet weather, the circumstances of Richard Coke's
inauguration were hardly auspicious.[1] As the Waco jurist and
planter himself recalled: "An universal conflict of jurisdiction and authority, extending through all the departments of government, embracing in
its sweep all the territory and inhabitants of the State, and every question
upon which legitimate government is called to act, was imminent and
impending. . . . Texas seemed on the verge of a convulsion."[2]

No one questioned that Democrat Coke had won a hefty majority of
the votes cast in the previous month's gubernatorial election.[3] Yet the state
supreme court had declared that election—which filled not only executive
but also legislative and county posts—unconstitutional and void. Republican
incumbent Edmund Davis refused to yield his office. The overwhelmingly
Democratic legislators-elect had nevertheless assembled in Austin and met
as the Fourteenth Legislature. As allies of Davis proceeded, with bayonets
fixed, to secure state offices in the Capitol, Democrats similarly reinforced the
legislative chambers upstairs. The self-proclaimed legislature, having seized
the election returns from a protesting secretary of state, swore in Coke. In the
meantime, some Republican members of the previous legislature gathered
in the building's basement and challenged those upstairs for recognition as
the state's legitimate lawmaking body.[4]

The standoff at the Capitol was only the most dramatic manifestation of a
broader contest. In various Texas counties local Republican officials likewise

refused to give way to their elected Democratic successors.[5] Clashes seemed to be brewing too on the streets of Austin. Democrats traveled to the capital city to support their cause, and they believed that Republicans were similarly streaming in. With African Americans prominent among Davis's supporters both within and without the Capitol, a sergeant at arms appointed by the de facto Democratic legislature reportedly warned the Radical governor: "Let a negro fire a gun, and the next shot will not be at them, but aimed directly at your heart."[6] The day after Coke's inauguration, rival bodies of troops briefly confronted one another at the local arsenal. Another armed crowd gathered downtown after reports filtered back that black militia had seized Austin's mayor during the incident. A prominent Democrat present at the scene later asserted that if fighting had actually commenced, "not less than 20,000 people would have been killed in two weeks—and Texas would not have recovered from it in fifty years."[7]

Rather suddenly, though, the state stepped back from the precipice. Outnumbered Republicans knew that without federal support all was lost. But the Grant administration refused to embrace their arguments as to the invalidity of Democrats' claims and would not provide troops to keep the peace in Austin. By January 19 Davis had surrendered his offices. Within days recalcitrant local officeholders seem also to have given way. Republican control of the executive had ended not with a bang, just a few huzzas offered Davis by black troops as he left office. More than a century passed before another Republican would serve as governor of Texas.[8]

This armed confrontation at the Capitol, often referred to as the Coke-Davis "Imbroglio," has traditionally been treated as the climactic finale of Reconstruction in Texas. For many historians it is what divided the period of Radical rule from a subsequent era of conservative hegemony.[9] Yet even in a state as overwhelmingly Democratic as Texas had become, Redeemers' assumption of power was too drawn out and complicated a process to be comprehended by a mere chronicling of this January standoff. The transfer of authority had begun well before the imbroglio. But even after Coke assumed office, many Democrats worried that their control remained far from complete, for the power that mattered in Texas was exercised not only in the governor's office but also in the legislature and at county courthouses, municipal buildings, and polling places.

When it came to redeeming state government, the true watershed had come fourteen months before Coke's inauguration, with the election of the decidedly Democratic Thirteenth Legislature in November 1872. Indeed some prominent Democrats took these earlier elections to mark Reconstruction's end. As the new legislature assembled in January 1873, the state's premier Democratic journal declared Texas "redeemed from the blighting rule of Radicalism and *permanently* so."[10]

This triumph had been long anticipated. The Republican grip on power had never been strong. Governor Davis's narrow victory in 1869 had come, in part, because many Democrats simply sat out an election that pitted the Radical against a more conservative Republican, Andrew Jackson Hamilton. The Republican majority in the Twelfth Legislature (1870–71) contained party members of both stripes, and the divisions between them would be compounded by disagreements over such matters as state subsidy of railroad construction. Democrats had been able in 1870 and 1871 to cultivate a powerful public opposition to various administration policies by building sometimes uncomfortable alliances with conservative Republicans anxious over the expense of Davis's programs and the extraordinary powers vested in the governor and his appointees.[11]

More than intramural conflict darkened Republicans' prospects, though. While Republican candidates did draw some support from erstwhile Unionists in North Texas and from German Texans, the party had proved unable to build a sizable and enduring constituency of white Republican voters.[12] It did enjoy a secure base among African Americans, but of the reconstructed states, only Arkansas and Tennessee had smaller percentages of blacks to total population in 1870 than Texas—and its western-flavored population boom promised to make the state only whiter.[13]

Barely eighteen months into Davis's administration, the Democrats had seemingly emerged as the majority party. In 1871, Democratic congressional candidates outdistanced Republicans by some 20,000 votes statewide. Republican officials complained that free and fair balloting had only occurred in, at most, twenty-five counties. But the scale of the Democratic victory and the fact that many polling places had been guarded by Republican police suggest how difficult it would have been to construct this majority wholly through fraud and intimidation. The key to Democrats' success lay in mobilizing the party's growing constituency. Its candidates had received almost twice the number of votes that conservative Republican Hamilton had won in 1869.[14]

The legislative elections of 1872 placed policymaking firmly in Democrats' hands. In the Texas House of Representatives, the Democrats gained some forty seats, securing a five-to-one majority. They took broad swaths of Central, South, and West Texas that previously had sent solidly Republican delegations to the House. The Republican lawmakers who survived came chiefly from a handful of black-majority counties. The turnover was less dramatic in the thirty-man Senate, where only a minority of members had been up for reelection. Nonetheless, of the eleven new faces, eight were Democrats. Five of these hailed from districts represented by Republicans in the preceding legislature. Among their gains Democrats had picked up German support, sending several formerly Republican German Texans to the legislature.[15]

The subsequent session of the Thirteenth Legislature—January–June 1873—merits close study as the pivotal episode of Redemption, remarkable for the thoroughness with which lawmakers dismantled Reconstruction government even as a Radical continued to occupy the governor's mansion. The Democrats' narrow 17–13 majority in the Senate would not permit the impeachment of Davis, which some had agitated for, but legislators drew a bead on the centerpieces of Reconstruction policy and strengthened their party's grip on various mechanisms of state power.

Democrats wasted no time in attacking the Republican law enforcement establishment. They quickly introduced bills voiding the 1870 state police and militia laws. The police law had created a state constabulary several hundred men strong, independent of local authorities and, because it was under the direct command of the governor and his adjutant general, largely independent of the now-Democratic legislature. The militia law had established the State Guard, also under executive control, and empowered the governor to declare martial law whenever law enforcement in a county was hampered "by combinations of lawless men too strong for the control of the civil authorities."[16]

For Republicans the 1870 measures had been justified by the widespread lawlessness besetting Texas—"a slow civil war" in Governor Davis's words.[17] The violence of the postwar period could be attributed, in part, to conditions of the sort that often bred criminality on the frontier. Weak and immature civil institutions and sparse population created abundant opportunities for robbery and rustling in many parts of the state. But, as importantly, many white Texans had fiercely resisted the political, social, and economic consequences of emancipation and black enfranchisement. The criminal careers of gunmen like John Wesley Hardin and Cullen Montgomery Baker, for example, had more to do with this violent opposition to Reconstruction than with the boisterousness of a lightly policed frontier. Hardin did, indeed, drive cattle to Kansas and claimed to have tangled with Wild Bill Hickok when he got there, but among his earliest and most noted victims were federal soldiers and members of the Reconstruction constabulary.[18] Hundreds of Texans—including freedpeople who had too aggressively sought to renegotiate class and race relations, black politicians and ministers organizing their communities, and white Unionist and Republican supporters of the new order—died at the hands of the unreconstructed. Local authorities often seemed powerless or, worse yet, disinclined to challenge such violence. By contrast, the state police made thousands of arrests in the first two years of its existence—far outnumbering those made by local authorities since 1865.[19]

Whatever their successes in enforcing the law, Democrats roundly attacked policemen as arbitrary, trigger-happy riff-raff who provoked or committed as much violence as they suppressed—or more. They said the state police operated as an oppressive political machine, called out during elections not to ensure fair balloting, but to browbeat Democratic voters. The militia law similarly concentrated a tyrannical power in the hands of the governor, permitting him to create a standing army officered by Republican politicos. Democrats especially condemned Davis's 1871 imposition of martial law in Hill, Walker, Limestone, and Freestone counties.[20] By 1873, Democrats had come to so detest the Republican constabulary that legislators tabled an invitation to attend the funeral of four state policemen killed by outlaws in Lampasas in an incident that had neither partisan nor racial overtones.[21]

Davis's police force does seem to have included some freebooters and rogues. Capt. Jack Helm, for instance, became known for his murderous brutality, and the force's first chief, Adj. Gen. James Davidson, embezzled more than $30,000 in state funds. But the frequency of Democrats' fulminations against "negro police" and—as the *Palestine Advocate* put it—"the nigger state guards of his excellency" suggests that they objected to the complexion as much as the character of law officers. Both police and militia were biracial forces, prompting Democrat Richard Hubbard to wail over white Texans having to vote "while your former slaves were placed there to insult you."[22]

Within a week of the legislature assembling, repeal bills were sailing through committee. Despite Davis's argument that rampant crime made a centralized, mobile constabulary necessary, Democrats voted unanimously to destroy the police force. The only detectable dissent came when a single German-born Democrat from Central Texas voted against overriding Davis's veto of this repeal.[23] Democrats showed a similar unanimity in destroying the Reconstruction militia. Only another German-born representative, lately a Liberal Republican, voted against a wholesale repeal of the 1870 law. After Davis vetoed that bill, Democrats—tardily persuaded that Texas required a militia of some sort—passed a narrower act eliminating the martial-law provisions of the militia law and the State Guard as a distinct gubernatorial force while allowing a reserve militia and frontier defense and drill companies to continue to exist.[24]

The consequences of abolishing these forces came quickly. Apparently, reprisals were either carried out or threatened against a number of policemen. The *Galveston Daily News* reported the lynching "on general principles" of one officer near San Saba. Two Limestone County men told the governor, "The Dimiecrat Party say that the[y] do in tend to hang us for Being on the Police." More generally, without the police the governor could do little to enforce order where local authorities could not or would not act: "I am as fully estopped from enforcing the laws or giving protection to peaceable citizens as though they had tied my hands."[25] Texans over the following years reported repeated incidents of political and racial violence—a campaign of murder and arson directed against black residents of Limestone County; killings in northeastern Texas intended to drive African Americans from their jobs at sawmills and saltworks; the gunning down of a Republican legislative candidate in Bastrop. None seem to have met with an effective response on the part of Texas authorities. "There is some good laws in this State," the wife of the murdered Bastrop candidate wrote President Grant, "but there is no Enforcement of them."[26]

Ironically, Democrats themselves stood to suffer by this vacuum of state authority. Newspapers bristled with cases of murder, rustling, feuding, arson, and vigilantism whose victims extended well beyond the ranks of African American and Republican Texans. The Democratic *San Antonio Daily Herald* claimed in 1876 that a "high carnival of blood . . . is reigning in various portions of Texas." Even the Redeemer adjutant general admitted: "The want of a well organized and armed militia is seriously felt at this time when it is apparent that in certain sections of the State the courts require military aid to enable them to try and punish offenders." Early in his first term, Richard Coke, like his predecessor, had to respond to pleas for aid by noting the governor's very limited powers to suppress criminality in the wake of the dismantling of the police and guard.[27] Even Democratic newspapers increasingly chose to blame Coke for this inability to enforce order.[28] Accordingly, Redeemers soon edged toward the reestablishment of a state constabulary, though one shorn of the objectionable innovations of the Reconstruction era. The new "Frontier Battalion" and "Special State Troops" would be all white and operate under the time-honored guise of Texas Rangers.[29]

Democratic legislators gutted a second crucial Reconstruction initiative even as a Republican continued as governor: public education. Only after

Radicals had taken charge in 1870 had Texas made a systematic and comprehensive effort to provide common schools throughout its length and breadth. The Reconstruction constitution of 1869 had dedicated proceeds from the sale of state land to education as well as one-fourth of the state's annual revenue and all the money raised by a one-dollar poll tax (that is, a capitation tax; voting was not contingent on its payment). Laws passed in 1870–71 also allowed localities to levy a 1 percent ad valorem tax for the construction and maintenance of schools. Republicans had built a centralized state establishment presided over by a superintendent and a board of education (including the governor) that exercised broad powers over curriculum, personnel, and school administration. The state superintendent appointed district supervisors (at first thirty-five, then only twelve) who in turn divided their territory into school districts and appointed five directors for each. By the 1871–72 school year, federal authorities reported, more than two thousand public schools served 125,000 Texans aged six to eighteen.[30]

Whatever its achievements, Democrats made the Republican school system a chief object of their anti-Reconstruction crusade, focusing on its centralization and expense as well as the oppression, extravagance, and corruption they claimed inevitably attended such an arrangement. State Superintendent Jacob C. DeGress had often favored Republicans in his appointments and in certain cases had filled places in such a manner as to promote the fortunes of certain factions within his party.[31] From this, Democrats constructed an image of the school system as a vast political machine. Unnecessary supervisory offices had been created to maintain party loyalists—"ignorant freedmen and low, mean white men"—at citizens' expense. They portrayed the State Board of Education as an "unmitigated despotism" whose authority over curriculum denied communities' right to guide their own children's upbringing. In making this complaint, Redeemers honored the principle of "local self-government" dear to Dixie Democrats while also tailoring their appeal to a population unusually diverse by southern standards. Texas' German and Catholic voters, like their immigrant counterparts in the North, worried that teacher certification and mandated curricula in public schools served as a means of forced assimilation to a native-born, Protestant standard. Tellingly, the Republican state school board had banned sectarian instruction in public schools.[32]

Democrats also attacked the school system in the name of a second cardinal principle—retrenchment. By the standards of nineteenth-century Texas, public education was certainly an expensive undertaking—in part because Republicans felt obliged to provide separate schools for black students.[33] The schools became a focus for Democrats' crucial argument that a chief sin of Reconstruction government was the burdens placed on taxpayers by venal politicians whose core constituency owned little of the sort of property that would make them subject to skyrocketing levies. Democrats damned the 1 percent school tax, charging that the money it raised had been frittered away by misdirection, incompetence, fraud, and peculation.[34] Arguing that the levy represented an unconstitutional delegation of the legislature's power to tax, and pointing out that the Reconstruction legislature had passed a second law seeming to limit this local taxation, Democrats had organized a crippling resistance campaign. Across the state, taxpayers crowded the courts seeking injunctions against the collection of the tax. Many simply did not pay. County governments sometimes refused to turn what had been collected over to school authorities.[35]

Legislators quickly moved against the most despised elements of the Radical school system, the statewide administrative apparatus and the 1 percent school tax, which had underwritten over half of the system's annual expenditures. The occasional dissents heard within the Democrat delegation usually came from foreign-born Central Texans. Lawmakers remolded the school system as far as the Reconstruction constitution allowed. The Thirteenth Legislature rendered the superintendency chiefly an advisory position, devolving the lion's share of authority over curriculum and administration to popularly elected county boards of school directors, who would subdivide their counties into districts that would elect their own school trustees. Democrats delivered on their promise of tax relief by, in effect, suspending collection of the 1 percent school tax due for the preceding year and further limiting the powers of localities to tax for support of their schools. They provided for only a 0.25 percent ad valorem levy for the construction and repair of schoolhouses and, should state funds not suffice, such taxation as was necessary to provide for four months of schooling annually—the constitutional minimum. Given that state funds had never covered more than a fraction of school costs, Democrats made public funding for anything more than four months unlikely. (Davis, by contrast, had wished to keep schools open for ten months annually.) Redeemers also eliminated the fines with which Republicans had enforced compulsory attendance. With an eye again toward ethnic politics, they made it somewhat easier for private schools to partake of public funds.[36]

The Redeemers' school laws had an immediate effect. By autumn 1873, newspaper reports indicated that private tuition-charging schools were proliferating, while a number of counties had few or no public schools.

Local officials were notoriously lackadaisical in reporting district statistics, but incomplete figures for the following two years suggest sharply declining school terms and expenditures per student.[37] In the end, though, the work of these first Redeemer legislatures represented merely a way station on a longer descent. Lawmakers uprooted fundamental components of the state's first functioning school system, but (as will be discussed in a later chapter) it quickly became evident that many Democrats supported a far more radical dismantling of educational finance and administration.

While a Republican still sat as governor, Democrats, with striking unanimity, had destroyed the twin pillars of Reconstruction government—Republicans' law enforcement and education establishments.[38] But the Thirteenth Legislature also pried away at what was left of Republicans' grip on the instruments of state power. Lacking the two-thirds majority in the senate required for impeachment, Redeemers nevertheless investigated the conduct of Republican state officials, most significantly School Superintendent DeGress. A special committee documented situations conducive to malfeasance—the handling of a great deal of state money, the employment of Republican party loyalists and those already on the payroll of other governmental bodies—more than it showed any actual wrongdoing. Legislators had to content themselves with expressing their wish that DeGress resign, though to no avail. Democrats would be surprised to find him still occupying a room in the Capitol a month after Davis had been driven from office.[39]

As a prelude to the following year's more comprehensive efforts, Democratic legislators also lit into several members of the Reconstruction judiciary. The case against District Judge John Scott went the furthest, proceeding to impeachment. Many Republicans under Scott's jurisdiction agreed that his conduct on the bench had been arbitrary, prejudicial, and even abusive. The judge failed to pursue charges of malfeasance lodged against county officers, ruled on a case involving himself as one of the principals, peremptorily ordered defendants from his district, and acquiesced (at the very least) in a system by which the district attorney would drop pending charges if the accused agreed to pay him the fees he would have received for a successful prosecution. But Republican senators, by displaying an atypical solidarity, made Scott's conviction impossible. Time ran out on the session without the senate even deliberating on charges lodged against other judges.[40]

Of far more consequence, Democrats moved against the mechanisms of executive power by which the Reconstruction regime had solidified its authority over considerable local opposition. In winning his very narrow victory in 1869, Davis had carried only 53 of 124 counties for which returns are available.[41] But Republicans had by no means conceded the vital functions of local government in the large portions of the state where they were clearly the weaker party, whether due to the small numbers of African Americans locally or to their opponents' use of nightriding and economic coercion. The 1869 Constitution and the Reconstruction legislature had centralized considerable authority in the governor, allowing for the Republican administration of counties and towns even in districts where the party was unlikely to win elections. The "enabling" act of 1870, for example, had given the governor broad, if temporary, discretion in appointing district attorneys and county officials, in filling vacancies in local offices, and in selecting the mayors and aldermen of incorporated cities. Although many of these powers had expired with the 1872 election, Davis had exercised them with vigor earlier, for instance, remaking municipal governments in Houston, San Antonio, and Brownsville.[42]

Predictably, Democrats railed against this appointment power as another example of the tyrannical "centralization" that, along with high taxes, constituted Reconstruction's greatest offense. The urgency they attached to abolition of what remained of the governor's appointment powers was evident in the fact that the first general law the 1873 legislature put on the books after providing for its own pay repealed the 1870 enabling act.[43]

Democratic legislators found other ways to circumvent the use of executive authority to ensure Republican survival at the local level. Voting solidly on most such issues, they stripped the governor of supervisory authority over elections. The governor, secretary of state, and attorney general could no longer act as a returning board, empowered to reject returns from localities should it determine that free balloting and a fair count had not taken place. Under Davis, the board had exercised these powers with untoward consequences for Democrats, for example throwing out returns from El Paso County that favored opposition candidates on the grounds that "mob violence, intimidation, and undue influence" had occurred.[44] The Redeemer legislature also divested the governor of his power to appoint election judges and registrars, leaving the supervision of polling to elected county officials and their appointees.[45] Such localization of authority would put elections in a majority of counties under the control of Democrats.

Other means of securing the Republican franchise likewise disappeared. Republicans had located polling places at county seats, believing balloting at a single site was more easily policed, whereas black and Republican Texans in more isolated rural districts and in Democratic counties would be subject to bullying should they have to vote in their own neighborhoods.[46] But the

1873 election law provided for just such precinct voting. At the same time, Democrats eliminated the harsh penalties established during Reconstruction against the sorts of coercion powerful men might work on voters, such as threatening to discharge them from employment, withhold their wages, or boycott their businesses. The new election law included more modest and vaguely worded sanctions against coercion, while it treated misdeeds on the part of voters themselves, such as multiple voting, far more severely.[47]

Democrats not only diminished what executive authority remained in Republican hands but also enhanced still further their own formidable power in the legislature. The Reconstruction constitution had mandated a new apportionment of election districts once 1870 census information became available. Since new district lines would be drawn, lawmakers, despite the objections of Republican senators (and a few Democrats), put all legislative seats up for election at the same time Texans voted for governor the next autumn—even though many senators and all house members had served only a fraction of their terms. This was likely, in a single stroke, to render the senate as overwhelmingly Democratic as the house.[48]

Significantly, though, Redeemers moved less aggressively and with less unanimity in this mandated reapportionment than they had in attacking executive authority. Their restraint might have been due in part to the power of thirteen Republican senators and a Radical governor to scuttle a nakedly unfair plan. More importantly, however, any very thoroughgoing gerrymandering may simply have seemed unnecessary. At least in the 1872 elections, Democrats had done strikingly well under the apportionment provided by the Reconstruction constitution, which had actually dissipated Republican strength by placing some strongly Republican counties, such as Brazoria and Matagorda, in the same district as counties with lots of Democrats. The Redeemer legislature chose to leave these districts, as well as eight others, as they had been drawn by Republicans. In several cases this involved Democrats' acknowledgment that the districts—in the lower Brazos and Colorado river basins—would remain Republican. Much of Texas' black population was concentrated in a number of contiguous counties there, and Democratic majorities were not likely to be achieved by any conceivable districting arrangement. But the Redeemers' "concession" of these counties ultimately served their party's purposes by packing a good portion of the state's Republican voters into just a few districts rather than allowing them to affect election results in a wider number of them.[49]

Reapportionment committees stacked with Democrats engaged in a number of the other classic strategies of gerrymandering. Counties where

Republicans, while not dominant, had won healthy percentages in recent elections (for example, Anderson, Houston, and McLennan) were joined with counties that voted more overwhelmingly Democratic, as if to guarantee satisfactory results. In some cases Democratic districts were overrepresented compared to Republican or contestable districts that had had approximately the same or even greater numbers of people in 1870.[50] Democrats also eliminated two single-county Republican districts by attaching them to adjacent counties that had been voting for Democrats.

In one instance, however, this last maneuver did not create a Democratic district but instead represented a complex transaction between the parties, one that illustrates a central theme in Texas' frontier redemption—the interests of the Democracy at large could conflict with those of Democrats in areas where party authority was less secure. Democratic legislators were eager to reward a conservative Republican senator, Webster Flanagan, whose aid had proved vital in a number of important matters, including the override of Davis's police-bill veto. They therefore redistricted in his interest rather than in the interests of the Democrats of his home county, Rusk. This county had voted for a Democrat in the congressional elections of 1871 and for Horace Greeley in 1872 and shared a district with Democratic-voting Panola County, boding ill for Flanagan's reelection. The 1873 reapportionment brightened Flanagan's prospects by joining Rusk not with Panola, but with Harrison, the Republicans' banner county in northeastern Texas.[51]

For most Texas Democrats, this abandonment of Rusk was a small price to pay to conciliate Flanagan. It did no harm to the party at the state level, as a new Democratic district created elsewhere in the state balanced its influence. The *Galveston Daily News* pronounced Rusk's sacrifice regrettable but "slight" as compared to "the general success and ultimate triumph of conservative principles."[52] But the Democrats immediately affected were of a different mind. The county's "known wants," a Rusk newspaper would sputter, had been "totally disregarded."[53] Tellingly, the largest bloc of votes against the apportionment plan came not from Republicans, but from Democrats representing counties given over to Republican districts or counties abutting such districts.[54]

This unhappiness over reapportionment merely hints at the divisions among Democrats that would mark—and occasionally seem on the verge of derailing—Texas' Redemption. Through the 1873 legislative session, Democrats voted solidly to repeal the central initiatives of Reconstruction and circumscribe the power of Republicans hanging on for dear life to the executive branch. But as likeminded as Democrats might be in detesting Reconstruction, they could divide bitterly over nearly everything else, including the lengths to which Redemption had to be carried, given that their party clearly enjoyed a statewide majority.

Through Reconstruction, Texas Democrats had differed among themselves over political strategy. As with other southern Democrats, some were persuaded of the need for a "New Departure," in which they would make their peace with the post-emancipation political order (including black suffrage) and cultivate the support of conservatives outside the party on the basis of a shared opposition to the Radicals' high taxes, alleged corruption, and excessive wielding of executive power. Men as different as the putatively "agrarian" Oran Roberts and the railroad enthusiast John H. Reagan favored a relatively conciliatory posture toward Congressional Reconstruction, at least early on. Others felt that principle and political interest would be better served by the party remaining in adamant opposition. By focusing its appeal on the red-meat doctrines of white supremacy and states' rights, the Democracy could turn out its voters in greater numbers while staying true to its traditions. Compared to some other southern states, though, this debate seems to have grown more muted in Texas after 1870, probably because the party's advantage had become so manifest that Democrats could expect to win elections on their own account without having to flirt with Republican dissidents. In 1872, Texas Democrats, after some argument, endorsed the Liberal Republican national ticket led by Horace Greeley, but they spurned any fusion at the state or local level with Republican conservatives.[55]

Instead it was the differences among Democrats over political economy that seemed, as the 1873 gubernatorial campaign loomed, to pose the most immediate obstacle to the further progress of Redemption. For all the unity legislators had displayed in destroying the state police and scuttling the Reconstruction school laws, Democrats fought fiercely among themselves (as will be described in a later chapter) over whether the state should honor a subsidy the Reconstruction legislature had promised to the International Railroad for constructing a line from northeastern Texas toward the Rio Grande. To further their conquest of state government, Democrats had still to win the governorship, but their selection of a nominee would very much be complicated by the considerable tension within the party over this issue.

The subsidies promised to several railroads during Reconstruction had proved tremendously unpopular with the general public. But many Democrats argued adamantly that Texas could not repudiate those obligations, however regrettable, without ruining its credit and thereby jeopardizing the further development of its frontier economy. As the gubernatorial campaign began, a number of the party's most prominent leaders and potential gubernatorial candidates publicly called for making good on the bonds. John Reagan—one of Texas' leading Democrats from his service as postmaster general of the Confederacy until his death in 1905—declared "repudiation" to be the campaign's paramount issue and insisted that the party's nominee favor the state honoring its promises to the International.[56] Other Democrats, however, seemed just as determined to deny the nomination to anyone supporting the delivery of even a portion of the promised bonds to the company. Dismissing Reagan's, and Richard Hubbard's, chances for nomination, State Senator D. M. Short told Oran Roberts: "No man in favor of paying the $10,000 a mile subsidy to the International can receive the nomination unless the Convention is made up of different material than the Legislature." A document circulating in Washington, Texas, committed signatories to deny their vote to any candidate who would not pledge himself against state aid in any form to railroads.[57]

With leading Democrats pledged to mutually irreconcilable positions on the issue, editorialists agonized over the possibility of a split in the party. Some worried that the Democratic convention might resolve against railroads, driving thousands of alienated conservatives to a Republican party that would firmly declare itself opposed to repudiation. Others, like the *Victoria Advocate,* predicted the International would control the convention, dictating its nominees. In that event the *Advocate* called for the formation of a third party centered upon the Grange, the farm organization that had established itself in Texas that very year. If the Democracy "continues to makes its bed with corrupt stock-jobbers," the paper fumed, "it deserves to be buried across the highway, face down, and ignominiously fastened by a spike driven through the body." One county convention south of Austin almost made good on the metaphor after "spicy debates" on the International question led to delegates pulling knives upon one another.[58]

At the last moment, though, Democrats of both persuasions paused, seeming to recognize that they risked squandering a sure opportunity to oust the Radical governor. By sheer force of will, it seems, delegates tempered their rhetoric on the railroad issue as the state convention gathered at Austin in September 1873. Avoiding a floor fight, the convention threw bones to every faction, resolving against railroad subsidies, against repudiation of "just and legal liabilities," for grants of public land to railroads, and for laws that would protect Texans "against oppression and unreasonable exactions" by railroads. Richard Coke may well have garnered the gubernatorial nomination precisely because of his ability to plot a course between the contending positions on the International issue. His chief rivals in early balloting were John Ireland and Charles DeMorse, neither known as friendly to railroads (Ireland had earned the nickname "Oxcart John"). But in the final rounds he beat out Tyler's Richard Hubbard, an International ally, who ultimately became his running mate.[59] Samuel Bell Maxey suggested Coke's strengths as a consensus candidate in describing him as "clear of Rail Road rings and opposed to repudiation." A *Galveston News* correspondent said that Coke was "a little wary and cautious on railroad matters, and . . . trims elegantly between the extremes." Supporting the "liberal encouragement" of railroads, Coke at the same time proved fluent in the language of anti-monopoly, insisting that the state had to guard against untoward accumulations of corporate power.[60]

Railroad subsidies did not present the sole threat to Democratic solidarity during this Redemption campaign. Prohibition had begun to roil Texas politics. By 1873 many Texans, both male and female, were devoting at least a portion of their civic energies to attending temperance meetings and joining temperance organizations. Given their numbers, one must assume that many were Democrats. The movement became explicitly political as adherents deluged the first Redeemer legislature with petitions calling for an "Ohio" law making liquor dealers liable for damages done by drunken patrons. In municipal elections in Gatesville, voters chose an "anti-whisky" over a "whisky" slate.[61] Yet many Democrats opposed prohibition, firmly believing that the state had no business intruding upon such private matters. But in addition to opposing paternalistic threats to "personal liberty," these southern Democrats surely recognized how Texas' ethnic complexity might skew the issue. The many Texans of German descent were known to be hostile to temperance legislation. Not surprisingly, party members from Central and South Texas, where the German population was larger, voted against an Ohio law in the senate, while all the Democrats who supported it hailed from North and East Texas (northern Texas would remain the state's stronghold of prohibitionism).[62]

The alcohol issue seemed sufficiently important to some Texans to eclipse the politics of Redemption. Some hoped for the organization of a prohibition party or at least resolved not to endorse any candidate unsympathetic to the cause. When the 1873 Democratic convention officially deplored "legal interference with the merely social habits of any class of citizens, natives or of foreign birth," a putatively Democratic North Texas paper declared: "If the Democratic Party is an anti-temperance party, it is time to have a new party."[63] No prohibitionist bolt occurred, but dry sentiment had become strong enough among Democrats by 1875 to prompt the Redeemers' constitutional convention to provide for local-option elections allowing communities to ban liquor sales within their limits. "Wets" and "drys" fought it out in the local arena in subsequent years, but the decided opposition of Texas' unusually large German and Latino populations seems to have slowed the progress of prohibition in the state.[64]

If a political caution born of Texas' ethnic complexity, and not simply a principled commitment to laissez-faire, encouraged Democrats to officially oppose prohibition during the 1873 Redemption campaign, the party found other ways to appeal to the state's comparatively large immigrant population. Throughout Reconstruction, they had sought to rally Irish and German Texans against what they suggested was the proscriptive nativism of Republicans. Democrats insisted on Republicans' Know-Nothing antecedents and declared their own interest in encouraging further European immigration and in making citizenship and the franchise easier for foreign-born whites to obtain. Democrats across the South proclaimed theirs as the party of the white man, but the presence of a substantial German population in old plantation counties like Colorado could give white-supremacy rhetoric a special twist in Texas: "the foreigner will never forget that the ignorant negro has been elevated above him, and given privileges under the Constitution that have been denied to sons of the heroes of Blenheim, Waterloo, Sadowa, and Sedan." Texas Democrats wished it known that their solicitude for white men knew no national boundaries. During the 1873 campaign, the chairman of the Democratic Executive Committee for the Galveston District declared: "The Democracy, influenced by a broad philanthropy—regarding the whole white race as constituting one common brotherhood—invites the foreigner to naturalization and to a full participation in all the privileges, as well as all the duties, of a common citizenship."[65] Such ethnic politics, directed at immigrant and Catholic voters, could make Texas Redeemers sound as much like northern as southern Democrats.

Another of Texas' distinctive features, its western dimension, also intruded on this campaign. With Indian raiding continuing in the state, Democrats west and south of the Colorado River clamored for protection. Prior to the convention one aspirant to the gubernatorial nomination, the old Indian fighter John Baylor, declared frontier defense—even during this season of Redemption—to be the campaign's central issue. The party officially extended its "deep and sincere" sympathy to suffering frontier families and pledged itself "to secure their speedy and adequate protection in the future, believing this to be paramount to all other duties."[66]

The most spectacular Indian incursion upon the state's southern politics in fact came during this Redemption campaign. It ought to have been difficult for Democrats to tar their Radical enemies as soft on Indians, for Texas Republicans had tried to take a firm hand. Governor Davis strenuously demanded that the federal government confine Plains Indians inside Indian Territory, confiscate their horses and guns, and compel them to live as sedentary farmers and adopt the ways of white people.[67]

Yet for all his adamancy, in October 1873 Davis released two Kiowa leaders, Satanta and Big Tree, who had been imprisoned in the Texas penitentiary for taking part in the grisly killing of seven teamsters two years earlier. Engaged in a steeply uphill battle for reelection, Davis must have known that freeing the two men would be hugely unpopular—even black and white Republican legislators had resolved unanimously against their pardon.[68] Yet under pressure from the Grant administration, which had promised Kiowas and Comanches that the pair would be freed if their people would remain peaceful, Davis returned them to Indian Territory without his conditions regarding confiscation and confinement having been met.[69]

This untimely reversal—Davis's most noted act in Texas' *western* history—can only be explained by his insecurity as a *southern* Republican. As a number of historians have recognized, Davis needed to ingratiate himself with federal authorities.[70] Texas Republicans understood the Grant administration to be the one friend they had to keep. Davis might not have even won his razor-thin victory in 1869 had federal soldiers not been deployed around the state, limiting their adversaries' opportunities to defraud and coerce, and military authorities not thrown out returns from several turbulent counties. After 1869, Republicans seemed only to grow more vulnerable. But they not only looked to the Grant administration to protect them against being overwhelmed or irregularly deposed but also to tip the balance in their own party's internal battles. As Carl Moneyhon has explained, the lesson party members drew from the 1869 election was that they would win their intraparty battles only to the extent that they secured outside intervention on the side of their faction. Accordingly, Texas Republicans sucker-punched and elbowed one another, competing for the favor of the Grant administration.[71]

Contemporaries sensed that Davis's release of the Kiowas had *something* to do with the politics of Reconstruction and Redemption. Before the release, rumors circulated that the governor hoped to trade the Indians for the removal of party rivals from lucrative federal patronage appointments, to obtain sufficient patronage of his own to influence the upcoming election, or to allow him a comfortable political afterlife when Redemption came.[72]

In fact, neither Davis's correspondence nor the episode's aftermath suggests any such deal. But both party and factional considerations must surely have counseled him against defying the wishes of federal officials regarding Satanta and Big Tree.

Handed this golden opportunity, Democrats had a field day. In immediate advance of the election, they could add Davis's knuckling under in the case of the Kiowas to their Reconstruction rap sheet of high taxes, "centralization," and "negro rule." When Indians raided in Mason and Burnet counties, partisan newspapers sneered "Davis' Pets on a Frolic." For its part the *San Antonio Herald* grew downright baleful: "when next the Kiowas come on a marauding expedition, as they assuredly will come, [Davis] may be judged for it, if found within the limits of our State, in a manner and by a tribunal unknown to Magna Charta."[73]

Hoping to complete their Redemption of state government, Democrats thus made the most of Texas' ethnic diversity and frontier concerns. But they seem to have really hit their stride during the fall campaign by waging southern politics, focusing their appeal on their time-tested anti-Reconstruction themes of retrenchment, local self-government, and white supremacy. "White line" rhetoric could unite Democrats where political economy might divide them.[74] In the heat of the contest, even the ostentatiously deliberate *Galveston Daily News*, which on other occasions might urge conservative property holders of both races to make common cause, published editorials suggesting that the election would ultimately decide whether the state would be governed by its white or its black population.[75]

For their part, Republicans, recognizing the deep divisions that existed within the Democracy over railroad subsidies, proved far less ready to drop the subject. Rumors that Coke supported a compromise by which the International would receive bonds for a portion of its planned construction had probably strengthened his position among company supporters at the convention, but it would cause him problems that autumn. Republican papers alleged an "International Railroad Ring conspiracy upon the Democratic camp," and both Coke and International director James W. Barnes had to go to some lengths to deny that he had been the company's chosen candidate at the convention.[76] Governor Davis emphasized how heartily Democrats in the Reconstruction legislature had favored lavish railroad subsidies, even to the point of overriding those he had vetoed. He chided the late Redeemer legislature for failing to pass a general law regulating railroad rates. Republicans also condemned Democratic lawmakers for offering railroads extraordinarily generous land grants, thus, in the words of one party newspaper, "depriving the poor man of his homestead rights." Republicans tried to build a larger case for Democrats legislating "in favor of the rich and against the poor" by citing their attempts to rewrite the state's landlord-tenant laws. At the same time, Republicans, noting many Democrats' animus against the International subsidy, warned businessmen of the dire economic consequences of repudiationists and former secessionists taking power.[77]

At this point, though, the politics of Redemption trumped both the divisions among Democrats and the Republicans' class politics. The unpopularity of railroad subsidies was apparently insufficient reason for the great number of Texans who had voted Democrat in 1871 and 1872 to do otherwise in 1873. Coke walloped Davis, receiving almost twice as many votes. Democrats won all but a handful of seats in both houses of the Texas legislature. Republicans would not again wield any very decisive influence in the legislature until late in the next century.[78]

The post-election imbroglio that yielded the Capitol standoff united Democrats all the more, albeit temporarily. This episode had its origins in certain ambiguities in the state's Reconstruction constitution. Democrats and Republicans had been arguing for some time as to when the current gubernatorial term ended. Davis and his supporters cited the constitution's declaration that the governor would hold office for four years "from the time of his instalment" and counted his term as beginning with the restoration of civil government in April 1870. Democrats noted that Davis had served, under military appointment, as provisional governor beginning in January of that year; pointed to an ordinance appended to the constitution that provided that officials' terms commenced "beginning from the day of their election"; and noted the constitution's expectation that the governor's term would begin the Thursday after the legislature assembled.[79]

After the December election a second obstacle emerged to the quick redemption of the executive branch. Republicans challenged the legitimacy of the election itself. The 1869 Constitution stipulated that elections "shall be held at the county seats of the several counties until otherwise provided by law; and the polls shall be opened for four days." The Democrats' 1873 election law, in substituting precinct for county-seat voting, had also provided for only one day of balloting. This latter act, the Republicans argued, the constitution did not permit, its wording and punctuation allowing change in the site of polling only. The arrest in Houston of one Joseph (or José) Rodriguez for multiple voting allowed Republicans to test the election's legality. Initiating habeas corpus proceedings before the Texas Supreme Court, Republican attorneys steered the justices toward a judgment on the legitimacy of the election by arguing that Rodriguez could not be held for violating a law that was unconstitutional. Democrats responded by insisting that political questions involving the elected branches of government should be decided by those branches—and by the popular will—not by the courts. They also argued that the state constitution mandated four days of voting only because of the inconveniences voters might experience having to travel to and from a county's single polling place. If the constitutional convention had empowered the legislature to change the *system* of voting, it would have had no reason to prohibit the legislature from changing the *period* of polling. Before the court, an odd spectacle developed in which a defendant's attorneys resisted the release of their client without a ruling on the constitutional issue, while prominent Democrats ostensibly representing the state demanded that, because the case had been gotten up for political reasons, the defendant either be sent on his way or, at most, be remanded to the court issuing the arrest warrant.[80]

At the beginning of the new year, the justices—Republican appointees Wesley Ogden, John McAdoo, and Moses Walker—voided the election. The constitution's placement of the phrase "until otherwise provided by law" in mid-sentence, followed by a semicolon, clearly allowed the legislature to alter the manner of voting but not the period over which it occurred.[81] Prominent Democrats quickly settled on a response. They would convene the new legislature on schedule, inaugurate Coke, and in essence present the nation with a completely organized, popularly sanctioned, de facto state government. Governor Davis, while accepting the election, "whether constitutional or not, as conclusive against myself," insisted that he would not recognize a legislature assembled in such a manner while also emphasizing his claim that his term be extended until April. He asked the contending parties to appeal to the president and Congress for guidance.[82]

Ultimately, federal authorities did defuse the confrontation, ending the armed standoff in Austin by refusing to intervene on Davis's behalf. The Grant administration could not but have been influenced by the apparent coolness of important northern Republican newspapers and politicians toward overturning an election seemingly so decisive. Railroads and other enterprises with interests in Texas and influence in Washington reportedly also counseled acquiescence in the de facto Democratic government as the best means to promote a healthy business climate. Davis had no choice but to vacate his offices, though he continued to contend that he was Texas' true governor.[83]

Even with a Republican still in the governor's mansion, Democrats had gone a long way toward destroying Reconstruction. Now in control of the executive branch, the party must have seemed to many to be sitting pretty. Not only did the scale of its victories in 1871, 1872, and 1873 seem to presage an enduring majority, but Texans also clearly recognized that white southern migration westward would further inflate Democratic margins.[84] But there were white conservatives who could not yet be certain that Texas had been made safe for the Democracy. Even as Democrats rose to statewide power, prominent party members could be understood to ask if Texas was indeed redeemed if they themselves were represented by Republicans, if Republican judges interpreted the law, if Republican officials administered the law in their own county or municipality, and if their fates could be decided by voters or by jurors they deemed incapable. The asking and the answering of these questions would constitute Redemption's second act in Texas, and it would show Democrats to be divided on issues of power—just as they were over the ends that power would serve.

2

Redemption's Second Act, 1874–75

The Judiciary and Local Government

Shortly after the Coke-Davis Imbroglio, the same Redeemer legislators who officially praised President Grant's refusal to intervene as "a high recognition of the inherent right of local self government" deposed Houston's elected municipal government, bringing Redemption to a city deemed by one Democratic newspaperman as "the Radical Carthage."[1]

The correspondent was perhaps exaggerating Republican strength there. Recent electoral battles in the city had been closely contested, bare-knuckled affairs, each party routinely accusing the other of cheating.[2] But Republicans had certainly proven competitive. Although Democrats had triumphed statewide in the 1872 elections, Republicans swept the city, returning Mayor T. H. Scanlan (an Irish immigrant) for another term and electing all but one of the city's at-large aldermen, three of whom were African Americans. Democrats, claiming they had been undermined by registration fraud, ballot-stuffing, and other chicanery, subsequently backed an effort to secure a new city charter from the state legislature that would provide for a fresh round of municipal elections. The charter movement also fed on concern over the city's fiscal condition, particularly its ballooning debt and bond issues—though these were largely the products of economic development strategies endorsed, at least in general terms, by many Houston Democrats. With a significant Republican minority in the state senate (including Houston party leader James G. Tracy) and a Radical still sitting as governor, the charter effort came to nothing in 1873. Houston Republicans seem to have been on the ropes through much of the rest of the year—beset by factionalism, the effects of the Panic of 1873 on the local economy, and a scandal involving aldermen's alleged solicitation of bribes to lift a yellow-fever quarantine against Galveston. Still, a number of party candidates outpolled Democrats in the city, though losing at the state, district, and county level.[3]

But with their party now controlling both the executive and legislative branch, Democrats would not have to endure another year of Republican city government. Houston legislators, including Decimus et Ultimus Barziza, went to work just as soon as Coke and Davis supporters stopped jostling one another in the Capitol's halls. The Fourteenth Legislature quickly passed a resolution forbidding Houston's mayor and aldermen from contracting debts, issuing bonds, or entering into contracts. Three days later legislators simply ousted Scanlan and the aldermen, granting Houston a new city charter and appointing a mayor and city council to serve until the next municipal elections, which were moved up from November to March. Not surprisingly, the appointees were local Democratic notables. The new mayor, James T. D. Wilson, a banker, was said to be "one of the largest property owners in the city."[4]

But these acts of the Redeemer legislature did not, it turned out, bring political peace to Houston. Democrats there immediately fell to squabbling over whether the appointed aldermen should presume to appoint a fresh set of city officers and differed more generally over fiscal and developmental policy. In the March elections, members of the deposed opposition joined disaffected Democrats on a "Citizens" ticket, reportedly supported by holders of city bonds (presumably eager that the Republican debt not be repudiated). Republican Scanlan came within ten votes of recapturing the mayoralty. His party continued to pack some punch locally. Houston's district would send a Republican delegation to the constitutional convention in 1875. That same year its Third Ward elected former senator Tracy to the city council.[5]

If this coup produced only mixed results, the manhandling of Houston tells us something important about Redemption. The process did not come to a final, triumphant close once Democrats captured the executive branch. In 1874 there remained within Texas distinct and potentially powerful concentrations of Republican power despite the Democrats' large statewide majority. Big electoral victories did not give Democrats immediate control over Texas' judiciary. Two of the three supreme court justices appointed under Republican governor Davis had time left on their terms. Under the current constitution, the state's thirty-five district judges would serve until 1878. Nor did the Redeemers' triumph necessarily place county and municipal administration in their hands. Republicans continued to be elected to office in some of the oldest and wealthiest districts. Fourteen counties had black majorities, and African Americans might yet win office there and even in certain precincts of predominantly white counties like Smith and Lamar.[6] Sizable black minorities and persistent Democratic factionalism in several of the largest cities might allow Republicans to win elections, as in Houston, or at least to sway elections, as in Galveston in 1873, when they allied with Democratic bolters to elect a mayor.

Few examinations of the South's Redemption have attended to the judiciary and local government, perhaps because this period is often treated as denouement—covered quickly as the final page of a Reconstruction saga rather than studied carefully as the foundation of many decades of Democratic rule. But to focus too exclusively on the executive and legislative branches of state government is to make the transfer of authority to Democrats appear simpler than it in fact was. Texas Redeemers enjoyed advantages that Dixie Democrats must surely have envied—a relatively small black population and only small numbers of white Republicans. That even they struggled with the judiciary and local government should be instructive to southern historians, for it suggests what an intricate task Redemption must have been everywhere in the South. "Redemption did not descend in a sudden rush of Democratic glory," Edward Ayers reminds us, "but arrived slowly, tentatively, awkwardly."[7]

No consideration of the foundations of Democratic hegemony in Texas—or anywhere in the postbellum South—can be complete without close attention to courts, counties, and cities because district judges, sheriffs, justices of the peace, mayors, and aldermen played central roles in wielding public authority. Indeed, they often impinged more directly on citizens' daily lives than either legislators or the governor did.[8] If federal and state institutions made the laws, one had to look chiefly to district courts and county authorities to implement and enforce them—particularly as the Reconstruction-era presence of federal agencies like the Freedmen's Bureau or the Justice Department diminished in southern communities. Texas' peculiarly southwestern circumstances only enhanced the significance of local officials. With the post-emancipation growth of tenancy and sharecropping, the spread of cotton cultivation farther into the blackland prairie, and the further development of an export-oriented cattle industry in South Texas, increasing numbers of Texans would be involved in more complex sets of legal and economic relationships, relationships that courts and local authorities might have to sort out.

District judges, each presiding over two or more counties, shouldered much of the responsibility of mediating disputes between Texans and punishing malefactors. The 1869 Constitution had granted district courts original jurisdiction in all criminal cases, all suits concerning title to land and enforcement of liens, and all suits, complaints, and pleas "when the matter in controversy shall be valued at or amount to one hundred dollars." District judges also exercised a general appellate jurisdiction over cases originating in local courts.[9] Their power under Reconstruction law to directly intervene in local governance lent them considerable political authority. District judges could oust popularly elected sheriffs, district clerks, and until reined in by the Texas Supreme Court, justices of the peace.[10] Early on, certain Davis appointees had tried to exercise this power vigorously. Mijamin Priest, for example, had removed a Democratic justice of the peace (the brother of future governor James Hogg) in Cherokee County on the grounds that Republicans could not get justice in his court, that he would not aid the state police, and that he treated black defendants more harshly than white. Judges' authority over the bonds that sheriffs and justices of the peace had to post before assuming office also vested them with considerable influence.[11]

Given these powers, Democrats' authority, even in those communities where they enjoyed overwhelming majorities, could not be complete as long as Davis appointees remained on the bench. Removing them and installing their own judges would in turn afford Democrats leverage over counties where Republicans remained in the majority.

Texans clearly recognized how crucial district judges were in shaping the fundamentals of civic and economic life. A Democratic leader in northeastern Texas emphasized the importance of securing a Democratic judge lest white conservatives in black-majority Harrison County be deprived "of all right to protect the rights of property and person within her borders for long years to come."[12] In a March 1873 petition, Washington County Republicans—both prominent white politicos and men unable to sign except with their mark—declared: "Because in the near future the government of our state, may temporarily pass out from republican hands . . . it may then in that event become highly important to honest and faithful republicans, to have the judiciary of our state as the protection of their liberty, and as a last resort for protection to life and property."[13] The deposing of Houston's municipal government in January 1874 suggests that Texans took the power exercised by county and city officeholders equally seriously. Local governments were charged with maintaining law and order, collecting taxes, and providing for schooling, relief, and such basic public works as roads. They were sufficiently consequential that, though their state's governor and legislature might be Democratic, many conservative Texans might yet feel themselves to be subject to "negro rule" or "mob rule."

Unfortunately for these Redeemers, Houston would not provide much of a model for dealing with local Republican officeholders. As crucial as local government was, the tools for manhandling it were limited. Legislative control over city charters made Houston vulnerable. But Redeemers had tied their own hands in 1873, when, to defend local Democratic majorities against a Republican state government, they had trimmed the governor's powers to appoint local officials and his ability to bypass local authorities in enforcing the laws of the state.

Yet deficiencies of will, and not just of means, left the Democratic take-over of the judiciary and local government incomplete. Some Democrats clearly wished to use the power seemingly guaranteed to their party at the state level to purge the judiciary or reshape government in communities where Republican voters—or even Democratic factions obnoxious to party leaders—predominated. But many others proved decidedly hesitant to manhandle the opposition to the extent political circumstance would have allowed. Some were simply sticking to their party's stated principles of local self-government, but Texas' frontier population boom, in strengthening the Democratic party statewide, also had an ironic consequence. With their control of the legislative and executive branches secure, and being in comfortable political circumstance in their own communities, many Democrats proved reluctant to go to extraordinary lengths to deal the coup de grâce to Republican power. This second round of Redemption thus created considerable tension within the Democracy, some members attaching enormous importance to completing the overthrow of Reconstruction by retaking the judiciary and local government and many others able to view things with much less urgency. This absence of single-mindedness is worth noting. It would be more characteristic of the party's approach to other of the vital issues confronting it than the unanimity and decisiveness evident in the destruction of the Reconstruction education and law-enforcement establishments.

> A halt:—at a small stone house, through whose open door one sees a curious blending of country-store, farm-house and post-office. Here the mail for the back-country is delivered. "Morning, Judge," from a lean by-stander, meditatively chewing tobacco, to an outside passenger. "Got them radical judges impeached yet?"[14]

This query, overheard by a Yankee journalist at a settlement south of Austin in the spring of 1873, certainly suggests that the problem of a Republican-appointed judiciary interested more than a small coterie of lawmakers and strategists. Newspapers rang with demands that Democrats use the power they had won to reduce this lingering bastion of Republican power. They called for a purge of the state judiciary "in order to give logical completeness and final efficiency to the curriculum of reforms decreed by the voice of the people at the election of last December."[15]

Democrats moved with unity and dispatch in dispensing with the judges who had interfered most directly with Redemption by declaring the 1873 election unconstitutional. In those same elections, Texans had ratified constitutional amendments restructuring the state's supreme court. One change, originating in the Democratic legislature the previous spring, increased the number of justices on the court from three to five. Redeemers understood the amendment to allow the appointment of an entirely new court rather than the simple addition of two new justices. The month before the election, candidate Coke was already plotting such a complete overhaul. After the legislature formally ratified the amendment in January 1874, the new governor quickly named five new justices. Although it was reported that the three displaced Republicans might challenge their unseating in federal court, the Democratic appointees took their seats without incident.[16]

The new court very much represented the return of an old order. Coke carefully ensured that sectional balance prevailed—dividing the seats among Democrats from East Texas, the coastal metropolises of Galveston and Houston, and the more westerly locales of Austin and San Antonio.[17] But that was about as much variety as was allowed. Four of the appointees, like Coke himself, had attended the 1861 secession convention, Chief Justice Oran M. Roberts as president of the body. All had served the Confederacy in one capacity or another—as soldiers, judges, or officeholders; one had been a Confederate congressman. Four held office during Presidential Reconstruction but had, in one way or another, run afoul of the new order. Roberts had been elected U.S. senator in 1866 but been sent packing by Congress. George Moore had served as chief justice of the Texas Supreme Court until he, like Associate Justice Richard Coke, had been removed by Gen. Charles Griffin, citing their hostility toward Reconstruction. Robert S. Gould and Reuben Reeves had likewise been removed in 1867 because, as district judges, both had effectively closed their courts rather than comply with Griffin's requirement that jurors swear they had not voluntarily supported the Confederacy.[18]

The district bench would not see the same clean sweep, though Democrats seemed just as exercised over the Davis-appointed district judges as by the supreme court. "In many instances," a *Galveston Daily News* correspondent fumed, "the district judges who preside in causes involving the property, estates, liberties and lives of citizens, are but judicial debauchery and stupid ignorance set over the people."[19] Yet in proceeding against these judges, Democrats acted selectively—so much so that the closest student of Reconstruction government in Texas has written, "The 'Democratic raid on the judiciary,' as the Republicans called it, resulted in few casualties."[20] Only thirteen of thirty-five district judges were proceeded against in one manner or another. The legislature actually removed only four of them and engineered the suspension of another.[21] But such modest figures, rather than implying the relative insignificance of the judiciary to Redemption, instead highlight divisions among Democrats, the variety of circumstances militating against wholesale displacement of the judiciary, and Redeemers' ability to secure the judiciary by means other than a purge.

The happiest of these circumstances—from Redeemers' perspective—was that an absolute reconstitution of the judiciary would not be required for party interests to be served. Although appointed by a Radical governor, district judges were never as uniformly devoted to advancing Republican interests as Democrats sometimes made it sound. Some possessed only very tepid allegiances to the "Party of Lincoln." A contemporary charged J. P. Richardson with habitually "wanting to be in with the ins," and indeed Richardson supported the Coke side during the imbroglio.[22] Other Davis appointees had straightforwardly broken with the party by 1873. William H. Russell got himself elected to the state senate as a Democrat that year.[23] James Masterson of Houston, who Republicans decided had feigned loyalty only to secure a judgeship, attended that year's Democratic state convention.[24]

Other judges, while they remained loyal Republicans, clearly met with Democrats' approval. Even party leader Coke excepted several Davis appointees from condemnation. Democrats praised Andrew P. McCormick of the Galveston-Brazoria District for his impartiality and ability. In a case before his own court, McCormick had embraced the Democrats' reasoning with respect to the election controversy of 1873.[25] Many Democrats seemed also to think well of Christopher Columbus Binckley, though as a wartime Unionist, he had once had many enemies in North Texas.[26]

Not only were wholesale removals unnecessary to create a judiciary more to Democrats' liking, they would not have been easy to accomplish. Under the state's Reconstruction constitution, the legislature could oust district judges by either of two methods. It could follow the familiar path of impeachment—the presentation of charges by vote of the lower house followed by trial in the upper house, a two-thirds majority being required for conviction. Under the "address" procedure, however, the legislature by a two-thirds vote of both houses could direct the governor to remove a judge "for incompetency, neglect of duty, or other reasonable causes, which are not sufficient grounds for impeachment."[27] Some Democrats saw in this second alternative a means to purge the judiciary without "exhaustive specifications." Unlike impeachment proceedings, under senate rules the body voted not on a series of individual charges, but on the single question of whether any of the charges in the address had been proven.[28] The legislature preferred address to impeachment in all but two cases, yet the procedure in the end did not allow a quick lopping off of judicial heads. Since the state constitution guaranteed the judges a hearing, the legislature had to follow a cumbersome process of taking testimony and hearing arguments in each case.

Even among the minority of judges proceeded against, though, only a handful would ultimately be removed. With Democrats enjoying a more than four-fifths majority in both the house and senate in 1874, Republicans could not obstruct removals as they had the year before, when the Thirteenth Legislature had managed no more than to suspend a single judge, John Scott.[29] In 1874 it seems to have been divisions among Democrats that reined in the proceedings. Redeemers did move with virtual unanimity in removing Henry Maney, J. B. Williamson, Mijamin Priest, and Simon Bolivar Newcomb. But no more than nine of twenty-six Democratic senators could be persuaded to sustain any of the charges against William Chambers. Thirty-two house Democrats voted against ousting Leroy Cooper.[30] After committee investigations, sufficient momentum could not be mustered to press further action against Tilson Barden in 1873 or James Burnett and John Osterhout in 1874. Charges against William Andrews appear not to have been considered at all.

Some Democrats believed address proceedings need only inquire into judges' "character and fitness," but others seemed to hew to a more rigorous standard by which actual wrongdoing or some irrefutable pattern of incapacity had to be demonstrated.[31] San Antonio's J. H. McLeary declared that while he would prefer to see every Radical judge dispensed with, he would not vote to sustain charges he did not believe were true. His colleague from Jefferson, Benjamin Epperson, likewise refused to be convinced by "perverted testimony" and passionate speeches, insisting: "No Legislature and no party, not even the Democratic party, could stand upon anything but justice and fair dealing."[32]

Generally, the charges entertained in 1874 did not resemble the rather damning indictment of Scott the previous year. In denouncing Reconstruction, southern Democrats made much of peculation and bribery, but as far as can be determined, none of the 1874 removal proceedings involved allegations of any very pervasive patterns—or any particularly lucrative acts—of official corruption. Judge Chambers allegedly pocketed $700 ordered paid over to his court, but it became clear that he had eventually deposited that amount with a court-appointed receiver. Democrats alleged that Cooper had received $100 from a defendant, but it seems that the man had stolen the judge's horse and the money had been paid as compensation.[33]

Rather than corruption or other high crimes and misdemeanors, the proceedings against district judges tended to rest on allegations of incompetence and partiality. In the cases of James Thornton and Martin Wheeler, the complaints linked incapacity to disability. Thornton's "physical debility and mental imbecility" meant that he could not perform his duties effectively.[34] But Redeemers usually emphasized a more culpable ignorance of the law. Believing that the judges had been selected because of their political loyalties instead of their merits as jurists, their Democratic enemies assumed them to be both unable *and* uninterested in rendering justice impartially.[35]

In charging incompetence, though, Democrats rarely resorted to dispassionate means of evaluating judicial performance, such as examining the appellate record to determine if a judge suffered an unusually high number of reversals in higher courts. Instead they might offer up a judge's inability to dispose of a large number of cases as evidence of incapacity—without noting how population growth, emancipation, or economic development might have increased the court's workload.[36] Assertions of popular opinion as to unfitness could be similarly vague. The "public sentiment" against Williamson that one witness cited was, he admitted, simply that of "the white element" of Harrison County; whites constituted less than one-third of the county's population.[37]

But a meaningful number of Democratic legislators appear to have discriminated among these charges of unfitness according to their relative strength. In the cases of three of those removed, several white Republicans agreed with a unanimous Democratic delegation that the judges' failings warranted their ouster. Legitimate cases very well could have been made for at least inquiring into these judges' competence. Newcomb had been trained in Canada and only arrived in Texas a year before his appointment to the bench. Even the single witness he was able to secure in his defense testified as to the shakiness of Newcomb's grasp of state law, at least early on. The judge allowed prosecutions for fornication to proceed in his court, apparently unaware that fornication was not an offense under state law. A witness called in Priest's defense—none other than Judge Cooper, who was being similarly worked over by the legislature—questioned his rulings on a number of points central to the proceedings.[38] Henry Maney had initiated a protracted duel with the Texas Supreme Court over their respective power and jurisdiction in contempt and habeas corpus proceedings, a confrontation that eventuated in the higher court jailing Maney for flouting its mandates and he in turn attempting to arrest his fellow Republican jurists for contempt. Not one Republican senator voted against Maney's removal.[39]

Judges who retained their seat, like Barden, Cooper, and Burnett, by contrast seem to have garnered more expressions of support from the people of their district, including Democrats.[40] The legislature seems also to have been less enthusiastic about proceedings, such as those involving Chambers and Burnett, that focused on a judge's actions in a single case or his hostile relations with one or two attorneys.[41]

Yet some Democrats' apparent willingness to discriminate between stronger and weaker cases for unfitness does not mean that merit alone shaped these proceedings. The affected judges typically had been politically active in some manner or another. Three district judges attended the 1872 Republican National Convention, and all of them—Chambers, Barden, and Williamson—subsequently faced proceedings. Six of the jurists had held important positions at Republican state conventions or in the state party organization.[42] Some had been activists at the regional level, attending party meetings, writing for party newspapers, or corresponding with Republican leaders in Austin concerning the well-being of the local organization. Judge Cooper had even put his name to the declaration that "the Republican party is dearer to us than all things of a public nature."[43] Maney's troubles began when he chaired a Republican meeting that formally condemned the injunctions employed by Democrats in their campaign of tax resistance against Reconstruction schools. He fined a number of lawyers, including well-known Democrat John Ireland, for contempt after they refused to argue injunction cases in his court, asserting the judge already had his mind made up.[44]

Democratic legislators, though, could not enforce a simple rule that political activism was prohibited to jurists, given that friendly judges like Russell and Masterson were showing up at Democratic conventions.[45] Instead, the charges suggested that judges had promoted, in an official capacity, the fortunes of their political allies and oppressed their political foes. Democrats accused Cooper, Priest, Williamson, and Newcomb of protecting Republican defendants by slanting charges to juries, setting aside guilty verdicts, excluding Democrats from juries, or blocking indictments.[46]

As in the matter of incompetence, a meaningful number of Democratic legislators seem to have made distinctions among these charges of partisanship. The case made against Judge Burnett focused almost exclusively on his resort to Davis's state police when local authorities or grand jurors failed to indict or detain those he considered to be suspects and his alleged role in the imposition of martial law in Walker County in 1871 (evidence suggests the judge had actually been reluctant to advocate that step).[47] But no one showed that Burnett exceeded or misused the authority vested in him by statute in 1871, and the case against him went nowhere. Cooper and Barden remained on the bench as well.

In the end it may well have been political conditions in a judge's district that determined how seriously Redeemers took the menace of his Republicanism. Democrats generally seem to have been able to tolerate Republican judges in firmly Democratic districts. They could also live with Republican judges, like McCormick, J. Livingston Lindsay, and William Burkhart, who presided over districts where Republicans were dominant or competitive, though only if those judges were less conspicuously active in politics. But being a conspicuous Republican partisan in a divided community spelled trouble.

Three of those removed—Williamson, Newcomb, and Priest—hailed from such turbulent districts, while the brawl that ousted Maney originated in Guadalupe, the one county in his district where Republicans were competitive. Such settings most likely magnified what may have been the genuine shortcomings of these men, and it may have made their political activities seem more malign than those of Chambers, whose southeastern Texas district was strongly Democratic. Where party feeling ran high and a judge was clearly identified with local Republicans, the tendency to attribute a partisan motive to actions that happened to serve a Republican's interests or discommode a Democrat must have been more reflexive. The fact that local politics was bitterly contested may have also increased the incentive for removal, given district judges' powers over local government and the administration of justice.

The large black and Republican majority in his home county of Harrison surely made Williamson an especially appealing target. Through the early 1870s, local conservatives recognized that Republican dominance in the county could not be challenged by electoral action. In 1872 they had not even bothered to nominate candidates for certain county offices. But the district judge, the county's most powerful Republican officeholder, could be reached by means other than elections—that is, the proceedings of a state legislature dominated by Democrats. His Democratic replacement could in turn exercise considerable authority over locally elected Republican officials. But Williamson's ouster did not offer Harrison Democrats permanent relief. Two years later the county's black majority elected him county judge.[48] The deposed Henry Maney was similarly elected Guadalupe county judge that same year.[49]

S. B. Newcomb of El Paso had as many enemies in his district as Williamson had in his, though far fewer friends. The intersections of regional histories in postbellum Texas were very much on display in the Newcomb case, for this Canadian carpetbagger who fell victim to Redemption served a borderland district with no history of plantation agriculture and relatively few African Americans. But if a number of the familiar constituents of Reconstruction-era politics barely existed in Newcomb's district, profound divisions emerged between Republicans and Democrats and between factions identifying themselves with the Radical and conservative wings of the state Republican party. In fact, Newcomb had been appointed to replace a judge gunned down in a burst of intraparty violence. Politicos vied not only for patronage and personal advantage but also for the support of the county's Latino majority, many members of which followed the lead of an apparently rather fearsome parish priest named Antonio Borajo. Newcomb had aligned himself with State Sen. Albert Jennings Fountain, a Radical whose battles with other members of the upper crust had yielded canings, shootings, and federal indictments. Such circumstances could only increase the predisposition of political enemies to attribute the judge's decisions to partisanship, and in fact, a number of the charges against Newcomb involved actions allegedly prejudicial to the interests of rivals like Democrat Charles Howard, conservative Republican W. W. Mills, and Borajo. Unfortunately for the judge, by 1874 his local support had evaporated, and Fountain had left for New Mexico. Governor Davis had received only 46 votes in the county to Coke's 447.[50]

Local political circumstances also probably made Mijamin Priest an appealing and easy target. Priest's East Texas district had no black-majority counties but a considerable black minority. Davis had won Nacogdoches County in 1869, and Republican candidates had been amassing respectable portions of the vote in San Augustine County. If Democrats dominated the district, they do not seem to have won their power easily or rested comfortably afterward. Evidence suggests that nightriding groups had been employed to suppress the black vote in Nacogdoches and San Augustine in 1869. Two years later Priest still doubted that elections could be conducted fairly. "The devil is in the White Camelias," he told Davis. In this district, where militant Democrats apparently felt they had to go to some lengths to secure their power, Priest had removed a Democratic officeholder, welcomed Davis's hated state police, and, Democrats charged, "made it a rule to favor all parties of African descent tried before him."[51]

In addition to ousted judges being political activists in badly divided districts, the other detectable pattern in the removals shows the imprint of Texas' ethnic diversity on its southern politics. In those proceedings where party solidarity broke down and roll calls were recorded, the handful of foreign-born Democrats seem to have been distinctly disinclined to support removals. Of the five foreign-born Democratic representatives, only Italian American Louis Cardis of El Paso voted to remove Cooper. The senate's only foreign-born member, Austrian George Erath of Waco, voted against the removal of both Cooper and Chambers. In the more partisan vote on Williamson's removal, German-born A. L. Kessler of New Braunfels and E. F. Schmidt of Houston along with Irish-born P. F. Murphy of Corpus Christi were the only Democrats to break ranks. In 1873, when Chambers submitted a petition asking that the charges against him be investigated and evidence published, a majority of native-born Democrats voted to table it, while all German-born Democrats voted against tabling.[52]

It could not simply be that foreign-born Democrats treated the cases with less urgency because they hailed from more politically secure communities. Several were from counties like Harris and Washington, where political competition was fierce. That the few dissents among Democratic legislators to the destruction of the state police and Republican school system similarly came from among the foreign born might suggest a less elevated partisanship on Reconstruction issues and perhaps a somewhat distinct set of political concerns.

If a meaningful number of Democrats seemed to scruple against removing judges in every case in which someone was unhappy with a Republican appointee, the party found other ways to extend its reach within the judiciary. A three-quarters vote could not be mustered for removal of Chambers and Cooper, but majorities did pass laws shortly afterward reducing the two judges' jurisdiction to the smallest possible territory. The legislature transferred all counties save one out of each of the judges' districts, commending the bulk of their population to the authority of two more congenial jurists.[53]

But lawmakers resisted fellow Democrats' demands in 1873 and 1874 that the districts of obnoxious judges Maney, Chambers, Williamson, Barden, and Burnett be entirely abolished.[54] Coke's attorney general and confidant

George Clark said that he opposed deposing of judges by eliminating their districts. Such a practice would allow a bare majority of legislators too much authority over the judiciary, thus encroaching upon the separation of powers and leaving any judge's tenure dependent "upon the political victory of their friends." Others warned that reducing the number of judicial districts would overwhelm the remaining courts.[55]

If scruples or considerations of convenience reined in Redeemers, they enjoyed other opportunities to remake the judiciary in their own image. Ten of thirty-five district judges resigned between late 1872 and 1874. At least five appear to have been under some pressure to depart—their resignations accomplishing what otherwise would likely have been attempted by formal proceedings. Two judges—Thornton and Wheeler—had addresses pending against them when they resigned. The Reconstruction legislature had already drafted articles of impeachment against John W. Oliver, and since that time he had jailed justices of the McLennan County Court in a political dispute and in turn had been declared insane by county authorities. The bars of their North Texas districts had called upon Judges Charles Soward and Hardin Hart to resign, which they subsequently did. Hart—a wartime Unionist and Freedmen's Bureau agent first appointed district judge in 1867—had hardly endeared himself to local Democrats with his interest in prosecuting the unreconstructed for the murders of Unionists during the war. He had lost an arm after being shot up in an ambush in 1869.[56]

Democrats controlled the filling of these ten vacancies, even those that occurred while Davis was still governor. Redeemer legislators did not hesitate to spurn men the Republican governor nominated as replacements. Davis himself wrote off certain prospective appointees as unlikely to be confirmed, and his correspondents fell to recommending the least objectionable Democrats.[57] Davis found himself reduced to recruiting from opposition ranks, soliciting Samuel Bell Maxey, termed by one Republican paper as an "ultra-simonpure-secession-anti-reconstruction Democrat." Maxey turned down Davis. Redeemers sent him to the U.S. Senate the following year.[58]

While the Democratic legislature purged only four district judges in 1874, Coke would have the opportunity—through removals, resignations, and deaths—to name fourteen more to his party's liking. Like his supreme court appointments, his district appointees possessed pedigrees in conservative politics. Edward Dougherty had been a member of the 1861 secession convention and, like Williamson's replacement, Matthew Ector, had served as a district judge and been removed by military authorities in 1867 for his hostility to Reconstruction. Three others—James H. Rogers, A. S. Broaddus, and

D. M. Prendergast—had likewise attended the secession convention. The latter two served as Democratic legislators in 1873. A. J. Hood and James A. Ware had sat on the Democratic state committee, Ware as recently as 1872. Priest's replacement, Richard S. Walker, had been a Confederate district judge.[59]

These changes—as well as the chilling effect the removal proceedings may have had on the partisan activities of the remaining Republican judges—undoubtedly allowed Democrats, within months of Coke taking office, to feel more secure in their power. At least one prominent Redeemer felt that the party had worked a profound transformation. When the legislature again assembled in 1875, Lt. Gov. Richard Hubbard noted a contrast with what had prevailed a year before: "Then our Judiciary was warped too often by political prejudices, if not wanting in the pure ermine of the bench—from the lowest to the highest courts the honored places of an illustrious line of great jurists were filled by domestic ignorance or foreign adventurers. But now a judiciary goes in and out from our temple of justice who know the law."[60]

Redeemers with the most at stake knew that a more congenial judiciary would not alone make their communities safe for the Democracy. Efforts to extend their authority in local government, however, would occasion direct and lively intraparty debate. More so than a purge of the judiciary, the means proposed to manage local government could seem to many Redeemers to contradict the stated principles of their party—not just some abstract standard of due process and fair play—and to impinge upon their own privileges. In his inaugural address Richard Coke had invoked his party's standard of local self-government, insisting that institutions exercising power over property and liberty should be seated close to the citizenry and directly accountable to it. The *Galveston Daily News* made clear that this principle meant more than just states' rights: "Centralization may be just as corrupt and pernicious with its centre at a State capital, as with its centre at the Federal capital. . . . The States must set an example of localizing self-government, as far as it can be localized in consistency with the public welfare."[61] In addition to preferring local to state authority, Democratic doctrine preferred elective to appointive officeholding. "Away with the appointive power," cried the *Houston Telegraph* in 1873. "It is a relic of kingcraft, and should never have a place in a republican government."[62]

Democrats had long preached local self-government, but the circumstances of Reconstruction in Texas had made the doctrine all the more attractive. Even in Republicans' best year, Davis had won majorities in fewer than half of the state's counties. Confident that they could win elections in most communities, Democrats bewailed the authority the Reconstruction regime exercised over local administration, which restricted communities' inherent right to select their own officers and determine their own affairs.

As the powers of the state began to fall into Democratic hands after the election of 1872, though, the most troubling challenges the party faced came not from a well-organized Republican party at the state level but rather from communities in which non-Democratic voters (or in some cases Democratic voters obnoxious to party leaders) existed in great enough numbers to decide local contests. Yet by enshrining local authority and the elective principle, the Redeemers had limited their ability to use state power to reshape local government where these opposition majorities prevailed.

Some Democrats were quick to point out these troubling implications of local self-government. A correspondent from an old plantation region noted how the "extravagant extension of the doctrine of 'home rule'" would commit "the government of the people of these counties to the hands of the ignorant and prejudiced class who were lately their slaves."[63] The *Austin Democratic Statesman* too emphasized the dangers in local empowerment: "When the whole State votes, as in creating the Legislature, the danger from the incapable and ignorant and lawless is not great. The power of this mob is then diffused. It is only terrible in local elections of local officers, as in Houston, Dallas, Luling, and other like places, and in certain counties of Texas."[64]

The deposing of Houston's city government illustrates the consequent flexibility of many Democrats regarding the principle of local self-determination. But some influential party members were not content to rely on the sort of legislative fiat exercised in this case, instead looking to more permanent structures of government to contain the threat of local opposition majorities. These conservatives would find, however, that many of their fellow Democrats could not accept more comprehensive responses to this local problem with as few qualms as they evidenced in overthrowing Houston's government. Unlike the ad hoc methods employed there, the institutional mechanisms being proposed would apply in their own communities and not simply selected Radical strongholds. Precisely because Democrats enjoyed secure majorities in the lion's share of Texas counties, and because the party's control of the state at large was not in question, such measures would offer few immediate advantages in most places while abridging Democrats' own enjoyment of local self-government. Should the alternative be to surrender their own privileges, many Democrats proved all too willing to concede certain districts to opposition rule.

In Florida, Louisiana, and North Carolina, Redeemers unwilling to endure majority rule in their own communities secured appointment rather than election of local officeholders.[65] Once a Democrat occupied the governor's mansion, such a system held considerable appeal to Texans in the comparatively small number of towns and localities where Democrats were not likely to win elections.

Rather than be so bold as to attempt to make existing elective offices appointive, these Democrats fought simply to retain the Reconstruction status quo when it came to district judgeships, the most significant unelected local post. Some party members couched their support for the continued appointment of judges in the need to prevent politicization of the bench.[66] But some of those anxious to keep the district judiciary appointive were willing to see supreme court justices elected by the state at large, indicating that the specter of a politicized judiciary concerned them less than the politics and ethnicity of the men likely to be elected in certain places. The *Galveston News* spoke with distaste of the prospect of "Sambo on the bench" in a number of "exceptional" districts. Referring to the "negro Counties," Guy Bryan (Speaker of the Texas House in 1874–75, Stephen Austin's nephew, and a college chum of Rutherford B. Hayes) cried: "For God sake, do not let the negroes select the Judges for these white people, do not by so doing force the whites to . . . cry out that their own people in the exercise of power are worse than the Yankee."[67] Under the Reconstruction system, a Democratic governor and senate would appoint "learned and enlightened" judges, another black-county Democrat said. Under an elective system, "there is nothing for us but despair."[68]

But this urge to retain an appointive district judiciary ran contrary not only to many Democrats' stated aversion to Reconstruction-era "centralization" and their positive enthusiasm for elective officeholding but also to precedent. Texans both before and immediately after the Civil War had elected their judges.[69] Accordingly, Democrats fell to fighting over this issue just as soon as their party controlled both the executive and legislative branch. When in early 1874 a committee of Democratic legislators undertook to rewrite Texas' constitution in lieu of holding a convention, it opted to continue gubernatorial appointment of district judges while making the supreme court elective. But the Democratic majority in the senate quickly amended this draft to render the judgeships elective. Significantly, almost all of the Democrats opposing this change came from counties or districts in which Republicans remained atypically competitive, scoring significantly higher than their statewide average in the previous December's gubernatorial balloting. Lawmakers soon scuttled the draft constitution entirely in favor of holding a convention, but in the event one could not be assembled, they prepared amendments to the existing document that provided for the election of both the district judiciary and the supreme court.[70]

Supporters of an appointed judiciary saw clearly that the demand for popular election had acquired a decided momentum. In private discussions at the beginning of 1875, four of the state's five supreme court justices confided to Galveston attorney William Pitt Ballinger that they preferred appointment but believed that citizens had been persuaded by politicians that judges should be elected.[71] Still, when Redeemers assembled a constitutional convention in September 1875 to forge an enduring post-Reconstruction order, some hoped popular election of district judges might yet be prevented. One Austin Democrat predicted "a *Serious Struggle*" on the issue, with "most of the intilect in the convention" favoring continued appointment.[72] Yet while both Ballinger and E. S. Rugely, a Democratic planter from the black and Republican coastal county of Matagorda, introduced resolutions calling for gubernatorial appointment of judges, both the judiciary article reported by committee and the substitutes for it entertained on the floor provided for popular election.[73] Late in the convention John W. Whitfield, a Democrat representing both Lavaca County and frequently Republican Colorado County, proposed, "as a last lingering hope for his district," that gubernatorial appointment of district judges be retained for the first four-year term under the new constitution. The measure was soundly defeated, its seventeen supporters tending to be Democrats who, like John Reagan, hailed from counties where Republicans remained unusually competitive (Reagan's county, Anderson, had voted 45 percent Republican in the last general election) or, like Ballinger, from the state's largest cities.[74]

Thus in contrast to Redeemer Democrats in a number of other southern states, Texans rather decisively opted for popular election rather than perpetuating the Republican system of judicial appointment.[75] John Ireland had explained his support for an appointed judiciary in 1874 by insisting: "While I believe the people of my district are in favor of the elective system, I believe they are willing to forego their own views to save our friends in other portions of this State."[76] Yet it seemed that in this state, made increasingly white and Democratic by frontier population growth, most Texans were in fact not willing to forego their right to elect officeholders to save Democratic "friends" in more competitive districts.

With the popular election of officials carrying the day, concerned Democrats offered a second strategy to, in the words of the *Austin Democratic*

Statesman, "secure trustworthy courts in southern and eastern counties" and "protect one-third of the State, and many of its richest towns and counties."[77] At the constitutional convention Whitfield proposed that the state be divided into five districts, each to elect one supreme court justice and five district judges, rather than a single judge being elected from each of twenty-five much smaller districts. This amendment, offered by a man who had led proslavery bands in Bleeding Kansas and served periodically as the border ruffians' delegate to Congress, embodied a second strategy familiar to both southerners and northerners interested in circumscribing the power of local majorities—expanding the territory from which officeholders would be elected.[78] Concentrations of Republicans in Texas tended to be localized, and any enlargement of the district and electorate responsible for selecting judges would in most cases draw in more of the state's large Democratic population.

Whitfield's supporters made their object clear. Fletcher Stockdale of Calhoun County (51 percent Republican in 1873) "alluded to the difficulties in the way of the election of judges in some localities, owing to the ignorance and prejudices of a certain class of the communities which ought not to control in judicial elections, and said that by his method it would be placed out of the power of local majorities to elect men to the bench who were inimical to the interests of the state." Whitfield indicated precisely who these incapable voters were: "his substitute was a plea for the black belt, in which he lived. If they voted that amendment down they would destroy the hope of fifteen counties, and put them under negro rule."[79]

Other Democrats at the convention proposed to delocalize elections in a second way—by providing for larger legislative districts. George McCormick of Colorado County (57 percent Republican at the last gubernatorial election) argued for the perpetuation of the Reconstruction system of electing multiple house members at large from each of the state's thirty-odd senatorial districts rather than the creation of smaller single-member representative districts. Under the at-large system, his typically Republican county had been represented by as many Democrats as Republicans since 1870 since it elected the legislators in concert with consistently Democratic Lavaca County.[80] In supporting multiple-member representative districts, John Reagan declared "that it must be evident to all the delegates that a large portion of their countrymen were incapable of self-government. On general principles he favored local option, but the situation in the eastern counties of Texas was peculiar."[81]

Democratic delegates proved less resistant to their colleagues' proposals for delocalized elections than to appointive officeholding, splitting more evenly on the Whitfield substitute.[82] Still, none of the proposals to enlarge judicial or representative districts was approved. Again, certain Democrats cited party doctrine in opposing measures intended to contain local opposition threats. In mandating single-member representative districts, the convention's apportionment committee invoked "local representation—a principle dear to an overwhelming majority of the people of Texas." John Henry Brown of firmly Democratic Dallas declared that while he would go as far as his conscience allowed "to relieve the afflicted sections," his party ought not, "because they had the majority, go back on the doctrine they had always taught."[83] Not surprisingly perhaps, this devotion to doctrine coincided nicely with most Democrats' immediate political interests. Of thirty Democrats who opposed the Whitfield measure, twenty-four hailed from counties in which Richard Coke had garnered over 60 percent of the gubernatorial vote in 1873 (two others came from newly established counties that had been carved from reliably Democratic territory).

Yet if the majority at the convention was ill-disposed to sacrifice community-based election of officeholders, it again demonstrated many Democrats' willingness, as in the case of Houston, to deal with local opposition majorities by ad hoc means. In this case they engaged in the time-honored (and still honored) Texas gerrymander. In constructing twenty-six judicial and thirty-one senatorial districts, the majority, where possible, parceled out potentially Republican areas among districts composed chiefly of safely Democratic counties. Districts ended up as oddly shaped as required to draw in the requisite number of Democratic voters. The V-shaped Fourth Judicial District, for example, extended awkwardly eastward and northward from the Republican fulcrum of Grimes and Walker to include the Democrats of Angelina, Trinity, Leon, and Madison counties. The Second Senatorial District linked Houston County, narrowly Republican in the last election, with a number of barely contiguous Democratic counties to its east. These elaborate efforts could hardly be justified as an effort to distribute population evenly since districts ended up being of widely varying size. Where Republicans were so numerous that they might overwhelm Democrats in adjacent counties—such as in the lower Brazos and Colorado river basins—they were quarantined in a handful of districts seemingly conceded to the opposition. Delegates drew their lines carefully enough, though, that where the Reconstruction constitution had created three black-majority judicial districts, the Redeemer document allowed just one.[84]

In the case of the smaller and more numerous representative districts, Democrats employed another means to circumscribe local Republican majorities. The convention allotted one representative for every 2,500 voters. Larger counties elected representatives on their own, but to provide for their excess population, they also were combined with adjacent counties to elect a second "floating" legislator. Delegates found ways to attach Republican counties, such as Harrison, to Democratic ones in such a way as to guarantee the floater was a Democrat. An anonymous newspaper correspondent, believed to be convention delegate William Neal Ramey of Shelby County, owned up to this strategy, terming one floater district "just a free-will offering to the white people of Harrison Co."[85] And exceptions to the rule of single-member districts were made in the case of Colorado County and black-majority Marion County, which may well have elected their own Republican representatives. They were required to elect multiple representatives in conjunction with adjacent underpopulated counties whose combined Democratic majorities would likely carry the district.

These various efforts served Democrats in Republican counties well. Gerrymandering resulted in black-majority counties like Harrison, Grimes, and Walker being presided over by Democratic district judges in the following years. And although Colorado, Marion, Grimes, Walker, Jackson, and San Jacinto mustered majorities for the Republican gubernatorial candidate in the subsequent general election, the districts in which they were situated sent Democrats to the legislature. The handful of Republicans in the next legislature came from either Republican quarantine districts or counties where Democratic factionalism had yielded a fatal round of ticket splitting.[86]

Embattled Democrats were not left with gerrymandering alone to contain the power of local opposition majorities, for their party was careful to make local officers subject to a variety of checks enforceable by a reliably Democratic state legislature and high court, an increasingly Democratic district judiciary, and even a community's wealthier citizens. These checks could be applied selectively, allowing the electoral choices of certain localities to be nullified without necessarily intruding upon the privileges of Democratic communities. While Redeemers made Texas' most powerful local office, the district judgeships, elective, they also made those judges easier to remove. The convention added a provision without precedent in Texas constitutions, allowing the supreme court, not simply the legislature, to remove any district judge who was incompetent or "shall be guilty of partiality, or oppression, or other official misconduct, or whose habits and conduct are such as to render him unfit to hold such office, or . . . who shall fail to execute in a reasonable measure the business in his courts." This put the fate of locally elected district judges in the hands of another body that, because it was elected by the state at large, was sure to be thoroughly Democratic.[87]

Redeemers also enhanced the power of the now more congenial district judiciary to deal with objectionable county officers. Their constitution expanded the scope of district judges' removal powers to cover all county officers. Furthermore, an earlier law of the Redeemer legislature ensured that a community whose electoral decision had been overturned by a district judge could not simply return a deposed officer to power. Passed over "strenuous opposition by the Radical members and a few Democrats," it provided that a person removed from a county office would not be eligible to hold that office for another two years.[88]

Redeemers enhanced district judges' authority over local politics in another important way. An 1873 law gave district courts jurisdiction—formerly held by county courts—over contested elections involving county officers, and the Texas Supreme Court subsequently ruled that district judges' decisions in these matters could not be appealed. An 1876 statute stipulated that "questions of fact which may be at issue between the contesting parties shall be passed upon by the court without the intervention of a jury." The same law discriminated against poorer and less well-connected officers-elect by allowing challengers to hold the office in question until any contest was settled should the contestee fail to post a bond of no less than twice the likely amount of fees to be realized during his term.[89]

The significance of Democrats vesting these powers in district judges, and of the 1875 convention's judicial districting ensuring that a number of Republican counties had Democratic judges, would be illustrated in black-majority Harrison County in 1878. Republicans apparently won that year's local elections. But the largely white and conservative Citizens party insisted that because a certain polling place had been incorrectly located, the votes cast there should not be counted—thus depriving Republicans of their majority. The losing Citizens candidates simply seized local offices and secured injunctions from District Judge A. J. Booty, a Democrat, intended to prevent County Judge J. B. Williamson from counting the vote from the contested precinct or issuing election certificates. The Citizens' nominee for county judge, George Lane, subsequently filed a contest to the reelection of incumbent Williamson. Judge Booty ruled against Williamson and against counting the disputed votes, effectively sealing the fate of Republican government in one of the party's surviving redoubts.[90]

Election contests, however, did not afford a universally applicable means of containing local opposition power. Their success depended on at least a plausible case for irregularity being made. The requirement that office-holders post security bonds, though, allowed challenges to the outcome of virtually any local election, and it seems to have been by this means, more than any other, that Democrats in the post-Reconstruction decades overturned the decisions of local majorities. The sums required for bonds could be hefty, particularly for officers who would handle tax monies. In 1873, for example, the sheriff of Marion County was suspended until he posted a new bond of $35,000. Even during Reconstruction, certain Republican appointees had found it difficult to make bond. Community members with sufficient wealth to serve as sureties could well be hostile to Radicals.[91]

While intended to promote official accountability, Democrats never shrank from employing bonding requirements as a tool to manipulate local politics. In 1875, while Harrison County was still under Republican rule, the conservative minority, in what one member called "an orderly and patriotic effort to rid the County of irresponsible officers and negros," had managed temporarily to unseat Republican sheriff S. H. Russell by challenging his bond.[92] Redeemers pressed a variety of measures whose cumulative effect was to render it still harder for local officers and officers-elect to make bond and to leave them more vulnerable to local enemies and the authority of the district judiciary. New laws allowed district judges more initiative to inquire into the sufficiency of the bonds of individual justices of the peace and sheriffs and to require those officials to give new bonds. The officers would be ousted if they failed to comply within twenty days. Individual citizens too could challenge the worthiness of a bond, and should they be unhappy with the action of a county government in approving a bond, they could appeal the matter to district judges. The new laws added the requirement that sureties be residents of an officer's home county. Sheriffs and justices could no longer look to patrons or political allies elsewhere for support, giving a community's property-holding elite greater say over who held office.[93] With the lion's share of wealth in black-majority counties residing in white hands, bond requirements worked particular hardship on African Americans. In 1874 none of the four black justices elected in Marion County could make bond. Neither could victorious black candidates in Wharton and Jackson counties two years later.[94]

Having won neither appointive officeholding nor at-large election at the 1875 convention, Democrats in black-majority counties seem to have become more systematic in using bonding requirements to subvert majority rule. In 1878 Grimes County Democrats promised to "discountenance" party members who supported the bond of any Republican elected to local office. From Brazoria County a Democrat correspondent reported shortly after the 1876 election: "It is doubtful if the Radical officers elect will be able to take their seats, as the tax-payers have unanimously resolved not to go on their bonds. Being outnumbered at the polls, our people have been forced, after ten years of quiet submission, to devise other means to throw off the heavy yoke of Radical rule." That same year a meeting of "white citizens and property owners" in neighboring Fort Bend County pledged to prevent their peers from acting as sureties on official bonds unless local Republicans backed their nominees for county judge and sheriff.[95] It would take another twelve years, the expulsion of local black leadership, and a dramatic shootout before Republican power could be destroyed in Fort Bend. But local Democrats used the bond device to seal their triumph, pledging party members to serve as sureties only on bonds of politicians approved by their Jay Bird Democratic Association.[96]

By early 1876 the legislature and executive branch rested firmly in Democrats' hands, and a new state constitution tailored to their specifications had been ratified. Yet the second act of Redemption had remained curiously incomplete. Those who sought most thoroughly to extend party authority in the judiciary and local government had met repeated frustration in the preceding two years. Here again Texas' frontier allure and western-style growth intruded on its southern politics. Its attractiveness to white southern migrants and the westward expansion of settlement within the state increased Democrats' numbers overall and in theretofore sparsely populated regions. But the very strength of their hold on Texas hindered the progress of Redemption in contested communities. Many party members in the vast stretches of the state that were politically secure simply would not surrender their own privileges in electing local officials to solve the problems of often distant Democratic brethren. Shortly after the Redeemers' constitutional convention adjourned in November 1875, the *Guadalupe Times* conveyed its regrets to those who would suffer the ill effects of an elective judiciary in "some of our poor counties that are ruled by negroes" but quickly added, "we can't help you." The *Rockport Transcript* of Aransas County—where Republicans garnered all of fourteen votes in the 1876 gubernatorial balloting—declared with respect to black officeholding, "the evil is not so great that a large majority of the people should sacrifice their preference to accommodate so small a section of the State."[97]

There had thus been no clean sweep of the judiciary, no perpetuation of appointive officeholding. Still, the less conspicuous strengthening of district judges' power in election contests and manipulation of bonding requirements would eventually allow a white minority to destroy majority rule in two Republican bastions—Harrison and Fort Bend counties—and to harass opposition officeholders elsewhere. But Democrats in black-majority areas and turbulent cities had always intended to work at more fundamental levels. Instead of simply limiting the power or thwarting the will of local electorates, they sought to alter their very composition.

3

The Ballot Box and the Jury Box

Redeemers and the Privileges of Citizenship

The integrity of the State is only compatible with perfect local independence, and this is only possible, under existing Federal codes, when the privilege of suffrage, in these districts, is restricted to tax-paying intelligence.

AUSTIN DAILY DEMOCRATIC STATESMAN,
FEBRUARY 27, 1876

Asthe *Democratic Statesman* suggests, it need not have been so difficult for Texas Redeemers to reconcile their principle of local self-government with their interest in extending party authority in places where a majority or large minority of adult males sided with the opposition. Should a sufficient number of the politically unreliable be eliminated from the electorate, "majority" rule might safely prevail. No issue more than voting rights shows the imprint of Texas' complicated social history upon Redemption. In their debates over disfranchisement in the mid-1870s, Texas Democrats sought to solve a southern problem, negotiated a complex ethnic politics without parallel elsewhere in the South, partook of a national anxiety about the implications of universal manhood suffrage in an era of growing wage work, and addressed the distinct political concerns of the state's burgeoning towns and cities.

If the heyday of southern disfranchisement came only after 1888, influential Texas Democrats had clearly been possessed of the ambition to "purify" the electorate from the dawn of Redemption and had made a concerted effort toward that end at the state's 1875 constitutional convention.[1] By the standards of the era, Texas' Reconstruction constitution had defined the electorate broadly. It conferred the franchise upon all adult male citizens twenty-one or older, provided they were sane and law abiding.[2] Following their party's capture of the legislature in 1872, prominent Democrats attempted to narrow that constitutional standard. John Ireland, whose home county of Guadalupe continued to sport an active Republican constituency, introduced measures in 1873 and 1874 intended to exclude from the franchise those who had not paid a poll tax. The abortive constitution drafted by legislative committee in 1874 allowed the legislature to mandate payment of a poll tax as a prerequisite for voting.[3]

The chief objects of the proposed suffrage qualifications are easily discerned. In seeking appointive officeholding and at-large representation, Democrats from black-majority regions had made no secret of their dismay over "negro rule." The *Galveston Daily News* probably spoke for many in declaring black suffrage a "preposterous experiment" and a "monstrous peril." Shortly after taking office Governor Coke made public note of "forty thousand unenlightened black voters, natural followers, in their simplicity and ignorance, of the unscrupulous trickster and demagogue, in some portions of Texas largely outnumbering the whites, and having equal privileges with them at the ballot box."[4] A poll tax would effectively limit that power, black Texans being far more likely than whites to be impoverished sharecroppers and laborers.[5]

Advocates of suffrage restriction, however, often identified their targets not as African Americans per se but as the "irresponsible" or the "non-taxpaying rabble."[6] Given the watchful eye many northern Republicans continued to cast upon the South, it made sense for Democrats to pay rhetorical obeisance to the Fifteenth Amendment and not agitate too nakedly for racial disfranchisement. But this race-neutral language had also surely been encouraged by the nature of their party's critique of the state's Reconstruction regime. Given the relatively small number of black-majority counties, the rapid growth of the white population outside those counties, the meager proportions of African Americans to whites through much of the state, and the absence of statewide black officeholders, the rhetoric of "negro rule" could not have been, for much of the Democratic constituency, a particularly germane critique of local conditions. While by no means swearing off racist harangues (or in some cases racial violence), Redeemers had often given primacy to fiscal arguments against Reconstruction, stressing the era's sharply higher taxes—allegedly the work of politicians elected by and answering to those whose propertylessness left them exempt from the ad valorem levies that funded much of state and local government. With this critique of Republican "misgovernment," it stood to reason that Democrats, in proposing to eliminate Reconstruction's local vestiges, emphasized the trimming of the power of the poor to impose taxes upon the propertied and debt upon the public. Many may well have equated exclusion of nontaxpayers with racial disfranchisement. Democrats tended to identify propertylessness with African Americans, white people being the "tax-paying element of the country."[7]

But some supporters of suffrage restriction made clear that the transient and propertyless Texans they wished to disfranchise included more than black Republicans, explicitly extending their arguments to include whites. One of the 1875 constitutional convention's most prominent supporters of the poll tax, John Reagan, had years earlier noted the "dangers to be apprehended from allowing all the ignorant negroes and whites to vote." During the convention the *Houston Telegraph* denounced "the low, groveling, equal-before-the-law, lazy, purchasable negro, who pays no taxes," but also asked: "Ought the miserable apologies for men with white skins, who exercise the right to vote only because it furnishes them with whiskey, be allowed to vote, if they don't pay the state a pittance for its protection and the privileges afforded them?" That same year the *San Antonio Herald* worried about universal suffrage reducing "taxpayers ... to a political serfdom ruled by ignorant negroes and worthless whites" and supported the disfranchisement of "the thriftless man, whether he be white or black." Alexander Watkins Terrell, Texas' most persistent advocate of suffrage restriction, was particularly adamant on the subject of black voters but made clear that his ultimate target was "the thriftless, idle and semi-vagrant element of both races."[8]

These white Texans who, with African Americans, were being targeted for disfranchisement in the mid-1870s seem not to have been angry farmers of the sort who later made the "agrarian revolt." At the time the first campaign to impose a poll tax climaxed in Texas in 1875, little existed in the way of an agrarian threat to the Democratic party. Hardscrabble white counties that became strongholds of populism in the 1890s were casting hugely lopsided votes for Democrats. The growing influence of the Grange *within* the party, it is true, distressed some cosmopolitan members. Yet as much as these Democrats might grouse at country bumpkins, the menacing images that would-be disfranchisers conjured up were not of marginal cultivators but of "the 'roughs' and riff-raff"; "the floating and irresponsible, who were here today and elsewhere tomorrow"; "the *gutter snipe-tramp & negro element*."[9] In warning against any very thoroughgoing application of its own party's principle of local self-government, the *Galveston Daily News* shuddered at the prospect both of "Senegambian blight in any place where ignorant blacks predominate" and of "the horrors of the Commune in any place where vicious and turbulent whites have the numerical preponderance."[10]

This image of Paris during the 1790s and 1871 was, of course, a specifically urban one. Certain suffrage reformers pointed to cities and some of the rowdier towns as a focus of this threat to the polity. In supporting measures to restrict the franchise, John Reagan spoke of the need "to protect towns and cities from the floating population." The "loafers and deadbeats" and "drifting multitudes" of the towns and cities likewise made the *Austin Democratic Statesman* nervous. In arguing for suffrage restriction, it pointed to "rabble-ruled communities . . . in which a white mob at one end of a city allied itself with a black rabble at the other," making clear that it feared more than just the freedpeople that had gathered in cities.[11]

The concern expressed about "worthless" whites illustrates the extent to which the movement for suffrage restriction in 1870s Texas not only addressed the South's distinctive circumstances but also participated in broader national currents. By raising up the specter of the "mob," Texas Democrats could sound as much like the genteel reformers of the North appalled by the fractious, class-ridden politics of their own cities as like southern Democrats beset by black citizenship. Echoing the Yankee elite, they invoked the interests of Texas' "best men" and conjured up images of the Paris Commune to express their anxieties about the political mischief propertyless voters might cause. They seconded demands being made in northern journals like *The Nation* and the *New York Times* that taxpayers alone (rather than the voting-age population at large) make decisions governing cities' expenditures.[12]

Except in border towns like Brownsville, there was little evidence in Texas during the 1870s of the highly developed machine politics that bedeviled the mugwump patricians of the North. But like those best men, Texas Redeemers also had to negotiate a political terrain whose ethnic complexities ranged far beyond the classically southern categories of black and white. As noted earlier, there was a significant Latino vote in South Texas, and cities such as Galveston and Houston had become home to a powerful ethnic politics, driven chiefly by German Americans, who either insisted that they be represented on party tickets or ran their own candidates. Yet it does not seem to have been the distinctive presence of a Latino electorate that accounts for the declared interest among some Redeemers in disfranchising whites as well as blacks. Texan racial thinking was such that the transient and propertyless among the Tejano population probably would not have been referred to as white.[13] And (as discussed earlier) the Democrats most immediately concerned seemed to have been more interested in mobilizing this vote than eliminating it. Finally, Tejano voters were not a distinctly urban constituency of the sort focused on by some disfranchisers. Among the largest cities of the state, only San Antonio possessed a sizable Latino electorate. And while that city's Democratic daily echoed the calls to limit the political power of "debased" whites as the crusade for a poll tax was peaking, the paper did not voice much concern over local Latino political activity.[14]

Nor does the presence of numerous European immigrants in Texas cities seem primarily to account for the interest in white disfranchisement. Democrats sometimes grumbled over organizing along ethnic lines.[15] But nativism seems not to have been as central an ingredient of the impulse to restrict the voting privileges of certain white people as it was among members of the Yankee elite, who worried that their cities were being surrendered to immigrant electors and their political bosses. As we have seen, Texas Redeemers behaved more like northern Democrats than northern mugwumps or Republicans in seeking to rally German and Irish voters by invoking a common white brotherhood, accusing Republicans of nativism, and seeking to ease naturalization procedures. At the same time the *Galveston News* shrieked of the horrors of the Commune, it greeted with apparent equanimity the election in 1875 of an immigrant Jewish clothier to the city council.[16] Had immigrant voting per se been the problem, one might expect a literacy qualification to have been offered up as a restrictive mechanism more often than it was. Instead, disfranchisers generally pressed a taxpaying qualification—a device that would reach a wide spectrum of poor Texans but not, for instance, many prosperous Germans.

What seems to have driven some Redeemers to embrace the language of Yankee patricians was that in Texas, as in northern cities, the expansion of a market economy had created large numbers of wage workers unattached to the land but invested with the franchise. The *sudden* growth of an urban laboring class in Texas during the Civil War and Reconstruction set it apart from much of the rest of the South. In the eleven former Confederate states, the percentage of population in urban areas grew from 6.9 percent in 1860 to 8.7 percent in 1880. In Texas the percentage of population in towns and cities more than doubled during the same period, from 4.4 to 9.2 percent. In fact the population boom in urban Texas outpaced even that in the countryside.[17] Entrepôts like Houston, San Antonio, Dallas, and Galveston expanded enormously as railroad construction tied Texas ever more closely to national and international markets. Both Houston's and Galveston's population nearly doubled between 1860 and 1870, while the number of persons census takers counted as engaged in manufacture more than tripled in the counties in which these cities were situated.[18] The growing laboring classes of these rapidly expanding, predominantly mercantile cities were not primarily composed of factory workers, however, but instead those toiling as common laborers; those moving things through the streets and on and off of ships and trains; those working in the building trades as carpenters, bricklayers, and painters; and those laboring on the lowest rungs of the commercial world as clerks. Some of these urban workers were African American, but very many of them were white.[19]

Railroads spawned a sizable working class of their own. With bursts of construction in the early and late 1870s, the number of railroad employees in Texas increased more than ten times—to over 7,300 persons—by the end of that decade.[20] These workers populated not only large cities but also the boom towns that railroads spawned—towns that contemporaries found on occasion to be as boisterous as the roughest city ward. For instance, Luling—known more recently chiefly for its annual "Watermelon Thump"—was in the 1870s a byword for rowdiness and mayhem. Tellingly, the *Austin Democratic Statesman* cited that town, together with Houston and Dallas, as an example of a community menaced by "incapable and ignorant and lawless" voters.[21]

Certain powerful Democrats in these cities and towns found reason to perceive a political threat in this growing working class. The propertylessness and transience that conservatives saw as principal threats to good government were also qualities seemingly identified with urban labor. In distinguishing between "the laboring and tax paying classes," the *Galveston News*, for instance, seemed to define workers as necessarily owning nothing.[22] While these men were almost certainly not as footloose or bereft of taxable possessions as many in the elite seemed to imagine, there does appear to have been a significant number of propertyless adults in Texas cities. In 1875 Dallas County and Harris County, which includes Houston, each had nearly seven hundred voting-age men listed on their rolls as owning no taxable property. Presumably, many more transients escaped the notice of the tax gatherer entirely.[23]

During the Reconstruction era, such propertyless citizens had grown not only in number but also in electoral weight. In Texas, Reconstruction's expansion of the political community had involved not simply black enfranchisement but greater citizenship rights for poor city dwellers too. Through the antebellum and war years and into the era of Presidential Reconstruction, the state's largest cities had limited the political participation of propertyless males, particularly transient bachelors, most commonly by placing various propertyholding or taxpaying qualifications on officeholding, but also, under certain charters by limiting the franchise to property owners and householders.[24] As late as 1866 only householders and owners of at least $100 of real or personal property could vote in Houston elections, while in Galveston one could not serve as mayor or alderman unless he held real estate within the city valued at $3,000 or more. Such qualifications were lifted, however, when the Reconstruction legislature rechartered major cities in 1870–71.[25] The political influence that unrestricted suffrage lent the urban laboring classes might be suggested by the fact that those listed in an 1875 Galveston city directory as laborers, transport and waterfront workers, and members of the building trades would alone account for some 43 percent of the 3,544 citizens who voted in that year's mayoral election. That proportion would increase considerably to the extent that artisans, those engaged in personal services, and clerks were added.[26] In Houston wage earners accounted for over one-fourth of the population by 1880.[27]

Just as Palo Duro followed closely upon the Coke-Davis Imbroglio, Redemption coincided with new expressions of discontent among this enfranchised working class. Texas experienced its first widespread strike, carried out by workers on the Houston & Texas Central Railroad, in 1872, just as Democrats were preparing to reclaim the legislature.[28] Amid the following year's gubernatorial election, Texas cities, like those across the nation, were rocked by the Panic of 1873 and the subsequent economic depression. Reports appeared in state newspapers of layoffs, wage cuts, destitution, and labor discontent.[29] Such turmoil surely enhanced an urban political uncertainty distinct from the concern that black enfranchisement had generated in old plantation communities. Houston Democrats found themselves worrying about the loyalties of their working-class constituents. In the selection of party nominees to the 1875 constitutional convention, the defeat of a candidate said to be popular with "the mechanics and working people" led to expectations of a bolt.[30] The anticipated divisions in a referendum over municipal subsidy of local railroad construction the year before were not between Democrat and Republican but "property holders and solid citizens" on the one hand and "the laboring, non-property-holding, and floating class" on the other (here again wage labor was identified with lack of property and transience).[31] In Austin, despite the city's substantial white majority, Democratic fortunes were undermined during these same years by a persistent factionalism that at least one correspondent attributed to declining party loyalties among working people beset by a depressed economy: "No city in Texas has more sorely felt the hard times than Austin, naturally creating dissatisfaction among the laboring classes who when out of employment and hungry pay no attention to party and will go for the man promising the most bread."[32] Not surprisingly, perhaps, the city's Democratic daily had become a sharp-tongued advocate of suffrage restriction—and one that emphasized the menace of white urban mobs.

Galveston, the state's largest city in the 1870s, best suggests how a burgeoning working class could disorder Democratic politics and how this—and not simply the concern to contain the electoral power of African Americans in plantation counties—might occasion a desire to restrict access to the ballot box. The city's Democratic organization was fractured by battles between a group led by Roger L. Fulton, a somewhat footloose newspaperman, and the so-called Strand Democracy, which was identified with the city's commercial elite (the Strand being a main thoroughfare in Galveston's business district). Both factions subordinated the partisan enmities of Reconstruction to their crusade against local intraparty enemies. After having lost out at nominating conventions, the Strand group bolted in the 1873 municipal elections, and Fulton's allies did the same in the 1876 county and district races. In both cases the bolters ultimately triumphed by teaming up with local Republicans.

The *Galveston News* itself could not really identify how the Strand Democracy and Fulton's followers differed on matters of policy, but Democrats of every stripe described the fault line in the language of class—the result of the arraying of "capital against labor" and the growing chasm "between the rich men and the poor."[33] Fulton's supporters derided the Strand faction, which in 1873 had nominated the president of a steamship company to oppose Fulton for the mayoralty, as "Monopolists." Fulton himself noted the opposition he provoked among the well off but insisted that "men who parted their names in the middle, wore swallow-tailed coats, always carried gold headed canes and always wore black kid gloves could not run the Democracy of Galveston."[34]

The Strand faction responded in kind, calling upon Galveston's property owners and taxpayers to rally themselves. In fact, the Fulton faction was far from exclusively a party of the dispossessed. At the bitterly divided county Democratic convention of 1876, delegates supporting the Fulton candidate for sheriff included several prominent attorneys as well as a factory superintendent.[35] But in suggesting the specific threat that their rivals posed, Strand men attacked their fellow Democrats with the same taxpayers rhetoric that their party had wielded against the Reconstruction regime: "To expect men who have their means invested in real estate, or who are engaged in the various enterprises which go to make up the commercial and financial institutions of

BEYOND REDEMPTION

the city, to sit idly by and see the management of municipal affairs pass under control of men whose only interest is in assessing and collecting taxes, no part of which they are called on to pay, would be simply absurd." A newspaper correspondent called on taxpayers to oppose candidates who manipulated "the votes of longshoremen, Dagos and negroes, who are thus made to control the city election without paying scarcely a dollar of taxes."[36]

Strand Democrats applied to workers of all colors a lesson that Reconstruction had hammered home with respect to freedpeople specifically. Universal manhood suffrage meant that men who paid little or nothing in ad valorem or license taxes might nevertheless play a large role in selecting the officers who would levy taxes upon the propertied and apportion the wealth thus expropriated.

But more than the prospect of redistributive politics seems to have quickened interest among urban elites in suffrage restriction. The working-class vote acquired a special significance because city elites were themselves divided. At the same time it raged about the menace of the propertyless, the *Galveston News*—an organ of the mercantile elite—wielded an equally fierce rhetorical battle against the local wharf company.[37] In Texas' rapidly developing urban areas, different factions within the business classes might compete among themselves not only for commercial advantage but also for public resources in the form of city contracts, franchises, or patronage. Leading citizens might also disagree over whether their own or their community's interests were better served by the city holding the line on debt and taxes or by further investment in public services and infrastructure in pursuit of even more rapid economic development. Accordingly, political bloodletting in Texas cities during the postbellum years was often occasioned by clashing interests or agendas *within* the entrepreneurial classes. Amid these sorts of divisions, working-class voters might provide the margin of victory to one or the other of the competing factions. In Houston and Dallas during the 1880s and 1890s, certain members of the business and professional communities broke with their brethren and made common cause with politically active working-class constituencies to back candidates with progressive developmental agendas. In Dallas, at least, these divisions clearly heightened interest in disfranchising propertyless and transient whites.[38] Suffrage restriction could be a means of preventing rivals within the elite from using the "floating" vote to their own ends—for instance to perpetuate a city government that awarded them and their friends lucrative franchises.

But whether urban conservatives were authentically appalled by the prospect of a Texas Commune or chiefly seeking to disarm their elite rivals, the problem remained essentially the same: the electoral power that universal suffrage had extended to propertyless or transient urban laborers, white as well as black. In the same 1874 session during which John Ireland pressed a poll tax, legislators attempted to create the sort of taxpayer veto over local expenditures advocated by some of the North's "best men." It passed a bill requiring that a majority of ad valorem taxpayers approve municipal spending that exceeded certain limits. Governor Coke felt compelled to veto the measure, finding that the state's constitution "treats all men as equal, as respects the question of suffrage, and leaves no discretion with the Legislature, to make distinctions between those who have, and those who have not property."[39] Redeemers' rewriting of the constitution would allow just such distinctions to be reintroduced into urban government while providing an opportunity to circumscribe the voting rights of African Americans.

The legacies of emancipation and urban growth would drive some Texas Redeemers to seek to abridge another privilege of citizenship. Proposals to redefine the electorate often came paired with calls to restrict the pool of jurors. The *Austin Democratic Statesman* deemed the "purification" of the jury system "quite as indispensable as that of the ballot box."[40]

In Texas, petit jurors dispensed justice to members of their communities, not only determining guilt and innocence but also sentencing those who had been convicted. Grand juries brought indictments and also exercised a more general oversight of the community, inquiring into matters of public concern, including in Galveston County in 1873 the adequacy of local anti-prostitution efforts (jurors recommended decriminalization).[41]

The state's 1869 constitution had provided for as broad access to the jury box as to the ballot box, defining all qualified voters as qualified jurors. The Reconstruction legislature directed that petit and grand jurors be selected at random from a list of county voters.[42] This promise of equal access was not always kept. African Americans sometimes complained of being kept off panels by county authorities.[43] Still, in many places the jury system proved to be remarkably open. Black Texans passed judgment on their neighbors not only in black-majority counties but also in places where white people outnumbered them, such as in Galveston, Houston, and Jefferson County. Even after the downfall of Reconstruction, W. P. Ballinger encountered black jurors in Galveston and nearby plantation counties. And Latino juries were the rule in certain Rio Grande counties.[44] This open jury system made many Democrats distinctly unhappy. It obviously irritated them that, as in the case of universal manhood suffrage, people they regarded as incompetent and

BEYOND REDEMPTION

irresponsible could make vital decisions regarding life, liberty, and property. Their tirades were often directed at African Americans, "Fifteenth Amendment jurors."[45] But, as in the case of voting rights, metropolitan newspapers sometimes explicitly extended their complaints to include "lazy whites" and "white vagabonds." In insisting that "the exclusion of the negro from the jury box is not enough," the *Austin Democratic Statesman* suggested: "We have suffered republicanism in America to go mad."[46]

Democrats' demands that the jury pool, in John Reagan's words, be "purged of ignorance and vice," seem most often to have anticipated exclusion of the illiterate.[47] As soon as their party took control of the Texas legislature in early 1873, Redeemers attempted to establish a literacy requirement for jury service. But Republicans still controlled enough seats in the senate to block a constitutional amendment to that effect. Democrats, however, did manage to pass a bill (by a strictly party-line vote in the senate) that allowed them to use their control of many county governments to affect the composition of grand juries. Under the new law petit jurors would continue to be drawn at random, but the county court and district clerk would handpick grand jurors.[48] A report from Houston the following spring suggests the power this gave local Democratic officials: "There is not a single negro on the Grand Jury at this term. During the late administration it was usual to put on four darkies, at least." But the law offered little of value to Democrats in districts in which Republicans still elected officeholders.[49]

Demands that the Constitutional Convention of 1875 recast citizenship thus were driven by the desire of white conservatives in Texas' relative handful of black-majority counties to be rid of "negro rule," by class divisions among white (and often Democratic) urban voters of the sort found in many Gilded Age American cities, and by a sense on the part of some Democrats that the state's jury system was too egalitarian. But the delegates did not serve these concerns equally well. Much of the support for suffrage restriction at the convention seems to have come from those wishing to rein in the electoral power of black and Republican voters, but the body ended up doing more to pacify urban politics.

Early in the proceedings DeWitt and Bexar county delegates submitted resolutions that the Committee on Suffrage consider limiting voting to those who had paid a poll tax or to those who had paid all the state and county taxes they owed. The committee complied, sending a suffrage article to the floor that provided that prospective voters "shall have paid all poll taxes due by him to the State and county."[50]

Yet the poll tax came to naught, dying at the hands of other Democrats. The convention accepted by a three-to-one margin a substitute for the relevant section of the suffrage article containing no such qualification upon the franchise. The convention then scuttled several attempts to reinsert a poll tax. Thirty-six Democrats (and eight Republicans) voted to table the most unembellished of these amendments, while twenty-seven party members (and one white Republican) opposed tabling. An ordinance that would have allowed the electorate to decide whether the legislature should be empowered to impose a taxpaying qualification on suffrage was tabled too.[51] In the end, the Redeemer constitution mimicked the Reconstruction document in authorizing poll taxes but not making voting contingent on their payment.

Democratic delegates explained their opposition to the poll tax variously. Some argued from republican principle. The "inevitable tendency" of such a restriction, declared B. D. Martin, a Hunt County farmer, "must in time result in transferring the political power of the State into the hands of the wealthy alone, and thus consign to slavery men who were made free and independent in the image of God." Others cited tradition: advocates of the tax were pressing a limitation upon the franchise that white Texans had never known, white manhood suffrage, except in municipal voting, having been the rule in Texas since its days as a republic. Still others saw fit to allude to the state's frontier and borderlands heritage: "To say that the men who rescue this land from barbarism; to say that the old, tottering veteran who struck down despotism; to see that man tremblingly approach the ballot box to exercise the right which he has purchased with his blood, and to tell him that he cannot vote because he has not a dollar in his pocket to pay his poll tax, is monstrous."[52]

Contemporaries tended to believe that Democratic opposition to the poll tax came from members of the Patrons of Husbandry, who made up about half of the party delegation to the convention. Immediately after the votes, the *Democratic Statesman* caused a stir by charging that more than thirty Grangers had conspired with Republican delegates to kill the poll tax. Patrons and Republicans both denied the charges, other newspapers quickly dismissed them, and the convention's rather desultory investigation failed to confirm the existence of any formal cooperation.[53] Yet there has been a tendency among scholars to follow the *Statesman* in identifying Grangers as the Democrats responsible for the defeat of the poll tax and for the shaping of the constitution more generally. Historian Seth McKay baldly asserts: "The Democratic opposition to the majority report making a poll tax qualification for suffrage came almost entirely from the Grangers." Subsequent scholars have taken him at his word.[54] The roll call votes tell a different story, though. Fourteen of the thirty-six Democrats opposing the poll tax on the most definitive vote were not Grangers, nor was Lipscomb Norvell, who introduced the substitute striking the tax. And although a significant majority of Grange-affiliated delegates did indeed oppose the poll-tax qualification, thirteen of twenty-eight delegates supporting it in a crucial vote seem to have been Patrons, including one of the men most identified with suffrage restriction—John Reagan.[55]

Rather than Grange affiliation, Democratic delegates' position on the poll tax seems to have been driven by political circumstances at home. In general terms, poll-tax advocates at the convention—Grangers and non-Grangers alike—more frequently hailed from counties where the Republican party had done unusually well in the last general election. The median Republican percentage in 1873 gubernatorial balloting had been 40 percent in the home counties of poll-tax Democrats—distinctly higher than E. J. Davis's statewide average of approximately 33 percent. Seventeen of the Democrats who participated in the convention's most definitive vote on the poll tax came from counties in which Republicans had scored 40 percent or higher in 1873. Fourteen of them backed suffrage restriction.[56] Democrats opposing the tax, however, tended to come from secure counties, the Republican median at the last general election being about 21 percent. The greater tendency of Grangers than non-Grange Democrats to oppose suffrage restriction probably stemmed chiefly from the fact that these delegates tended more often than their non-Grange peers to come from uncontested counties.[57]

As with appointive officeholding and at-large elections, Democratic delegates from politically noncompetitive, predominantly rural counties stood to reap no immediate rewards from suffrage restriction, given their party's pre-eminence both at the local and state level and the absence of an internal threat from a turbulent urban electorate. Furthermore, many of them had reason to regard the poll tax as actually detrimental to party interests. Some thought that, like Reconstruction-era voter registration, it would offend Democrats' sensibilities by requiring them to abase themselves before election officials in order to exercise their rights as citizens. Dallas's John Henry Brown became particularly agitated on this score, one newspaper reporting: "MR. BROWN said he was pregnant with a speech and desired to be delivered. He said there were three things he hated, the jailor of Napoleon on St. Helena, the registration law, and the infamous police bill under Governor Davis. And now, when they had gotten rid of the registration act, should they pass a law similar in effect, forcing every man to carry his pass in his hand? The people would curse them from one end of the land to the other."[58]

But the poll tax might also actually bar some white-county Democrats from the polls. Overwhelmingly white and Democratic counties—often represented by Grangers and frequently situated on the blackland prairie or in West Central Texas—were at some point in the process of shifting from open-range stockraising or the cultivation of grain and food crops for local consumption to more intensive cotton production for distant markets.[59] White herdsmen and cultivators, whether largely self-sufficient or engaged in commercial production, routinely might not have had enough cash on hand to make even a one-dollar poll tax very easily borne, given oft-depressed staple prices, the reliance of cotton farmers on credit, and the existing ad valorem tax burden. J. Morgan Kousser has demonstrated how vulnerable cultivators might have been to disfranchisement, estimating that per capita income of residents of the former Confederate states in 1880 was only eighty-six dollars. The *cash* income of farmers, particularly those caught up in the crop-lien system, would likely have been considerably less than that. At the convention, delegate W. T. G. Weaver pointed out that in his North Texas district, propertyless transients were not the only people who might lose their right to vote to a poll tax. Referring to recent hard times, he alluded to "numbers of the most respectable citizens who had not a dollar in their pockets and could not afford to enjoy the luxury of a cup of tea."[60]

With the Greenback and Populist insurgencies of later years, shrinking the electorate in certain white-majority counties might serve Democratic interests. But in the early and mid-1870s, those white farmers were among the Texas Democracy's most loyal constituents. The poll tax was too blunt an instrument to strike at its intended targets—African Americans and the rowdies and rounders of towns and cities—without also injuring citizens few Democrats wanted to keep from the polls.

Democrats found that they could reconcile their differences over suffrage when it came to more targeted measures aimed explicitly at those too poor or footloose to pay property taxes while exempting hardscrabble cultivators. The convention embraced restrictive devices that urban conservatives, including William P. Ballinger of Galveston, Jacob Waelder of San Antonio, and Charles West of Austin, pursued more avidly than (or even instead of) a poll tax—that is, specific limitations upon the electoral power of poorer city dwellers.[61] Delegates initially balked at an article restricting voting in towns and cities to men who had paid all taxes due the municipality and allowing only freeholders to vote "for the creation of debt for the improvement of such town or city, or for other purpose." But when Charles DeMorse, an outspoken opponent of a poll tax, proposed a more carefully drawn substitute guaranteeing male residents of incorporated cities and towns the right to vote for municipal officeholders but allowing only local property owners to vote in elections "to determine the expenditure of money or the assumption of debt," the measure passed by a three-to-one margin. Along with the nearly unanimous backing of poll-tax supporters, the DeMorse proposal won the support of some two-thirds of Democrats who had voted to discard a statewide poll tax.[62] The convention also provided that any school tax cities and towns chose to levy be approved by a two-thirds vote of taxpayers.[63]

While hardly as comprehensive as most suffrage reformers seemed to desire, the winnowing of the population eligible to participate in bond elections went to the heart of urban politics. In many cases the bonded debt of Texas cities had climbed considerably during Reconstruction. In subsequent years these frontier municipalities continued to grow rapidly, creating further demand for the expansion of basic public services. A central public-policy issue was the extent to which city resources would be applied to paying existing debt, to serving immediate needs through the enhancement of urban services, or to pursuing additional developmental projects to accelerate local growth.[64] The electoral limitations mandated by the Redeemer convention allowed the propertied additional authority in determining to which of these purposes their wealth would be put while preventing the manipulation of the "floating" vote when they divided on these matters. The "laboring, non-propertyholding" class could not block developmental projects, on the one hand, or, on the other, saddle cities with bonded debt that property owners alone would have to pay through their taxes.

If white-county Democrats proved less resistant to restrictions on urban voting than to a statewide poll tax, so too did they accede to jury "reform." Very early in the proceedings, a Democrat from black-majority Matagorda County offered a resolution to exclude all those who could not read and write English from Texas juries. Such efforts faced the determined opposition of Republicans, who sought to maintain the Reconstruction standard of allowing all eligible voters to serve as jurors. The Democratic delegation stood equally united on the other side. While proponents of suffrage restriction had often in the same breath called for "purification" of the jury box, Democratic opponents of the poll tax apparently did not see the issues as necessarily linked. None of them raised any objection to jury restriction on the floor of the convention, and one, DeMorse, explicitly endorsed excluding the illiterate.[65]

The convention thus eliminated the constitutional guarantee that all voters could serve as jurors, leaving it to the legislature to establish qualifications for jury service. Democratic lawmakers wasted no time in imposing a literacy restriction. They were led by State Sen. Alexander W. Terrell, a Travis County lawyer who in subsequent years would also spearhead renewed efforts to impose a poll-tax qualification for voting.[66] The law passed in 1876 required jurors—"so far as practicable"—to be literate except in communities where a sufficient number of literate citizens were not to be found. But it also employed other means to render the jury system less open and egalitarian, giving local officials greater latitude in excluding even the literate. Rather than having jurors drawn by lot, it provided that district judges (which the convention, as we have seen, went to some pains to ensure would be Democrats) and county judges would appoint three "intelligent" citizens who would handpick citizens "of good moral character, of sound judgment," and "well-informed" to compose the pool of potential jurors.[67]

The consequences of the law could be easily predicted. Over three-quarters of the state's adult black males could not write in 1880, compared to less than one-ninth of their white counterparts.[68] While county governments still in Republican hands might impanel literate black citizens, the new law had a markedly restrictive effect even in these communities. Donald Nieman has found not only that the numbers of black petit and grand jurors in Washington County substantially declined after 1876 but also that the class background of African Americans who did serve changed. Prior to the literacy requirement, a majority of black grand jurors had been laborers. Subsequently, they tended to be professionals and artisans and more frequently mulattos.[69] While careful studies do not exist for other Texas communities, the results of the 1876 law was unquestionably far more profound in the vast majority of counties where white Democrats controlled jury selection. Within seven years of white conservatives redeeming black-majority Harrison County, for instance, a local paper reported that African Americans no longer served on juries.[70] Testimony from a number of court proceedings around the turn of the century in which black defendants challenged indictments or convictions on the grounds that their African American peers had been kept off grand or petit juries indicates that since the 1870s, even qualified black citizens had been routinely excluded in counties as varied as Grayson, Harris, Galveston, Tarrant, and El Paso.[71] African Americans must have felt this exclusion deeply, for the issue repeatedly surfaced in political campaigns dominated by or aimed at black Texans. In the early 1880s, Republican platforms contained planks challenging the

Democrats' jury laws. In the 1890s Texas Populists soliciting black support often promised equal access to the jury box.[72]

The extent to which the 1876 law worked to keep the white "rabble" off juries is not immediately clear. In 1870, census enumerators had found several hundred white males of voting age unable to write in each of a number of firmly Democratic counties, including Collin, Hood, Hopkins, Hunt, and Kaufman.[73] And by 1890 Texas courts were interpreting the law's requirement that jurors be freeholders or "householders" as excluding propertyless males who were not heads of families.[74] The Redeemer laws also affected justice in the state's less "southern" precincts, for courts interpreted them to disqualify those who could not understand, read, and write English as opposed to German or Spanish. In at least one Rio Grande county, though, court proceedings continued for a time to be translated for Spanish-speaking jurors. When called to task by higher courts, the county's district judge explained, "this being a sparsely populated country, the test of reading and writing had been dispensed with."[75]

If efforts to secure a poll-tax restriction, appointive officeholding, and at-large voting failed in these early years of Democratic restoration, urban conservatives and those in black-majority counties had been able, in the case of jury service and the municipal franchise, to begin to reverse Reconstruction's expansion of the political community. These Democrats were not inclined to look on the bright side, however. The convention's work proved to be controversial, so much so that Democratic leaders found that they could not make support of this Redeemer constitution a test of party loyalty or include an endorsement of it in the party's 1876 platform.[76] Democrats found various reasons to dislike their new constitution, but many of the expressions of dissatisfaction focused on the elective judiciary and universal male suffrage; the critics, in essence, aggrieved that the party had not used its power at the state level to contain the threat posed in some localities by opposition constituencies. Even some of the constitution's most prominent supporters acknowledged its failure in this regard. Governor Coke called for its ratification but also its quick amendment to provide for a poll tax qualification on voting and an appointive judiciary.[77]

In February 1876, Texans approved the Redeemer constitution by a large margin (136,606 to 56,652), but at least 14,000 Democrats who voted in the same election to reelect Governor Coke failed to support it. Some appear simply to have shrugged off the ratification referendum. But in many counties the vote against the constitution exceeded the vote for the Republican gubernatorial candidate, the much-harassed Judge William Chambers, indicating that some Democrats joined Republicans in actually seeking its defeat. Suggesting the role that universal suffrage and elective officeholding played in this dissatisfaction, anti-ratification votes considerably outnumbered Chambers votes in a number of black-majority counties—Matagorda, Brazoria, Marion, and Washington. Other counties that seem to evidence unusually high numbers of Democrats opposing the constitution—Fayette, Bastrop, Robertson, and Victoria—had white majorities but also relatively large black populations, atypically competitive Republican minorities, and convention delegates who had supported a poll tax. The largest numbers of Democratic anti-ratification votes, however, appear to have come from a number of Texas cities. Total anti-ratification votes exceeded the Republican vote for governor by 1,294 in Harris County (Houston), 746 in Galveston County, and 490 in Bexar County (San Antonio).[78]

Cosmopolitan Democrats had a number of reasons to be unhappy with the constitution. But as much as any other element, metropolitan newspapers complained of its provisions for unrestricted suffrage and an elective judiciary. The *Galveston News* steamed: "Nothing, not even the straightest and most patent processes of centralization, could tend more directly to the wreck of our republican institutions than the application of the principle of local self-government to local sub-divisions where circumstances are essentially unsuited to its safe exercise." The *Austin Democratic Statesman* was not reassured by the limitations placed on the franchise of the urban propertyless, arguing that while taxpayers alone could vote on the expenditure of municipal money, they would never consent to paying for railroads, hospitals, or sewers as long as "rabble-chosen thieves, . . . the *products* of universal suffrage," would handle the funds.[79]

The constitution's ratification can be seen as the close of Redemption's second act—one marked by the Democrats' conflicted efforts to extend their authority in the judiciary and at the local level. The party had secured a hegemony at the state and district level that would endure through much of the twentieth century and had written a constitution that, though much amended, would remain in force in the twenty-first century. Yet the very success of Redemption's first round—the capture of the state government—had restrained the party from pressing its advantages during the second, at least to the extent that Redeemer elites in cities and black-majority counties desired. The very security most Texas Democrats enjoyed made the fate of the state's more contested communities a less momentous problem, something that they would not sacrifice their own political privileges to address.

The pattern established at the 1875 convention persisted through the next quarter century. Lawmakers repeatedly turned back efforts to provide for statewide suffrage restriction. In 1879 the legislature did pass a law requiring that ballots be printed on plain white paper with no identifying mark by which illiterates might distinguish among party tickets. But that year and through the 1880s and 1890s, lawmakers shot down the poll-tax proposals of A. W. Terrell and his allies, though not always as decisively as had the constitutional convention.[80]

But the Democrats of black-majority areas had hardly been left defenseless. They profited from gerrymandering and various checks on locally elected officeholders. And holding the lion's share of community resources, they could make their power felt without question. In some places it seems, their patronage and control over bonds allowed them to arrive at mutually beneficial accommodations with potential opposition leaders. "Fusion" arrangements divided the spoils, allowing white Democrats to hold certain county offices and ceding others to Republicans by prior agreement.[81] Some black Texans almost certainly voted freely for Democrats—because they found that party more attuned to their material interests; because they were disillusioned with a Republican party that took their vote for granted; or simply because they thought it wise to side with their communities' most powerful white men.[82] But the control the white elite exercised over local land, labor, and commerce also allowed Democrats to dictate certain black voters' political choices. A Republican leader declared that in his county, "colored people that the Democrats hire for wages, the male portion of them, as a general rule, are compelled, under threat of losing their positions, to vote the Democratic ticket."[83] A Louisiana man bragged to the Democratic gubernatorial candidate in 1878: "I have quite a vote I can cast in the shape of a negro element on my plantation in Texas, all of which you shall have the benefit of."[84]

Yet a number of black-majority counties continued to sport active Republican organizations and a critical mass of less pliable black voters. In such circumstances, having failed to secure suffrage restriction or appointive officeholding, Democrats resorted to more desperate expedients to solidify the sort of authority in their own communities that they had probably expected to win upon Reconstruction's collapse. In the twenty years following the constitutional convention, they would fight a protracted third round of Redemption.

This third round would involve county-by-county efforts to displace unsympathetic officeholders and nullify opposition majorities, Democrats' operating principle being "by any means necessary." By the end of the 1880s in a number of important instances, and by the beginning of the twentieth century in virtually every case, citadels of Republican and third-party strength had been reduced by fraud, intimidation, or outright violence. Harrison County was an early casualty. As discussed in the preceding chapter, a "Citizens party" led by white conservatives had used the incorrect placement of a ballot box in 1878 to accomplish what historian Randolph Campbell has labeled a "virtual *coup d'état.*" Two years later the conservatives won outright majorities, but forty-five members of the Citizens party subsequently pled guilty in federal court to election violations. Initially, the Citizens party made an effort to court black voters, but by the 1880s it increasingly excluded them from its primaries. Eventually, party members went so far as to expel ten prominent African Americans from the county. The effect of their efforts is apparent in Democratic gubernatorial candidates' sweep of the county in 1884 and 1892, though Republican presidential candidates won healthy majorities (conservatives were leery of tampering with federal elections and had little reason to since their state and congressional district would inevitably go Democratic).[85]

Democrats in other counties followed suit. Local circumstance dictated the timing of their emergence, but by the end of the century, virtually all black-majority counties sported political organizations like the Citizens party. Such groups—the Jaybird Democratic Association in Fort Bend, the White Man's Union in Wharton and Grimes, the Tax Payers' Union in Brazoria, and the Citizens' White Primary in Marion—pledged members to support the organization's nominees, selected in white primaries, and promised to shun any white politicking independently of the group.[86] But Redemption could not have been achieved by the mere establishment of white man's parties and white primaries had those counties' African American electorates remained cohesive and active and had opposition parties remained in place.[87] The establishment of white men's organizations frequently coincided with the destruction of their opposition's local political infrastructure. In a number of counties, local opposition leaders were driven from their communities or simply murdered. In 1886, after black Republicans shot a white man participating in raids on Washington County polling places, three of them were lynched. Shortly thereafter, Democrats forced several white Republican leaders to flee the county. One later told the U.S. Senate that several hundred black voters had likewise been run out of the county.[88] In both Grimes and Fort Bend, the assassination or expulsion of local black leaders was followed by dramatic courthouse shootouts that left leading white enemies of local conservatives either dead, badly wounded, or thoroughly convinced that it was time to get out (as well, it seems, by the exodus of a good number of black residents of both counties). The assassination of a Populist sheriff and a subsequent courthouse siege similarly finished off third-party rule in white-majority but firmly Populist San Augustine County.[89]

These developments did not go entirely unchallenged. Until the inauguration of Grover Cleveland in 1885, northern Republicans controlled the appointment of federal judges, attorneys, and marshals, who might on occasion interest themselves in civil rights and voting rights cases in the South. The early years of Redeemer rule thus saw a number of Texans indicted under the Enforcement Acts for violations that included "bulldozing" voters.[90] Likewise, many of the most spectacular attacks on local Republican organizations brought federal action. After the 1878 elections in Harrison County, five Citizens party members stood trial for interfering with black citizens' right to vote. The 1886 election violence in Washington County yielded not only an investigation by the U.S. Senate but also federal prosecution. Two of the black leaders driven from Fort Bend in 1888 had their day in federal court. One, Charles Ferguson, won a substantial out-of-court settlement. Yet judges and juries in Texas typically proved none too eager to punish voting-rights violations. Most of the cases ended in verdicts of not guilty (including the 1878 Harrison County and 1886 Washington County cases) or brought only nominal fines.[91]

Despite this occasional federal interference, Democratic elites by 1900 had established their political dominance in black-majority counties in a piecemeal and extralegal fashion—not with the aid of the state but *despite* the universal suffrage and local self-government enshrined in the Redeemer constitution. In the same decades, urban conservatives similarly extended their authority but did so, by contrast, with considerable help from other Democrats.

The Redeemer constitution's exclusion of the propertyless from municipal-bond and school-tax elections had not entirely quelled turbulent factionalism and complex class politics in many of the state's major cities. With its lingering power to elect local officeholders, the urban rank and file continued to discomfit and divide the Democratic leadership. Republican Jacob DeGress, the *bête noire* of Democrats while head of the Reconstruction school system, won reelection as Austin's mayor in 1877 when pitted against both a regular Democrat and a "Workingmen's" candidate.[92] In Houston a labor-supported candidate defeated incumbent Democratic mayor and business leader William Baker in 1886. In Galveston, party lines continued to be confounded through the later 1870s and 1880s, with R. L. Fulton cultivating alliances with black Republicans, most notably Norris Wright Cuney, the ranking African American in the state GOP; Cuney himself served during the 1880s as a city alderman from a white-majority district.[93] The emergence of statewide third-party and independent reform efforts complicated urban politics as well. Dissident Greenbackers helped elect mayors in Dallas and Austin. In the mid-1880s Knights of Labor and supporters of the Farmers Alliance made common cause in Fort Worth, electing an antimonopoly mayor who served several terms.[94] In neighboring Dallas organized labor and nascent Populists participated in an Independent coalition that in the early 1890s kept the local Democratic organization at bay—at least for a while.[95]

Amid this persistent contention, legislators, like convention delegates in 1875, aided cities with devices that they refused to impose on the state as a whole, including property qualifications for officeholding, voter registration, the secret ballot, and at-large elections. As early as 1876 the legislature passed a charter for Dallas stipulating that its mayor and aldermen be owners of real estate within the city. Similar provisions were inserted into Houston's charter in the 1880s. The reimposition of property qualifications certainly shrank the pool of potential officeholders—by 1890 fewer than one-third of families living in Texas cities with 8,000 or more residents owned their own homes.[96] An 1891 law targeted the electoral power of transient citydwellers in another manner. Applying only to cities with 10,000 or more inhabitants, the law stipulated that when someone's right to vote was challenged at the polls, election judges would not accept his vote unless "he proves by the oath of one well known resident of the ward, that he is a qualified voter at such election and in such ward." In the Dallas municipal elections of that year, the law yielded several hundred challenges. Alicia Rodriquez has found that of the challenged voters who can be identified, the large majority were either African Americans or white workers.[97]

Shortly afterward, the legislature authorized voter registration in the state's largest cities. During Reconstruction, Democrats had vehemently attacked voter registration as degrading and subject to political manipulation. Accordingly, the 1875 constitutional convention prohibited this practice, though there had been some support for exempting large cities from the ban (and thus, said one delegate, stand by "the men who owned property" in them).[98] In 1891, however, voters approved a constitutional amendment pressed by Dallas Democrats in the wake of the defeat of the party's mayoral candidate largely by the vote of heavily black and working-class white precincts. The measure permitted registration in the largest cities only.[99] Subsequent legislation allowed the establishment of voter registration in cities of 10,000 or more provided that 500 citizens in a city petitioned for such. A secret-ballot measure—originally introduced by a black-belt Democrat and intended to apply to the state at large—was incorporated into the law, its operation likewise restricted to the largest cities. Communities immediately subject to these measures of the early 1890s included Dallas, Galveston, Houston, Austin, Laredo, San Antonio, El Paso, Fort Worth, Denison, and Waco.[100] Significantly, few of these cities appear to have had powerful Republican organizations. Between 1876 and 1890 no Republican gubernatorial candidate carried *any* of the counties in which these cities were situated. In only two, Houston and Waco, did African Americans represent more than about 20 percent of the male voting-age population. Clearly, different political problems were being addressed by these laws than the ones plaguing Democrats in old plantation counties.[101]

Scholars have documented how voter registration and "Australian" ballot (requiring voting in secret using official ballots rather than party tickets) measures operated—and were intended—to restrict suffrage. They made the greatest demands on certain classes of voters, making it harder for illiterate citizens to cast their ballots freely and establishing prerequisites to the exercise of the franchise that might easily be neglected by the transient.[102] While these changes certainly addressed very real problems familiar to any student of Gilded Age politics—including multiple voting and voter intimidation—such abuses in Texas were widespread in the countryside as well as in urban areas. Yet registration and the secret ballot were instituted in cities alone. Their effect appears to have been variable. A careful study of San Antonio shows that registration produced no immediate decline in voter turnout in that city, while another of Dallas suggests registration and the secret ballot were factors in the pacification of municipal politics, keeping people away from the polls or nullifying the votes of those who had failed to cast them by the letter of the new laws.[103]

The shift toward at-large elections—similarly targeted only at cities—also pacified urban politics. When in the early rounds of Redemption some Democrats had sought to have officeholders elected across larger, and presumably more Democratic, expanses, the many party supporters living in politically secure counties had refused to sacrifice their own constituents' preferences for local self-government. But when at-large elections could be imposed on urban areas by means of municipal incorporation laws and not on the state as a whole, resistance to them diminished. As early as 1885 Galvestonians apparently targeting Norris Wright Cuney had persuaded the legislature to replace ward-by-ward election of alderman with a system by which councilmen would represent wards but be elected by the city as a whole. Galveston partially restored ward election in 1891. But in 1895—prompted, it seems, by the city's business community—lawmakers revised the charters of not only Galveston but also Houston, as well as the general laws for municipal incorporation, to mandate at-large alderman elections. This worked to the decided advantage of Texas' "best men," for as a prominent Houstonian later put it, a successful citywide candidate must be of "sufficient standing and reputation to be known throughout the body of the city as a fit man." Certain occupational and ethnic groups often concentrated in specific districts, and politicians who might command majorities in those neighborhoods but not citywide would thereafter be excluded from municipal government. Under the at-large system, Galveston, whose wards had continued for two decades after the end of Reconstruction to elect black and white working-class alder-men, all but eliminated African American representation in its governing bodies and reduced white laborers' electoral clout as well.[104]

The city-commission system, adopted in the following decade, is usually counted as a "Progressive" reform. It brought greater efficiency to certain of these cities and undeniable improvements in local finance and public services. But in many respects it also realized conservative ambitions dating from the 1870s. The system not only institutionalized at-large election of aldermen but also in many cases rendered previously elected municipal offices appointive. The system emerged in Galveston in the aftermath of the devastating hur-ricane of 1900 and quickly spread to Houston, Dallas, Fort Worth, Austin, and El Paso. Commission government was typically the pet project of these cities' businessmen and typically opposed by organized labor.[105]

The "Galveston" system would come to govern cities across the nation, securing Texas' place on the cutting edge of a national reaction against rough-and-tumble urban democracy. The state since the 1870s had imposed on its cities just the sort of restrictive devices that "reformers" of the urban North cherished: taxpaying qualifications on municipal voting, at-large representa-tion, the secret ballot, and voter registration. Yet Texas at the same time was slower than other former Confederate states to arrive at statewide de jure disfranchisement. From the very moment Redemption made it a possibil-ity, some Texas Democrats had pursued suffrage restriction for the classic "southern" reasons, wishing to strike at African American voters, thus hob-bling Republican strength and ending "negro rule" in black-majority counties. But the frontier dynamism of its demographic and economic growth and the declining proportions of African Americans to total population had retarded progress in Texas toward statewide suffrage restriction. Democrats hesitated when it came to restrictive mechanisms that could not be implemented selectively and thus might discommode some party voters in politically secure areas. Only as the political reliability of rural white-majority counties began to diminish late in the nineteenth century did Texas as a whole begin to catch up with its cities in limiting the political power of certain classes of citizens.

PART 2

~

The Political Economy
of Redemption

4

Retrenchment, Development, and the Politics of Public Land

T exas Redeemers argued over more than just the lengths they had to go to secure their power. They also divided over the ends that power would serve. Many Texans demanded that state and local government act to advance their material interests. The state itself had enormous needs. Deciding whether and how government would address those interests and needs would produce just as much conflict among Democrats as the question of suffrage or an elective judiciary.

Democrats did display a certain single-mindedness, though. Like other southern Redeemers, they served the interests of white landowning farmers. Their actions demonstrated the very real consequences of Redemption for daily life when Democrats revised landlord-tenant laws, handing landowners more authority over the growing ranks of tenant farmers and sharecroppers. Redeemers enhanced the lien landlords held for their tenants' rent and supplies and gave them effective control of their renters' entire harvest—not simply, as under earlier laws, a portion equivalent to what they were owed or the specific crops (for example, cotton or corn) in which rent was to be paid.[1]

As soon as they took control of the legislature, Democrats attempted to rewrite landlord-tenant laws, passing a bill by an essentially party-line vote. But a Republican still held the governorship, and he not only vetoed the bill but also attempted to make it an issue in the subsequent general election, terming the effort an attempt "to legislate in favor of the rich men against the poor of all classes and colors."[2] The following year, though their party now held the governorship, Democrats passed a somewhat less onerous bill, perhaps because even some of their own party members hesitated to grant landlords undivided authority. The lien in the bill that Governor

Davis had killed covered all of a renter's property; the 1874 lien applied only to crops and to property and stock furnished by the landlord. Still the new law stipulated that landlords' (but not merchants') liens would override the state's longstanding homestead exemption, which prevented a portion of an individual's property from being seized for payment of debt. It also gave landlords effective control over the disposition of everything the tenant grew by prohibiting the removal of any crop without a landowner's permission.[3] Like Redeemers elsewhere, Democrats surely revised landlord-tenant laws with an eye chiefly to giving landowners greater control over a freed black labor force (Shack Roberts, a Republican legislator and former slave, certainly thought so). But the intensification of cotton cultivation and, by the 1880s, spread of landlessness in the white-majority blackland prairie made these laws of broader application and enduring consequence.[4]

Texas Redeemers also served landowners' interests by restoring the ceilings on interest rates that had been abolished during Reconstruction. Scholars have found that in the Deep South small rural producers generally supported usury laws. But the interest in such laws expressed by a heavily indebted blue-blood planter, Moses Austin Bryan of Washington County, might suggest the sort of Texan who could expect to benefit most from them—those actually borrowing money rather than borrowing in kind from a furnishing merchant, as smaller farmers and tenants enmeshed in the crop-lien did.[5] Some Democrats, such as newspaper editors solicitous of local commercial interests, spoke dimly of governmental encroachment on the free market and opposed efforts to restrict interest rates.[6] But such limits seem to have been popular within the party, for at the 1875 constitutional convention, Democrats voted fairly overwhelmingly in favor of limiting the rate of interest to 12 percent between contracting parties and 8 percent in the absence of contract provisions.[7]

Texas Redeemers also contributed to the postbellum South's piecemeal move away from traditional open-range practices by which livestock grazed at will, even upon the unimproved property of others. The Reconstruction legislature had reaffirmed antebellum laws requiring that crops be fenced against the intrusion of livestock. But in 1873 and again in 1876, Democrats passed legislation allowing communities, by majority vote, to impose "hog laws" requiring smaller stock be penned (presumably in deference to the state's large-scale stockraising industry, cattle were not made subject to such laws).[8]

The best-known fencing controversies in postbellum Texas—the fence-cutting "wars" of 1883—had a decidedly western cast, pitting against one another ranching grandees who enclosed their own pastures with barbed wire; cattlemen who fenced public or even other individuals' lands; smaller stockraisers who depended on the open range; and farmers who did not want cattle trampling their crops but who in turn did not want to be denied access to water or grass by cattlemen's wire.[9] But in the first years of Redemption, fencing issues more frequently paralleled controversies elsewhere in the South, with freedpeople in black-majority counties understanding themselves to have much to lose from hog laws. The requirement that pigs, sheep, and goats be penned in made it far more difficult for the landless or petty proprietors to keep stock since many could afford neither pasturage nor fencing materials. This left them fewer alternatives to working as laborers or tenants for a landowner.[10] A Washington County memorial, twenty-nine of the seventy-five signers of which were labeled "f.m.c." (presumably "free men of color"), termed the 1873 legislation "*oppressive* to the Laboring man—and the poor—and beneficial only to the opulent and the rich." The district clerk of Grimes County remarked: "There is not a Colored man in this co. so far as my information extends but what is opposed to this law." Even the *Galveston Daily News,* that reliable spokesman of the mercantile community, recognized the class biases in such legislation, conceding, "such a law would compel many poor persons to abandon stock raising."[11] But hog laws only grew more comprehensive, the exemptions provided for many counties in 1873 being eliminated by the more overwhelmingly Democratic legislature of 1876.

The evolution of convict leasing also clearly served certain landed cultivators. Texas had begun to contract prison labor to private parties during Reconstruction. Under the Redeemers the proportion of convicts working outside the prison increased and their chief employers changed. During Reconstruction, it appears, prisoners labored almost exclusively for railroads being built through the state. Upon Democrats taking control, prison administrators—faced with the virtual suspension of railway construction following the Panic of 1873—began renting out increasing numbers of convicts for agricultural labor (including to the head of the Texas Grange). Even after extensive railway construction resumed in the late 1870s, the largest private employers of leased convicts remained planters. This bound labor force came to play a central role in the production of sugar in Texas.[12]

Convict leasing offered an instance of state government promoting economic development in Texas without cost to itself. Strategies for promoting growth that, by contrast, required investment of public resources divided Redeemers much more badly than landlord-tenant, usury, or fencing legislation did. If securing Democratic power in towns and counties with large opposition electorates had been inhibited by the Redeemers' own principles of local self-government, their choices with respect to promoting economic growth would be complicated by the vigor of their fiscal argument against Republican government. During Reconstruction, Democrats had encouraged Texans to believe the worst about taxation and state spending. Tax rates had historically been low in Texas and levies haphazardly assessed and collected.[13] Sharp increases in state and local taxation by the early 1870s undoubtedly created real hardship. Democrats could score rattling political successes by cultivating the impression that higher taxation and increasing public debt was largely unnecessary and attributable chiefly to the corruption and irresponsibility of Republican officeholders and their propertyless followers. As one Cherokee County newspaper put it, "the Radical party alone is responsible for this increase of our burdens."[14]

Such arguments could paint Democrats into corners, though, for the unprecedented levels of taxation and spending in the postbellum years were more than the result of Republican extravagance. Just maintaining antebellum levels of per capita spending in the post-emancipation era would presumably have entailed greater tax bills for larger number of Texans or greater indebtedness for the state, for prior to 1861 the assessed value of slaves had nearly equaled that of real property.[15]

Texas' western aspects also complicated the southern politics of retrenchment. Frontier defense constituted one of the largest single categories of state expenditure during Reconstruction, and Redeemers likewise felt compelled to deploy forces to check Indian raiding and cross-border banditry along the Rio Grande.[16] More importantly, as frontier settlement spread and population grew far more dense, state and local spending also had to grow to create or maintain essential material and institutional infrastructure and fund an expanding judicial system. Local tax bills had to cover the construction or improvement of courthouses and jails.[17]

Democrats had accomplished their "southern" goal of Redemption by forging a politics of retrenchment, yet they stood to anger or inconvenience citizens if they did not meet the rapidly growing state's frontier needs. So if they condemned Reconstruction taxes to build and maintain roads and bridges as "unjust and odious," they had to find other ways to get this vital work done: fines, the labor of those imprisoned for misdemeanors, and the forced contribution by able-bodied men of several days' worth of work a year provided a start.[18]

The tensions between the demands of Texas' development and the Democrats' commitment to retrenchment were most acute in the matter of railroads, understood by all to be the locomotive of economic growth. Unlike most southeastern states, Texas had yet to fully utilize vast stretches of its best agricultural land, much less develop the capacity for large-scale exploitation of its other natural resources. Plantation agriculture had been concentrated in the state's eastern and coastal fringes. The commercial possibilities of the rich blackland and Grand Prairie regions had gone largely unrealized before the Civil War. Few of the state's rivers could be regularly navigated any considerable distance from the coast. And while oxcart transport had been extensively developed, it proved too slow, irregular, and expensive to allow large-scale shipping of bulky staple crops to distant markets. Prairie farmers had accordingly concentrated more on cultivating grain and other food crops for local consumption. Stockraisers did produce for more distant markets, but with their footloose, open-range methods, they hardly made optimum commercial use of the land.[19]

As well as anyone, Redeemers knew that only the extension of railroads would allow the state to fully exploit its natural wealth. Railway construction had begun in Texas two decades before, but only during Reconstruction had lines reached much beyond the coast and the northeastern corner of the state. Their further extension would be essential to connect with out-of-state lines, afford better access to markets, distribute settlers to underutilized agricultural areas, accelerate the transition to staple-crop cultivation (which seemed to offer the most immediate prospect of prosperity), and expand trade in East Texas timber, South and West Texas cattle, and the mineral resources Texans expected to find scattered across the state.

For all this rich potential, Texans could hardly assume private profit-seeking alone would get railroads built. Construction into freshly populated territory did not promise immediate dividends. One Texas railway executive estimated in the 1870s that companies averaged an annual income of $4,300 per mile of track, while the typical cost of constructing that mile had been $40,000. Relatively few Texans could afford to wait for distant rewards, and Yankees remained wary of unsecured investments in the reconstructed South. Like other Americans at similar thresholds in their region's development, Texans seeking accelerated economic growth understood that prosperity might depend on bringing public resources to the aid of internal improvement.[20]

By the latter years of Reconstruction, however, the politically feasible ways by which state government might promote railroad development had been rather narrowly defined. Before the Civil War a number of prominent Texans had urged a plan by which the state itself would finance, construct, and operate a railway—as New York had done with the Erie Canal. This option was spurned.[21] For lawmakers in the 1870s, the choice was between public aid to private companies or no aid at all.

The state's options were further restricted even within these narrow parameters. Democrats' anti-Reconstruction politics of retrenchment had helped make certain forms of public subsidy of private corporations prohibitively unpopular. Texas' Reconstruction legislature had in 1870 and 1871 passed a number of bills promising to donate $10,000 or more in state bonds to individual railroad companies for every mile of track they constructed. Support had been bipartisan; indeed, Democrats had generally backed them in higher proportions than Republicans.[22] But the two most conspicuous of these laws—one subsidizing the International Railroad for construction of a line from Northeast Texas to the Rio Grande via Austin and San Antonio, the other funding two northern Texas lines (later the Texas & Pacific) for building west to a transcontinental connection—met popular opposition. There had been allegations of bribery in the passage of the legislation, and Democrats' growing drumbeat against rising taxes and increasing state debt had surely made the public sensitive about spending of any sort, particularly since the state seemed to be lavishing gifts on what Texans might be excused for seeing as Yankee monopolies. (The T&P board was increasingly dominated by Philadelphians and the International by New Yorkers.)[23]

Despite their party's complicity in passage of the subsidies (and Governor Davis's opposition to them), Democrats did their best to assimilate the anti-subsidy backlash to their larger attack on Reconstruction by portraying the unpopular laws as part and parcel of the Radical "extravagance" they excoriated.[24] This carried a price, though, for Democrats with railroad connections—including two of the party's more eminent leaders. James Throckmorton, who had been deposed as governor with the onset of Radical Reconstruction, was a director of the T&P. Although John Reagan would later become famous as one of the architects of federal regulation of railroads, during the first years of Redemption he was identified (mistakenly, he always insisted) as an International lobbyist. Reagan had been involved in local efforts to bring the railroad to his hometown of Palestine and subsequently did legal work for the company. Throckmorton's and Reagan's political careers would be hobbled for several years by these associations, a fellow Democrat at the 1875 constitutional convention even attacking Reagan as a "special apologist of corporations."[25] In vying to be the state's first Redeemer U.S.

senator in early 1874, neither man could muster a majority, the *Houston Age* arguing that Throckmorton's "advocacy of the railroad combination upon the treasury and public domain of Texans . . . is in violation of the first and best principle of Democracy. . . . The people desire a man in the United States Senate who has no connection with railroads." Legislators finally settled on Samuel Bell Maxey, a man unencumbered by conspicuous association with either of the unpopular subsidies.[26]

Financial support of railroads proved so politically problematic that by the summer of 1872, both parties had sworn off it. The Democratic state convention opposed "all moneyed subsidies to private corporations by the State government" as "unsound in principle and dangerous in practice." Democratic newspapers notably enthusiastic about economic development and party leaders personally interested in railroads—such as Civil War–era lieutenant governor Fletcher Stockdale, Rep. William Herndon, and even Throckmorton himself—likewise proclaimed their opposition to such subvention.[27] The Redeemer legislature in 1874 was even moved to repeal an 1871 law allowing towns and counties to issue bonds to railroads or subscribe to their stock in order to encourage companies to build their lines through or locate their shops and offices in the community.[28] A number of communities had voted such subsidies, Dallas managing to effect the intersection of two trunk lines within its boundaries by such means.[29] But as the bills became due, this local support had also became party to Democrats' politics of retrenchment. Just as they refused to pay school levies, many citizens would not pay taxes to make good on their community's railroad pledges.[30] Overlooking the role party members had played in sponsoring or approving local subsides, Democrats portrayed them as part and parcel of the Reconstruction politics they deplored, one legislator asserting that they had been granted in many counties "where an irresponsible class, paying no taxes, was in the ascendency."[31]

Yet this issue remained far from settled. More than any other, the protracted controversy over whether the state should honor the subsidy promised the International Railroad illustrates how the clash between the frontier imperative of development and the southern imperative of retrenchment might fracture the party of Redemption. Indeed, one Democratic legislator suggested that more feeling had been manifested on the matter than on any other issue.[32] As noted, the International question had in 1873 divided Democrats otherwise united in wrecking the Reconstruction education and law-and-order establishments. It threatened to render any gubernatorial nominee unacceptable to a good portion of his own party. Richard Coke's early ability to finesse the International imbroglio seems to have had a good deal to do with his emergence as Texas' most important Redeemer Demo-crat. In the 1874 congressional races, the central contest in northeastern Texas occurred not between Democrats and Republicans in the general election, but between two veteran Democrats for their party's nomination. One denounced the International subsidy, while the other, hailing from Jefferson, the company's northern terminus, supported compromise.[33] Dragging on for over two years, the International controversy became a central episode in Redemption-era politics, which like the debate over suf-frage, revealed some of the elemental dynamics of the post-Reconstruction Democratic party.

Democrats opposed both to honoring the subsidy as originally conceived and to any compromise involving the issuance of bonds in lesser amounts echoed the arguments of two *Republican* state officials, Comptroller A. Bledsoe and Attorney General William Alexander, who had ignited the controversy by refusing to forward bonds due the International for track it had completed. The original incorporation act, they said, had been un-constitutional. By making it the responsibility of the comptroller to levy an annual tax to pay off the bonds, the law bypassed the legislature's and local officials' role in appropriation and tax assessment. The two men charged that the bill's passage had been secured by bribery. And besides, the public ought not be taxed for the benefit of a private corporation.[34] But Democrats went further, assimilating these arguments into their party's broader denials of the legitimacy of Reconstruction government. The Reconstruction legis-lature had not represented the state's taxpaying population. The actions of carpetbaggers, scalawags, and "ignorant negroes recently emancipated from the cotton fields of the Colorado and Brazos" could hardly be binding.[35]

In challenging the International subsidy's constitutionality, however, Democrats also articulated notions of the proper role of government and the legitimate objects of taxation considerably more sophisticated than their party's shorthand equation of taxing and spending with corruption, extravagance, and propertylessness. The state, they said, might justifiably tax the populace for such purposes as charity, education, and frontier defense, the standard being, as one Cass County legislator put it, "is it for the benefit of the whole people or use of government." But the advantages railway con-struction might bring a community by no means rendered railroads public institutions entitled to public funds. Instead, they were simply groups of private individuals organized for personal profit. Taxation to meet the In-ternational bond payments thus represented the seizure of the property of one citizen for the benefit of another.[36]

Those Democrats wishing to resolve the standoff by issuing bonds to the company for at least a portion of its construction argued just as passionately. Sometimes they answered their opponents' constitutional arguments forthrightly, pointing to a string of federal and state court decisions affirming the right of governments to tax in support of railway development. Even if privately owned, the courts had reasoned, railroads operated as public highways, being incorporated, granted eminent domain, and regulated by state authority. The public interest would be served by travel and transport to markets being made cheaper and more convenient, and if necessary, the state could contract with private concerns to accomplish these objects.[37]

If some defended the legitimacy of money subsidies, supporters of the International typically proved far more sensitive to the prevailing political winds. Rather than assert the virtues of taxation for internal improvement, these Democrats denounced the original legislation and subsidies in general but insisted upon the ill effect refusal to pay would have upon the state. Even Democratic graybeard Ashbel Smith, whom International officials relied upon for support, thought it best in public statements to suggest that while he opposed the original subsidy and suspected it to have been secured by bribery, he believed Texas had to make good on obligations contracted by its legally constituted authorities.[38] Other Democrats likewise dwelt on the iniquity of "repudiation" instead of bucking their party's dedication to retrenchment. Whether or not the Reconstruction legislature had represented white property owners, the contracts it made as Texas' official lawmaking body could not be dismissed by subsequent legislatures without damaging the credit of the state. In the moralistic language so common to nineteenth-century discussions of finance, compromise advocates repeatedly invoked the state's sacred pledges and good name: "The financial integrity of a state is as sensitive as is a maiden's honor—once soiled, always doubted."[39]

By raising the horrors of repudiation, compromise supporters conjured with what apparently was a powerful sentiment among Texas Redeemers. Despite the centrality of retrenchment to Democratic politics, Redeemers proved consistently unwilling to carry their arguments against the legitimacy of Reconstruction taxing and spending to the same logical end as other southern Democrats. The state might drag its feet in meeting its obligations to pay public-school teachers or holders of state warrants. It might refund outstanding bonds at lower interest rates. But unlike almost every other former Confederate state, Texas never categorically repudiated or scaled large portions of its postwar bonded debt.[40] Even those who claimed the subsidy laws were unconstitutional tended not to propose that companies be sent away empty handed.

The shying away of most Texas Democrats from outright repudiation might suggest another instance of the state's frontier aspects intruding on its southern history. Texans could more comfortably adopt a rigid posture against repudiation, the state debt being relatively low and hardly as unmanageable as elsewhere in Dixie. But Democrats likely also recognized that given the relatively primitive state of Texas' transportation, industrial, and financial infrastructure and the enormous potential of development, it could ill afford to alienate northern capital.

Another important dynamic in Texas politics tapped by compromise supporters was intrastate sectionalism. In a state so large and so varied, it was by no means surprising that the first loyalty of legislators and their constituents might be to their immediate region rather than to the interests of Texas in the abstract. Throughout the Redemption-era debate over public subsidy of economic development, advocates on both sides of various questions often played on a longstanding suspicion among many Texans that resources of their own region had gone, or might go, to support development that primarily benefited distant parts of the state. During the International controversy, opponents of a bond compromise sometimes asserted the injustice of taxing the people of one region for the benefit of roads built in another.[41] But it was legislators and editors friendlier to the subsidies who most assiduously played the sectional card. To date, state aid had mainly helped Central and Northeast Texas and coastal entrepôts, the support given the Houston & Texas Central Railroad, for instance, having lifted Houston out of its "native swamp." It would hardly be fair to citizens living south and west of the Colorado for the state to repudiate support for a trunk line promising to cross that river and continue on to the Rio Grande.[42]

The International controversy even prompted some trans-Colorado Democrats to broadcast their suspicions that their section might be better off as its own state, directing its resources exclusively to its own needs rather than being governed by lawmakers ignorant and heedless of its interests. Over the course of the debate, support for the division of the state, a goal that since the end of the Civil War had been associated primarily with Radicals, seemingly increased and grew more bipartisan. "Nothing short of the International in running order to San Antonio shall prevent our dividing the state," proclaimed the *San Antonio Daily Herald*. By the time the Redeemers' constitutional convention wrapped up its work, the newspaper's editors seemed eager to be rid of their fellow Texas Democrats: "we have neither love nor respect for Texas or her Government; no more than we would have for any other merciless tyrant."[43]

Sectionalism alone did not govern the politics of economic development, however. South and West Texans themselves differed over the International. Division sentiment seemed to center in San Antonio—the last of Texas' long-settled mercantile cities to be without rail service. Some lawmakers and newspapers elsewhere in the southern and western parts of the state could be far less friendly to the International. They may, like John Ireland, have supported rival railroad projects or, like the *Victoria Advocate,* spoken for districts tapped by other lines.[44] But opposition also emerged among those living western or borderlands lives. According to one South Texas correspondent, the International's enemies might include the man who "has little land and large stock interests, and is afraid if the road is built the country will be settled, and his stock range curtailed."[45] A northern journalist claimed that San Antonio's Tejano elite opposed railroad development, having little desire for closer ties to the rest of the United States, and that even some merchants feared that once the city enjoyed rail connections, they would lose their trade with Mexico and with federal military outposts to more distant suppliers.[46]

Amid these bitter divisions, Democrats struggled with the International over three legislative sessions. The year 1873 saw only stalemate. The state senate embraced the company-sanctioned compromise—bonds at $10,000 per mile for construction between Jefferson and San Antonio (amounting to about $3.7 million of the $6 million originally promised)—while the house insisted upon substituting public land for bonds.[47] With the party's sweeping victory in that year's elections leaving the matter entirely in Democrats' hands, lawmakers moved cautiously in the next session. Both chambers concurred on the compromise allowing bonds for construction between Jefferson and San Antonio but added a proviso requiring the state supreme court to affirm the legality of the subsidy.[48] If Democrats hoped that by referring final judgment on the matter to the court they might evade ultimate responsibility for saddling the state with either an unpopular subsidy or the stigma of repudiation, they would be frustrated. The court booted the question right back to the legislature, disavowing jurisdiction over the issue.[49] As lawmakers returned once again to Austin in January 1875, they found themselves importuned by what Governor Coke described as "the most powerful lobby ever congregated in Austin."[50] The International had begun to miss interest payments on its own bonds because of the tardiness of state aid, and company officials insisted that it would go into receivership were a bond settlement not quickly effected. Whether persuaded by these pleas or by the bribes that the Speaker of the House believed had been handed out, the legislature by the smallest of margins passed another bill offering up to $3 million in bonds for construction between Jefferson and San Antonio.[51]

As legislators tussled, the governor had been making a journey of his own. During the campaign, Coke had had to deny that he was cozy with the International. In his early months as governor, Coke remained officially silent but suggested privately that he might accept a bond compromise under certain conditions. But his heart hardened toward the International as he became convinced that the company's friends were besmirching the state's reputation among New York investors, inhibiting the sale of bonds necessary to fund the public debt. Although the irrepressible *Victoria Advocate* might still chide the governor for "his evident complicity in the International Railroad robbery," Coke's attorney general, George Clark, went before the supreme court rehearsing the familiar arguments against the subsidy. By the time legislators met in 1875, the governor was ready to publicly declare against a compromise involving issuance of bonds.[52]

This shift may well have marked an important juncture in Coke's development as one of the most successful Texas politicians of his era, the International controversy once again advancing his career. His own enthusiasm about economic expansion, as revealed in his support for state promotion of immigration and, indeed, his final settlement of the International controversy, appealed to developmentally oriented Democrats. But the International fracas allowed him to hone the anti-monopoly rhetoric that surely contributed to his high standing among Grangers. Coke clearly recognized the rewards this might bring, writing early in 1875: "I am all right with the people if I can keep the *politicians* and RR men from tricking them." He told the legislature that he looked forward to the day when "capital and monopoly, rather than the people, shall cease to be the ruling power of the government," and "the farmer and producer is emancipated from thralldom to the manufacturer and capitalist, and labor meets its legitimate reward."[53]

So, when the legislature passed its bond compromise, Coke carried out a promise to "veto h—l out of it."[54] In a lengthy message the governor reiterated the longstanding anti-compromise arguments (without making clear why he had not embraced them so directly earlier). The subsidy involved taxation for private benefit, not the public good; the legislature that passed it had not represented the taxpayers of the state. Flexing his anti-monopoly muscles, he argued that far more important than settling the bond question was establishing that the government of Texas belonged to the people and not "rings, jobbers and plunderers."[55]

But Coke in fact was ready to settle the three-year dispute, with a generosity that would give readily of the state's wealth so long as it did not make for identifiable increments in citizens' tax bills. Given that the bond compromise had passed far too narrowly to permit override of his veto, the governor could recommend what the company had always rejected—public land. The legislature quickly granted the International twenty sections (that is, twenty square miles) of land per mile of rail constructed. It also exempted the company's property, including its capital stock, land, and land certificates, from state, county, and municipal taxation for twenty-five years.[56]

The company quickly accepted these terms, and the controversy that had had Democrats screaming at one another for two years or more ended. Coke insisted this liberal settlement would "cost the people nothing," and indeed no one's taxes would go up immediately by virtue of it.[57] But a number of editors and legislators pointed out that in the long run the settlement could cost Texas plenty, perhaps more than the bond subsidy would have. The state could end up giving the company millions of dollars worth of land. Over the course of twenty-five years, the taxes that otherwise would have been due on those lands, as well as on other company property, seemed likely to amount to millions more—revenue that might have lightened other taxpayers' burdens.[58]

The International controversy suggests how contested public promotion of economic development could become, but its resolution perfectly illustrates how Redeemers would ultimately manage the conflicting demands of retrenchment and development. In accepting what it had long spurned—a bounteous grant of public land—the company allowed Texas Democrats to play their ace in the hole. Public land would be the linchpin of Redeemer political economy, for it seemed to allow the state to encourage development and serve public needs without making the sorts of demands on taxpayers that Democrats had made almost prohibitively unpopular.

That these southern Redeemers could base their developmental strategies almost entirely on public land was a legacy of Texas' borderlands history. When this one-time dominion of Mexico surrendered its independence in 1845, Texas had remained, by the terms of annexation, in complete control of its vast public lands. By contrast, in other states outside the original thirteen—and portions of those constituted as states in their own right (Kentucky, Tennessee, Maine, Vermont, and West Virginia)—the federal government exercised ultimate authority over the public domain. Certainly it did not hoard this land but instead turned a good deal of it over to the states, though usually with some conditions on its use. Florida and Alabama gave public land to railroads. Arkansas sold it to settlers to raise money for internal improvements and schools.[59] But neither the earlier landed states nor the ones later granted portions of the federal domain ever had at their disposal anything remotely approaching the almost 182 million unappropriated acres with which Texas entered the Union. Democrats redeemed a state that in 1873 still had under its control some 84 million unappropriated acres as well as land already reserved for the benefit of public schools, a state university, and asylums. This unparalleled wealth of public land and the exclusive authority the state exercised over it combined to make Texas' situation unique in the nineteenth century.[60]

The availability of this land allowed many state Democrats to believe that they could underwrite economic development and public welfare without requisitioning to any great extent tax dollars or creating long-term debt. Texas certainly was not alone in attempting to subsidize services and accelerate development by means other than taxation. Georgia, New York, and North Carolina tried to make the most of revenue generated by dividends from state investments and various federally generated windfalls.[61] But the sheer extent of Texas' landed resources seems to have bred particularly extravagant expectations and persuasive promises.

State leaders developed a number of strategies for putting these lands to public purposes. The government sold acres to private parties and used the proceeds to pay state expenses. It invested the proceeds of land sales and devoted the dividends to public services like education. The state also hoped to speed settlement and economic growth by giving away land or selling it cheaply to homesteaders. It also granted land to private individuals or companies in return for the performance of some task for the state, such as building its pink granite capitol building in the 1880s. Finally, Texas granted land to private companies for activities deemed to be in the public interest though pursued for private profit. The companies in turn could use the land as security for loans or sell it and make use of the proceeds.[62]

A measure passed in 1854 charted land policy as applied to railroads. Every company constructing twenty-five miles or more of track would receive, in addition to right of way, sixteen sections of land for every mile completed (one section equaling 640 acres). These land grants, unlike federal ones, were rarely made along railroads' routes. Instead companies received certificates entitling them to locate their grants wherever unappropriated land was available. They would receive land in alternate sections, the intervening plots being reserved for the state, though surveyed at company expense. The railroad in turn would be required to sell the land, preferably to settlers, within twelve years.[63]

Land subsidies naturally became the strategy latched onto by those Redeemers most interested in promoting economic growth as money subsidies
became politically impossible. If such grants represented a transfer of public
resources to private hands, these resources at least were not drawn from the
pockets of taxpayers. But as attractive as this strategy might be in evading
the untoward consequences of their party's fiscal argument against Reconstruction, developmentally oriented Democrats could not simply decree a
return to antebellum practice. The Reconstruction constitution had banned
land grants except to individual settlers. Some seemed to feel that monetary
subsidies would be far more effective in accelerating growth, while other
Democrats and Republicans had not supported subventions of any sort. Radical leader Edmund Davis felt that Texas would be better served by reserving
the entire public domain for homesteads and school endowments (opponents
suggesting that Republicans wished to fill the public lands "with negroes to
perpetuate their power").[64] But as the Democratic drumbeat against taxing
and spending grew, the Reconstruction legislature passed a resolution in
1871 to amend the constitution to allow internal-improvement land grants.[65]
In the same 1872 elections that put Democrats in control of the legislature,
Texans endorsed this amendment by a large margin. Legislators then voted
officially to ratify it in early 1873.

Supporters of the amendment promoted it as a means to render existing
subsidy arrangements harmless through the substitution of lands for the
promised bonds.[66] In the case of the Texas & Pacific grant, public land did
indeed spare Democrats the agony they went through with the International.
The T&P's need for an extension of the construction deadlines set in its
charter made it far more agreeable to a substitution of land for bonds. The
Reconstruction legislature had granted the company's predecessors up to $6
million in bonds or—should the constitution be amended—twenty-four sections of land per mile built, but it had required construction to be completed
to Fort Worth by the beginning of 1874, a deadline the company had come
to believe it could not meet. Laws passed by the Democratic majority in 1873
substituted the maximum constitutionally permissible land grant—twenty
sections per mile—for the donation of state bonds. The acceptance of this
substitution being portrayed as a concession on the part of the company
(though Throckmorton later indicated that he and T&P chief Thomas Scott
welcomed and even worked for the land-grant amendment), the legislature
in turn extended the deadlines for completion of various portions of the line
and affirmed and extended the reservation of a large swath of Texas within
which the company would have first claim on land.[67]

Together, the land-grant amendment and the 1873 T&P bill had relieved citizens of an imminent tax burden. But a majority of Redeemer lawmakers clearly saw land grants not simply as a means to escape bond obligations without categorically repudiating them but also as the basis of a broad strategy for development. While the Reconstruction legislature had favored only a few of the railroads it chartered with money subsidies or tax exemptions, its Redeemer successors promised land subsidies to virtually all of the lines they incorporated. The Thirteenth Legislature (1873) not only chartered fifteen roads, giving all but a short tap road sixteen sections of land per mile constructed, but it also amended the charters of twelve already incorporated companies to provide the land subsidies missing from the original legislation. Such bills attracted overwhelming bipartisan support.[68] The Fourteenth Legislature incorporated twenty-six companies in 1874–75, promising all land grants (typically sixteen sections per mile).[69]

Yet if land subsidies allowed Democrats to reconcile developmental aid and retrenchment, their adoption did not allow them to create categorical consensus within the party. Some Texans clearly harbored doubts about Redeemer land policy. The land-grant amendment had been approved by 62 percent of voters in 1872, but twenty-eight counties had opposed it by majorities of over 80 percent—and many of them were firmly Democratic. A seeming lack of interest on the part of the press during the ratification campaign obscures the nature of these voters' objections. The heavy vote against the amendment in counties along the projected route of the International might have stemmed from residents' fear that the substitution of a less valuable land grant for bonds would retard construction. But opponents in counties on the western fringes of agrarian settlement in Central Texas, such as Coryell, Comanche, and Bosque, may have resented the prospect of frontier land subsidizing construction in distant and more thickly settled eastern and northern Texas. Stockraisers in those counties, particularly those operating on the open range, may have viewed railroads not as a boon but as a threat. Their product could walk itself to market, but as railroads raised land values and encouraged population growth, herds would become more difficult and expensive to maintain.[70]

The minority of Democratic legislators who in 1873 opposed final ratification of the amendment or the T&P compromise did record their concerns over land subsidies. Amendment opponents on occasion questioned the benefits of the sort of economic growth railroads would foster. Rep. John Ireland "did not think it impossible that the state could become great without railroads; the states North and East are now under the iron heel of railroad monopolies. Our descendants, and mayhap ourselves, will realize the curse these moneyed corporations will prove to be."[71] But those against the amendment or the T&P compromise frequently indicated through word or deed that they were displeased less with railroads or economic development per se than with those who stood to benefit most immediately by the grants— "foreign" corporations run by New Yorkers and Philadelphians. However leery he might have been of "moneyed corporations," Ireland initiated several railroad-incorporation bills that included land subsidies. Neither he nor most of the others who had opposed the amendment voted against very many of the over two dozen bills the Thirteenth Legislature subsequently passed granting lands to railroads other than the T&P.[72] Significantly, these grants typically went to lines projected as predominantly Texas concerns. The suspicion of land grants only to the extent that they served what were perceived as non-Texan institutions partook of a broader pattern in the politics of economic development in the state. Even those most enthusiastic about public promotion repeatedly demonstrated their concern that it not benefit out-of-state interests at the expense of Texas businesses.

If opponents of the land grant amendment and the T&P compromise failed to articulate any very consistent hostility to the principle of land-subsidized economic growth, they did raise an issue that would become central to Democratic politics in the years after 1876: the finitude of the public domain. Many Redeemers seem to have treated public land as an inexhaustible resource, an endowment so vast that it could be applied to a whole range of purposes—internal improvement, public works, settlement, education, debt service—with few unpleasant choices having to be made among them. But from the dawn of Redemption, fellow Democrats reminded them that, as large as the state's supply of land might be, it was hardly unlimited. In favoring one use for its land, the state was necessarily limiting the amount available for other worthy purposes. In the case of the T&P compromise, critics focused on how the reservation of thousands of square miles for that company privileged railroad development over the interests of homesteading settlers. While the house tabled proposals allowing settlers to preempt land inside the reserved territory, it tacitly acknowledged the need to safeguard other interests it wished served by the public domain. Before ratifying the land-grant amendment, it passed a law reaffirming the antebellum practice of requiring railroads to survey their grants in alternate sections and directed that the intervening plots be set aside to benefit the state school fund.[73]

Redeemers also hoped to reconcile development with the politics of retrenchment by seeking federal aid for state railroad projects. Legislators, state and federal officeholders, and even the Texas Grange urged upon the federal government developmental strategies that they anathematized and ultimately banned at the state level.[74] These included the United States guaranteeing the payment of interest on the T&P's bonds, though the proposal's congressional opponents argued against such aid in rhetoric similar to that employed by Texans against the International subsidy.[75] After he was elevated to the U.S. Senate in 1876, Richard Coke, the most important foe of the International bond subsidy, introduced bills providing that the United States underwrite other railroads' construction along routes similar to that of the International.[76]

Some Democrats addressed the apparent contradictions in their enthusiasm for federal railroad aid, usually suggesting that while they could not approve such aid in principle, sectional justice demanded southern projects get the sort of support railroads serving the North had received.[77] However justified, federal aid comported with the politics of retrenchment, for even if the United States had to pay the interest on railroad companies' bonds, no immediate or easily identifiable costs would be imposed on Texans for which Democrats might be punished.

Besides the underwriting of railroads, Texas Redeemers had other choices to make with respect to promoting economic growth. Some southern states exempted from taxation certain enterprises, including manufacturing and mining operations, to encourage industrial development. Some spent money to attract settlers.[78] As great as its developmental needs were, however, Texans proved less liberal than some other Redeemers when it came to such strategies.

It is telling that what modest discontent emerged with the final International settlement focused on the tax exemption rather than the generous land subsidy. Land giveaways had proved politically safe, but tax exemptions for industry found little favor. The Reconstruction legislature had passed a law exempting manufacturers of cotton and wool products from taxation for five years.[79] Some Democrats—even men none too sympathetic to direct expenditure of state revenue for developmental purposes—subsequently supported the extension of exemptions to include other sorts of manufacturing enterprises and to apply over longer periods of time. As in other discussions of the state's role in economic development, these Democrats often stressed the importance of cultivating indigenous enterprise. Texas should not have to depend on northern concerns for the processing of its raw materials and the production of the finished goods its people consumed.[80]

But having howled about the iniquity of taxation, many Democrats could hardly have relished the prospect of explaining to rural constituents why they remained subject to a state tax rate still set at Reconstruction levels while industrialists and entrepreneurs were relieved of such burdens. Also, as loathe as they may have been to admit it in their eagerness to be rid of the vexed International controversy, many Democrats realized that tax exemptions amounted to at least an indirect subsidy. Having relinquished revenue, the state had either to spend less or require more of those individuals and firms still subject to taxation. Two years before the final International settlement, a Democrat-dominated senate committee derided a proposed general tax exemption for railroads as contemplating something close to the state building railroads and then donating them to private companies.[81]

Given this sort of opposition, bills proposing to encourage indigenous industry by exempting manufacturers died in both 1874 and 1875. In the most definitive legislative vote on the matter—an 1875 motion in the house to postpone indefinitely an exemption bill—Democrats split 39–31 in opposition to the exemptions. Those from more urbanized districts provided the most consistent support for the measure. Democrats from black-majority counties were split, suggesting again the difficulty of identifying any single "planter" stance on development policy in Texas.[82]

Active state promotion of migration to Texas from elsewhere in North America and from Europe enjoyed broader support than either tax exemptions or cash subsidies for railroad development. Some boosters focused on the state's labor needs, seeking to replace or at least augment the African American labor force in plantation counties with what they regarded as a more dependable and less politically problematic white population.[83] But there were "western" as well as "southern" reasons for aggressively courting immigrants—filling in the wide-open spaces even more quickly, thereby raising land values; developing natural resources; generating more tax revenue; cultivating a larger domestic market; and acquiring more clout in national politics. Texans of German and Central European backgrounds seemed eager for the company of greater numbers of their countrymen.[84] Thus conservatives from black-majority counties, foreign-born Democrats, and representatives of more thinly settled regions west and south of the Colorado River might unite in pressing the state to further action in promoting immigration.

But immigrant aid also fell victim to the politics of retrenchment. The Reconstruction regime had established the Bureau of Immigration to distribute promotional literature and arrange for discounted passage to the state. The

1869 Constitution broke with Texas precedent by actually authorizing the expenditure of state revenue to pay an individual immigrant's travel expenses.[85] But Democrats, even those supporting such aid, criticized the Republican agency as the same sort of wasteful patronage mill as the educational and law-enforcement establishments. William H. Parsons, the state's immigration agent in New York, seems to have been particularly unpopular among Democrats. The brother of Haymarket martyr Albert Parsons, he had led a brigade of Confederate cavalry during the war but rather tardily converted to Republicanism during Radical Reconstruction.[86] Sweeping the bureau clean of Republican appointees, though, was not enough to reconcile other Redeemers to this promotional strategy. Although a number of prominent Democrats opposed to money subsidies for railroad development supported increased expenditure for immigration—most prominently Governor Coke and Oxcart John Ireland—Redeemer legislators whittled away at the state's effort, eliminating appropriations first for the agents in New York and Europe, then for southern and western agents. By 1875 the legislature funded only the superintendent's salary and the printing and distribution of promotional pamphlets.[87]

Opponents of state immigration aid usually stressed that they welcomed outsiders. Given the energy their party had given to cultivating Texas' German and Irish population and its official welcoming of whites from every land, nativism would have hardly been fitting. But spending tax money to encourage immigration was, in their view, neither proper nor necessary. The sheer quantity of public land and its liberal homesteading laws assured that Texas could attract all the settlers it required by—at most—simply letting the world know of its attractions.[88] In this case too the state's land reserve allowed Redeemers to believe that they neither had to spend nor do without.

Texas Redeemers had to not only set government's course in the promotion of economic development but also determine what control it should exercise over the agents of that development. While the proper mechanisms for regulating railroads would be the source of much debate in the 1880s, the principle that they ought to be regulated by public authority seems to have generated less disagreement in the 1870s. Ample precedent plainly existed. During the Republic period and the first years of statehood, Texas had written clauses into its earliest railroad charters either reserving to the state the right to regulate rates charged by the companies or actually stipulating maximum charges. In 1853—before any lines operated in the state—the legislature enacted a comprehensive regulatory law allowing it to prescribe passenger and freight rates on any railroad, though mandating that the rates set had to allow the company a per annum net profit of 12 percent on its capital stock. The law also required companies to build at a uniform gauge, locate their principal offices at some point on the line, and follow certain safety practices. In subsequent years the legislature passed laws requiring a majority of the directors and officers of lines benefiting from state land grants or loans to reside in Texas and restricting stock watering. The regulations do not seem to have borne heavily on Texas companies, as even railroaders acknowledged. The legislature hardly seemed anxious to exercise its powers to mandate maximum rates. Still these antebellum provisions clearly indicate that the principle and objects of regulation enshrined in the Redeemer constitution had been anticipated several decades earlier.[89]

With railway construction accelerating during Reconstruction, Texans' thoughts turned again to regulation. Republican governor Davis called for general laws regulating rates, while his Democratic successor recommended that in granting charters the state be careful to reserve the power to challenge "oppressive" charges and to "subordinate railroad corporations to the supremacy of the government."[90] The same lawmakers who provided for generous land grants wrote regulations into those same charters. House Democrats, in particular, seemed anxious in 1873 to provide for more uniformly restrictive charters—first through the amendment of bills from the floor, then by the establishment of a special railroad committee to review all legislation. The provisions the committee incorporated reaffirmed the right of the state to regulate rates, prohibited roads from consolidating with parallel or competing lines, and placed conditions upon companies' disposal of lands granted by the state, such as restricting sales to other corporations. Such regulatory amendments appear to have been approved with relatively little debate. In both 1873 and 1874, the lower house also passed bills stipulating maximum rates for passengers and freight, but these died in the senate.[91]

This strength of regulatory sentiment among Redeemer Democrats has sometimes been taken as an index of the power of "agrarians" in the party. But in Texas as elsewhere, the constituency for railroad regulation extended far beyond the farm. Historians have noted the interest of certain business groups in regulation immediately prior to the establishment of the state railroad commission in the 1890s.[92] But that sentiment had also been evident during the first years of Redemption, when the fundamental powers of post-Reconstruction state government were being charted. Various business groups, particularly merchants, wholeheartedly supported the extension of railway lines but proved eager to ensure that the vital connection between marketplace and hinterland be made on advantageous terms. Merchants across Texas complained bitterly when they believed railroads had damaged their business through extortionate rates or discrimination against their communities. They lent their voices to a growing demand that lawmakers act. In 1874, for instance, a committee of the Galveston Cotton Exchange drafted its own bill to regulate railroads and forwarded it to the legislature.[93]

The *Galveston Daily News* offers a case in point. The premier newspaper of the state's largest city vigorously endorsed various means to accelerate Texas development, from railroad land grants to state aid to immigration. As the organ of a powerful mercantile community, this enthusiasm was understandable, but the paper expressed the vulnerability merchants felt as well. Unable to rely on inland navigation to expand its hinterland, the island city's prosperity and future growth depended upon railroads, most of which were owned by out-of-state interests and some of which were headquartered in rival Houston. The *News* remained ever sensitive to rates that might make Galveston a more expensive port to do business with and redirect trade through out-of-state entrepôts like Saint Louis. When it felt the livelihood of the business community threatened, it wielded an anti-monopoly rhetoric as fierce as anyone's. "The time has come," the paper declared, "for a stern and inexorable repudiation of the idea that there can be such a thing as absolute private ownership in an essentially public high way." In attacking the Houston & Texas Central for channeling trade to Houston, it railed against "the tyrannical pretensions and exactions" of the railroad, insisting that "the day has gone by when a transportation company, chartered as a common carrier over a public highway, can impose arbitrary terms upon merchants and planters."[94]

Many Democrats followed the lead of these business allies, including those personally interested in railroad expansion. Even James Throckmorton endorsed state oversight.[95] This willingness of developmentally oriented Democrats to sanction regulation would not necessarily mature over subsequent decades into any very consistent embrace—or even routine acknowledgment—of the public's claims on private enterprise. When public authority seemed likely to intrude on local business prerogatives, such as when official weighers were appointed in Galveston and other commercial centers to assure farmers that their cotton was fairly valued, the *News* and like-minded journals denounced paternalistic intrusion into purely private business transactions, invoking the Democratic doctrines of free trade, individual liberty, laissez-faire, and "the magnificent rule of '*Caveat Emptor.*'"[96] Others forthrightly opposed regulation. The *Austin Democratic Statesman* insisted, for instance, that competition and not state intrusion was the best way to contain costs and prevent discrimination, and Houston's cotton exchange memorialized against regulation later in the decade.[97]

Clearly, though, the growth of an enhanced regulatory role for the state did not necessarily take place over the objections of "New South" Democrats eager to modernize Texas. Instead many developmentally minded Redeemers took up regulation and anti-monopoly rhetoric. In doing so they built an enduring relationship between the state and private enterprise, one based not on laissez-faire but on various forms of public intervention intended to cultivate in-state business interests and rationalize commerce to their advantage. The fact that insurance, the other large business enterprise to fall under more comprehensive state regulation during the Redemption era, was also to a significant extent carried on by out-of-state firms, seems to confirm this tendency. In calling for legislative action in this area, Governor Coke asked for laws that would protect Texans from the shady practices of insurance companies headquartered in distant cities and "at the same time assist in the organization and development of home institutions of like character."[98] While many Redeemers seemed to anticipate the further growth of a primarily extractive economy, supplying staple crops and raw materials to the nation and the world, they did not relish the prospect of a "colonial" economy in which out-of-state interests would derive the larger share of the benefits.

As Democrats prepared for their constitutional convention in 1875, the vice president of the Texas & Pacific urged longtime politico and railroadman Benjamin Epperson to run for a seat in the body: "our friends . . . deem it of *very* great importance to the State, and to all who are interested in railways and other property in the state, that the *best men* should have a hand in framing a new constitution."[99]

Indeed, the convention's significance could not be overstated. Democrats would have the opportunity to codify the political economy of Redemption, writing their preferences with respect to taxation, public promotion of economic growth, and corporate regulation into the organic law of the state. But that would involve making choices among the positions staked out by party members. Most accounts of the convention imply that it generally chose the least generous of the alternatives before it. Agrarian delegates associated with the Grange, it has often been suggested, triumphed over a more developmentally oriented and cosmopolitan faction of Democrats to create a distinctly restrictive and tight-fisted document.[100] Michael Perman tells us that developmentally minded New South Democrats were "routed" at the convention, making for a constitution that, in the words of *The New Handbook of Texas*, "was adequate for a rural people engaged principally in subsistence farming, but not for an urban-industrial-commercial society."[101] Yet a close examination of the proceedings, the choices before the convention, and the political context in which delegates worked tells another story.

Redeemers had already cut the taxes they had howled loudest about in making their fiscal argument against Reconstruction—local levies for schools and roads. But drafting a new constitution offered the opportunity to dedicate the state in a more comprehensive way to retrenchment. Indeed, many Democratic delegates came to Austin convinced that their most important task was to bind the hands of public officials when it came to taxing, borrowing, and spending of any sort.[102] Accordingly, the Redeemer constitution capped the state ad valorem tax rate at 0.5 percent and that of counties and most towns at 0.25 percent—though it exempted taxes necessary to pay existing public debts from these limits and, given the expanding state's infrastructure needs, allowed counties to tax an additional 0.5 percent to pay for the construction of public buildings. Lawmakers could not expand the state debt by more than $200,000 to supply deficiencies in revenue—except in the event of invasion, insurrection, or war or to pay the current debt. Delegates cut executive, legislative, and judicial salaries; reduced the size of the very expensive district judiciary; and provided for biannual rather than annual sessions of the legislature (as well as reducing gubernatorial terms to two years).[103]

Certain Democrats, both within and without the convention hall, resisted the reductions in official salaries, complaining that the savings generated would be rather small while at the same time the meager pay would discourage the most competent men, at least those without independent means, from holding office. More generally, Governor Coke worried in private that the new constitution would "fit too tight for comfort," and the *Galveston Daily News* remarked wistfully that there was more to government than cutting taxes.[104] But the cap on the state property-tax rate encountered little resistance within the convention, perhaps because rather than enforcing actual rollbacks, it was in fact a rather modest guarantee that the rate would not exceed the highest levels of Reconstruction. Some sentiment developed among Democratic delegates to raise or even eliminate the ceiling on local levies, but the most divisive tax question did not involve the incorporation of specific maximum figures into the fundamental law.[105] This issue derived not from the politics of retrenchment but from Texas' position as a growing western state. Delegates fought over whether the state's many absentee landowners would have their taxes assessed and collected in the county in which their property was situated, at Austin, or in the county in which they resided. Representatives of counties, particularly near the frontier, that possessed large tracts of land owned by nonresidents complained that, being beyond the reach of local authorities, many wealthy men and non-Texans evaded taxation, leaving a disproportionate portion of the burden to be borne by actual settlers, many of whom were of humble circumstance.[106]

As for the state debt, as low as the $200,000 maximum may have been, much of what opposition emerged to it came not from delegates who found it too constricting, but instead from those who supported an even lower ceiling, those who did not want the government to be given *any* power to borrow to supply deficiencies in revenue, and those who opposed even the leeway given the state in defending itself from insurrection or invasion.[107]

The convention's actions on debt partook of more general, if often overlooked, patterns. If delegates made a constitution decidedly more parsimonious than its Reconstruction predecessor, they often chose the less, not the more, restrictive alternative offered them. And while many accounts suggest delegates affiliated with the Grange voted as a bloc, Patrons proved as divided on debt as they were on suffrage.[108] Some Grangers supported the $200,000 ceiling, some supported a $100,000 limit, and some evidently wished the state be given no further authority to contract such obligations. Similar divisions emerged on tax issues, about one-third of Grangers voting at some point to allow absentee landowners to pay property taxes to the state comptroller rather than in the counties in which the property was situated or to allow counties a maximum ad valorem tax rate of 0.5 percent instead of just 0.25 percent. In fact only on the issue of reducing the salaries of state officials does one encounter the circumstance that much of the historical literature would lead one to expect to find across the board—almost all Grange delegates clustered on one side (the lower rate) and almost all unaffiliated Democrats voting on the other, more generous side.[109]

The same patterns prevailed with respect to economic development and corporate regulation. The Redeemer constitution declared railroads to be common carriers and public highways subject to legislative regulation; prohibited the state, counties, and municipalities from aiding railroads or other corporations through money or bond subsidies or the extension of credit; limited the legislature's power to exempt corporations and their property from taxation; and prohibited the state from appropriating money to maintain an immigration bureau or to bring in settlers.[110] Some attacked such provisions, worrying that the state would be perceived as hostile to progress.[111] But the constitution would seem in fact to have embodied as liberal a developmental policy as was politically feasible, incorporating as it did much of the Redeemer legislatures' strategies. Corporate tax exemptions and local subsidy of railroads had already been all but killed off by the politics of retrenchment. Spending to promote immigration had dropped steeply. With the exception of the aborted compromise on the International question, no Texas legislature had offered a money subsidy since Redemption had begun.

For the most part, the prohibitions on various revenue-based growth mechanisms generated little obvious controversy at the convention. When a committee reported an article banning monetary subsidies, no one sought to amend it. Little opposition emerged either to the prohibition on the legislature exempting corporations from taxation.[112] Only the question of state investment in promoting immigration to Texas occasioned substantial floor debate. Illustrating the diverse constituency for enhanced immigration, Democrats from cities, plantation counties, and South and West Texas joined foreign-born and Republican delegates in fruitlessly pressing for a state commitment of some sort—if only a bureau to collect and disseminate information.[113]

Democrats most eager to promote growth suffered a bitter defeat on the issue of immigration, but not on what had become the cardinal Redeemer development strategy. The chief decision the convention had to make with respect to state subsidy of economic growth was not between rewarding railroads with public money or merely with public land, as some historians seem to assume, but between granting land or nothing at all. In this matter the so-called New South Democrats were not routed but actually triumphed.

No one took the floor to argue for money subsidies at the convention, while forceful and eloquent voices were heard denouncing the granting even of land to railroads. Their arguments often echoed those employed against the earlier bond subsidies: invoking the dangers posed by "foreign corporations" and "a grasping, rasping set of monopolies" as well as the iniquity of using the state's wealth to benefit a few private citizens. But the anti-subsidy faction also tried to turn the goal of development against their opponents. Texas' growth depended on "hardy pioneers" attracted to the state by the very lands pro-subsidy forces proposed to squander on corporations.[114]

For their part, pro-subsidy Democrats tried once again to make land grants serve the politics of retrenchment, in this case by arguing that taxes would fall as railroads, by promoting immigration and economic growth, made the population larger and wealthier.[115] Land grant supporters also resorted to the familiar strategy of appealing to sectional justice. Eastern as well as western delegates argued that West Texas, South Texas, and southeastern Texas should have the same opportunities as northeastern and Central Texas had enjoyed to profit from state-supported construction. John Stayton, a South Texan, put such appeals to the test by proposing that what land was left to be granted be reserved for construction south of the Colorado River, west of Dallas, and in the southeastern corner of the state. The Stayton measure, however, generated little support among pro-subsidy delegates whose districts did not, at least in part, stand to benefit, and it ultimately failed. So did future Populist leader Thomas Nugent's effort to end land subsidies to railroads altogether. While pro-subsidy spokesmen frequently claimed their opponents hailed from areas already well served by railroads, fully half of those voting to ban land grants came from western, southern, and southeastern areas that Stayton's proposal suggested lacked adequate service.[116]

Ultimately, the Redeemer convention confirmed the existing policy of granting sixteen sections per mile of track constructed by railroads, the companies required to resell granted land within twelve years. But rather than directing such subsidies only to those deemed deserving by the legislature, it mandated that general laws be established making land available to all companies that could meet certain conditions.[117]

The convention endorsed another railroad-friendly policy that had been embraced by the Redeemer legislatures, providing for the extension of construction deadlines set in railroad companies' charters. After the Panic of 1873 slowed construction on existing roads and prevented the financing of projected ones, the T&P—termed the "Micawber of the prairie" by the *Dallas Herald*—had led successful efforts in 1874 and 1875 to secure general extensions.[118] In lopsided votes the constitutional convention twice rejected measures that would have barred the legislature from granting such extensions. Instead delegates passed an ordinance, introduced by one of their most conspicuous Grangers, that extended pending charter deadlines for all railroads through the end of the next session of the legislature, duly empowered to grant further relief.[119]

Delegates evidentially found little contradiction in being generous to railroads in terms of land subsidies and time extensions while also empowering the legislature "to correct abuses and prevent unjust discrimination and extortion." Consistent with his position in years past, John Reagan spoke vigorously for railroad development. But he also voted for the regulatory provisions and afterward became well known for his efforts in Congress to establish federal regulation of railroads.[120] The railroad article made general a number of the regulatory provisions Redeemer lawmakers had routinely inserted into individual charters, such as reserving to the state the authority to set maximum rates and prohibiting company consolidations with parallel or competing lines. Expressing the sensitivity to external control of railroads apparent even among the developmentally minded, the convention also prohibited the merging of Texas lines with those chartered out of state. A few did argue against the government's right to interfere with railroads and other corporations that had already been chartered. Delegate Fletcher Stockdale—the vice president of the Gulf, Western Texas, & Pacific Railroad—insisted the state "might . . . as well say what profit the Capital Ice Company should make, as say what profit should be derived by railroad corporations." But efforts to reduce the legislature's regulatory powers garnered no more than eight of seventy-five Democratic votes.[121]

The convention's railroad decisions do not in themselves contradict traditional portrayals of this constitution as the "master work" of the Texas Grange.[122] Most Grangers appear to have been commercial cotton farmers and thus had every reason to support rate regulation, though not necessarily any direct interest in opposing the further extension of railroads.[123] The state Grange's "Worthy Master," W. W. Lang, in a speech delivered shortly before the convention, had insisted: "The interests of the farmers are too closely twined with transportation companies for them to act inimical towards railroads. We want railroads, and where we have no navigable rivers must have them."[124] Still it is by no means clear that the convention's actions can be regarded as primarily the work of Grangers. They voted overwhelmingly in favor of the regulatory article, but non-Grange Democrats supported it by a better than two-thirds majority. The provisions had not been introduced by a Patron, and the committee majority that reported them was evenly divided between members of the order and nonmembers. While Grangers had introduced measures banning money subsidies to railroads, the article prohibiting them had been reported by a committee dominated by non-Grangers. Nor did Patrons always vote with greater unanimity on railroad matters than they did on suffrage or the state debt. While they represented a majority of those supporting the effort to ban land grants, a majority of Grangers voted against it.

Grange and non-Grange Democrats alike had written the politics of retrenchment into the organic law of the state, rendering tax-based growth strategies not merely politically impossible but also constitutionally impermissible. Yet the convention perpetuated what had already become a favored means of promotion among Democrats, generous land grants and

116

time extensions. This mixed legacy seems to have led to wildly varying perceptions of the constitution. Some Texans felt the convention had served at least certain railroad interests too well. They cited the T&P's interest in the extension ordinance and suggested what restrictions the document did contain had been placed there to discourage the emergence of new roads that might compete with the existing giants. "This New Constitution . . . ," one broadside argued, "says, 'Texas, we hand you over to the Texas Central, the Great Northern, and the Texas Pacific Rail Road monopoly made by us.'"[125] In the years immediately following the convention, much criticism of the constitution's development policies would focus not on their miserliness toward corporations but on their being too generous in allowing millions of acres of the public domain to be granted to railroad companies rather than reserving it exclusively for yeoman settlement or public education.[126]

But other Texans drew very different conclusions, one delegate assuming the "Rail Roads, & other speculating & monopoly interests" would oppose ratification of the constitution.[127] Republicans and some Democrats believed it would label Texas as anti-development and hostile to both immigration and outside investment. "Like a devil-fish," the *Austin Democratic Statesman* groused, the constitution "throttles all improvements."[128] Displeasure with the ban on immigration aid and other revenue-based growth mechanisms may have contributed to the phenomenon noted in the preceding chapter—a relatively large number of Democrats in Texas' urban counties apparently voting against ratification of the constitution their party had made.

These Texans were surely correct in seeing their new constitution as miserly regarding the powers of state. But its parsimony should not be taken as evidence of the power of the most agrarian or least liberal faction of the Democratic party. It instead illustrates how limited the choices were that Democrats of any stripe could entertain in the 1870s. While Democratic delegates did not inevitably choose the most penurious alternative, they had no alternative but to be penurious. As their party took power, even those members most dedicated to economic development found themselves required to abjure money subsidies to railroads, a generously funded educational system, and deficit spending.

But developmentally minded Redeemers could take parsimony to such extremes because they assumed their vast public lands would do much of the work that other states had to accomplish through taxation or deficit spending. Facing politically insupportable levels of tax and debt, Arkansas Democrats had the year before also written a restrictive constitution for their growing state, paring the powers of government and prohibiting the lending of state credit or the issuing of interest-bearing bonds except to accommodate existing debt. But without the option of unrestricted land subsidy, the constitution had to be somewhat more liberal than that of Texas. In contrast to its neighbor, Arkansas allowed tax exemptions for mining and manufacturing enterprises, established an immigration bureau, set maximum state and county tax rates at twice the Texas levels, and allowed communities broader authority to tax for schools. Elsewhere in the South, Redeemers also felt compelled to write higher tax ceilings into their constitutions than did Texas Democrats.[129]

Nevertheless, many Texans remained none too impressed with their Redeemer constitution. In the course of the proceedings, the *Waco Examiner,* identified as the Grange organ, asserted that the purportedly Grange-dominated convention was filled with drunkards, while the *Fredericksburg Sentinel* labeled it a "body of clowns."[130] Yet these drunkards and clowns had created a constitution that remained in force, though much encrusted with amendments, into the twenty-first century. The choices they made between acceptable and unacceptable uses of the power their party had won would forge an enduring relationship between the state, business, and economic development. Both Texans' dependence on natural resources to get the state's public work done, in preference to the Reconstruction alternatives of taxing and spending, and the goals of state regulation would long survive the era of Redemption.

BEYOND REDEMPTION

5

Redeemer Democrats and the Politics of Social Welfare

Texas occupies the anomalous position of having the best school fund and the poorest school system in the United States.

ENCYCLOPAEDIA BRITANNICA,
9TH EDITION (1888)

I n redeeming Texas, Democrats not only charted the role government would play in promoting development but also had to define its responsibilities in cultivating the state's human resources. As in most states, public education represented the signal effort in this regard. Indeed, as measured by expense, common-school education would be the single most important endeavor in which Texas government engaged. "There is no statute so universal in its application as a school law," the Redeemers' state superintendent of public instruction pointed out, "since it involves in its execution the social and financial interest of each and every citizen in the Commonwealth." A modern authority writes of the post-Reconstruction decades: "The politics of education . . . is central to any discussion of the distribution of government services in the South in this period, for state and local government there provided no other services, except possibly the courts, which directly affected large numbers of people or which could possibly have redistributed societal resources from race to race or class to class."[1]

Many forward-looking Texans in the 1870s saw better education as a vital aspect of progress. Prominent Democrats stressed the importance of a good school system in creating a more skilled labor force and attracting settlers. Some also saw schooling as a means to cushion the effect of developments that had made elite Texans nervous. It accelerated social mobility, thereby providing "a medium of conciliation between capital and labor." And if conservative white Texans had to reconcile themselves to universal suffrage, universal enlightenment might mitigate its consequences. "Without the conservative virtue which a right education will impart," the *Galveston Daily News* warned, "the elective franchise, unqualified and unconfined, must prove a destroying monster."[2]

These Democrats thereby linked popular education to two issues of greatest moment in the 1870s: economic development and the extension of conservative authority in the wake of Reconstruction's collapse. And as with economic development, the role the state played in schooling its citizenry would be crucially shaped both by the rhetoric of retrenchment that Democrats had employed against the Reconstruction regime and by Texas' unique and uniquely abundant reserve of land. As in their grappling with local opposition majorities, Democrats' education policies would be profoundly influenced by their declared commitment to decentralization. The choices Redeemers made in the 1870s and 1880s with respect to public education and government services, as with economic development and citizenship rights, would have enduring consequences for public life in Texas.

In its crucial Redemption campaigns of 1872 and 1873, the Democratic party had officially dedicated itself to providing a "common school education to every child in the State." The party's 1873 standard bearers, Richard Coke and Richard Hubbard, spoke in favor of public schools on the stump (though in debate Governor Davis forced Coke to admit that he, like many Democrats, had refused to pay his school tax).[3] But such broad statements of principle left crucial issues unsettled: state versus local government's responsibilities to fund teaching, administration, and schoolhouse construction; the proper sources of such funding; the initiative the state should exercise in actually establishing schools in individual communities; and the degree to which it should maintain some oversight regarding curriculum and personnel.

In addressing these issues Democrats might look to antebellum precedents for guidance. But those precedents could be cited to counsel both generosity or stinginess and inertia. Early on, Texas had allotted resources for education with an openhandedness other American states could not match. The republic had granted to each of its counties four square leagues of public land (approximately 18,000 acres) that could be leased or eventually sold to support a primary school or academy.[4] In 1854 the state had deposited into a school fund U.S. bonds worth $2 million it had received upon settling its boundary with New Mexico during the Compromise of 1850. The annual interest on this fund would be distributed pro rata to counties according to their population of free white people between the ages of six and sixteen. Later in the decade proceeds from the sale of unappropriated state lands and of the alternate sections surveyed by railroads and other recipients of public land grants were also directed to the school fund. Eleemosynary institutions were similarly supported, prospective asylums for the insane, the blind, and the deaf and mute as well as an orphanage each receiving land grants of 100,000 acres. The lunatic asylum also had $50,000 worth of the federal bonds set aside for its benefit.[5]

Despite this rich endowment, no educational *system* actually emerged in antebellum Texas—at least, not in the sense of a uniform establishment of community schools hewing to some common standard of instruction. The vast bounty yielded relatively little in terms of revenue that could be put to immediate use. Land remained easily available in Texas and its price low; receipts from land-scrip sales between 1856 and 1861—$155,687.85—did not generate substantial interest income for the schools.[6] Despite these meager returns, Texas proved reluctant, as in the case of economic development, to impress individuals' wealth to meet public needs. It would not levy a school tax. The Constitution of 1845 did earmark one-tenth of the annual state revenue for educational purposes. But this money would chiefly pay for the schooling of indigent and orphaned children, parents with sufficient means having to shoulder at least a portion of their children's teachers' salaries.[7]

Insufficient resources did not alone account for the state's failure to advance beyond the ad hoc schooling of some children. Antebellum laws did not arm it with much initiative in assuring that communities, which had to furnish their own buildings, actually established schools. The government did little more than divvy up state money among what schools happened to exist. Salaries, lengths of terms, and apparently curriculum were determined locally.[8] While localizing all initiative in establishing and administering schools, the laws made virtually no provision for local taxation to support education; only a few cities and one county were even authorized to levy school taxes. Nor did every community make much of an effort to secure its share of the state school funds apportioned between 1855 and 1861 or to profit off the public land reserved for each county.[9]

If the antebellum precedents with respect to schools left only the faintest institutional legacy—beyond the establishment of the school fund—they did establish meaningful patterns. The state saddled communities with the responsibility of actually providing schools but had not given local governments the taxing authority to fund whatever efforts the community deemed necessary. While a generous portion of the state's landed resources remained dedicated for the benefit of education, the state had proved closefisted in applying current revenue to immediate needs.

The early postbellum years saw few departures from these patterns. The erstwhile secessionists and conservative Unionists who controlled the 1866 constitutional convention inserted more imperative language in the new document, mandating that the legislature should, "as early as practicable, establish a system of free schools throughout the State," and provided for a state superintendent of public instruction. Yet a reservation of a specific portion of the state's annual revenue was eliminated, and while the existing land endowment was affirmed, only half of the proceeds from the sale of the public domain, rather than the full amount, was earmarked for the school fund, which was to benefit white children exclusively. Although the new constitution permitted it, the Eleventh Legislature (1866) failed to institute a separate education tax. Initiative in establishing schools and curriculum remained localized. The legislature did allow counties to tax themselves for educational purposes but only so that indigent white children might attend school. The relatively small amounts of tax revenue that could be raised in the African American community would alone fund black education.[10]

The school system created in Texas by Radical Republicans in 1870–71, by contrast, had made a clean break with antebellum precedents. In calling for "the gratuitous instruction" of all Texans between six and eighteen for at least four months each year, the Constitution of 1869 mandated what never before had been attempted—a statewide effort funded by the citizenry at large. Republicans, while allowing segregated facilities, for the first time expanded the state's educational efforts to include black children while channeling a far more generous proportion of the state's tax revenue to education. The constitution authorized a separate state levy for schools—a one-dollar poll tax—and also reserved fully one-fourth of the proceeds of general taxation for schools. The Davis government neatly reversed antebellum practice by transferring a great deal of initiative in the founding and equipping of schools, as well as in curriculum and personnel, to the state while allowing the tapping of community resources by means of local property taxes.[11]

Given their pointed attacks on the Republican educational bureaucracy, the campaign of tax resistance they had orchestrated against the school levies, and their more general pledges of tax relief, spending cuts, and decentralization, Redeemer Democrats would seem to have obliged themselves, once in power, to edge Texas back toward less state and community tax support and simultaneously more localized administration. During the first years of Redemption, though any move backward would be constrained by the Reconstruction constitution. As described in an earlier chapter, Democrats had initially to content themselves with slashing local school taxes and devolving authority over curriculum and personnel from a state bureaucracy to locally elected county boards.[12]

Democratic lawmakers displayed a good deal of unity in shepherding through this initial reorientation. Yet no consensus reigned within the party at large regarding the state's proper role in education. Prominent party members apparently believed their colleagues had gone too far in dismantling the existing system. They worried that the 1873 legislation made public education vulnerable to local apathy and parental indifference and, in providing for only four months of instruction, displayed a stinginess unworthy of Texas. Some Democrats embraced, at least tentatively, principles embodied in Republican laws: compulsory education, active state oversight of community efforts, an expansive definition of the scholastic population to include all children between six and eighteen, and gratuitous public education that recognized no distinction between those whose parents could afford to pay tuition and those whose parents could not.[13]

Perhaps the most important of these school-friendly Democrats was Orlando N. Hollingsworth, the man Redeemers had selected to replace Jacob DeGress as state superintendent of public instruction. Hollingsworth had sat in the state legislature in 1873 and, during its deliberations, seems not to have vigorously opposed his party's new school law. But within a year of becoming superintendent, he plainly felt it was defective. In his first annual report, he complained of the absence of uniformity and efficiency in a system governed by local officers possessing varying degrees of commitment, competence, and expertise while subject in some places to popular opposition. He also argued, in effect, that schools would need more money to operate at the minimal standards allowed under the existing constitution. He recommended a statewide property tax for the benefit of education, levied at or near the general state tax rate enforced under the Republicans.[14]

But if some Democrats felt that the 1873 school law had gone too far, many others believed it had not gone far enough. Some of this latter group thought that, as worthy a project as public education might be, Texas could not afford even the scaled-back system proposed in the new legislation. Governor Coke, while asserting the importance of education to "the material growth and the political and moral health of a State," wished to reduce the number of children eligible for schooling and agitated for a more bare-bones curriculum, cuts in teachers' salaries, and further caps on local school taxes.[15] Other party leaders called for a fundamental rethinking of the state's obligations. Some sought to eliminate the reservation of a portion of the annual revenue for education. Rep. James Throckmorton advocated a return to the antebellum system of utilizing the existing school fund and landed endowment chiefly to pay for the education of the indigent and distributing only what remained of the proceeds among the rest of the student population.[16]

Some Democrats simply objected to school taxes on principle. John Reagan had complained that the Republican school system levied upon white Texans for the benefit of black Texans. But he and other Redeemers objected to more than the fact that white dollars went to black education: "I could never see the right that I had to make another man pay for the education of my children." The *Austin Daily Democratic Statesman* seconded this sentiment in contending that the man paying taxes that went toward the education of someone else's children "is not only wrongfully robbed, but the strongest incentive to honest industry is removed from the path of him whose children become the beneficiaries of this public charity."[17] Yet even Democrats who viewed educational taxation as an unjust confiscation of one man's property for another man's use tended not to argue against common schools per se. They typically suggested that they would accept, even welcome, public education if it were paid for by proceeds from public land, for such funding did not involve the redistribution of private wealth.

That formulation provided a patch of common ground for Redeemers. The interests of all Democrats would be served by the substitution of revenue derived from land for tax revenue in funding schools. (Governor Coke hoped that education might eventually be funded entirely from nontax sources.)[18] Those Democrats who supported more comprehensive public efforts might approve general taxation for education in principle, but having often joined in the denunciations of the Radical school system as too extravagant and centralized, they had contributed to the public's expectation of tax relief.[19] At the very least they had acquiesced in the reduction of local school taxation—and in the 1871–72 school year, local monies had provided over 60 percent of educational funds spent.[20] Land offered a politically safe way to make up this lost funding. As with economic-development subsidies, public land might reconcile the political imperative of retrenchment with some semblance of state activism.

Consequently, Redeemers between 1873 and 1876 enlarged the public schools' landed endowment and endeavored to generate more income from it. As indicated in the preceding chapter, when the Thirteenth Legislature revived internal-improvement land grants in 1873, it also restored the policy of reserving alternate sections of the surveyed land to the benefit of the school fund. Redeemer legislators also put portions of the existing public school and university endowments on the market.[21] Their constitutional convention not only reaffirmed existing reservations of funds and property to the permanent school fund, as well as the alternate-sections arrangement, but also reserved one-half of the remaining public domain for sale or lease to benefit the school fund. The 1869 Reconstruction constitution had mandated that the proceeds from all sales of public land be directed to education but had placed no restrictions on the portion of the public domain that could be given away rather than sold. The Redeemers' constitution, while affirming railroad land grants and homestead donations, sought to place a vast acreage beyond the reach of either homesteaders or corporations (this reservation, though, existed in the abstract, not as a portion of territory actually marked off). In contrast to the 1873 school law, though, the constitution restored the Reconstruction practice of directing land proceeds to the permanent fund rather than including them among immediately available school funds—meaning only the interest could be utilized.[22]

The reservation of half of the public domain provoked relatively little controversy at the convention. Only fifteen of seventy-five Democrats seem to have made an effort to delete the provision. This small band included an odd assortment of delegates supporting both a more and a less aggressive state posture toward education, but the concentration of South and West Texans among them suggests that much of the opposition stemmed from fears that insufficient land would remain to subsidize railroad development into underserved regions or encourage frontier settlement.[23]

In perpetuating earlier reservations of public land and its proceeds and making additional provisions of its own, the Redeemer convention earmarked far more acreage to schools than the federal government granted to any single American state to support education and eleemosynary institutions. Indeed, had they been contiguous, the 52 million acres of public land that Texas ultimately reserved for schools and asylums would have been larger in area than many states.[24]

At the same time Redeemer legislators had put university and school lands on the market in 1874, they also provided for the sale of lands granted to the lunatic, blind, and deaf and dumb asylums.[25] But the experience of the asylums would not be strictly comparable to that of other public services intended by Democrats to be supported, at least in part, by the public domain. Except during 1874–75, spending on asylums, in contrast to spending on public schools, did not dip substantially below Reconstruction levels through the balance of the 1870s.[26]

Democrats took a distinct approach toward public institutions that served the disabled rather than the populace as a whole. The asylums had been the object of anti-Reconstruction rhetoric, Democrats charging waste, extravagance, and corruption in their management.[27] Yet Redeemers tended not to portray the administration or funding of asylums as fundamentally illegitimate in the same way many of them deplored the centralization of the Reconstruction-era school system or questioned the very use of tax revenue for mass education.

Several factors probably account for the state asylums being spared the worst of retrenchment politics. In the first place, having been established at the end of the antebellum period, these institutions were not identified as products of the Republican regime in the way the school system was. Nor did they present the same sort of dilemmas for a party that had pressed tax resistance and budget cutting, being nowhere near as costly as education. Most importantly, asylum spending did not encounter the ideological obstacles that common-school funding did. Even those Democrats with the most diminished sense of the proper realm of state action placed charity, at least of a limited sort, within those bounds. Thus many Democrats generally hostile to the use of tax revenue for mass education had conceded that the state might pay the tuition of orphaned and very needy students in existing private institutions. Like impoverished children, mentally or physically disabled adults who lacked the means for proper care were legitimate objects of state spending, while children whose parents might conceivably provide for their education were not. Suggestive of the distinctions made between educational and charitable efforts, Govs. Richard Hubbard and Oran Roberts later in the decade pressed the legislature to cut educational spending but at the same time called for increased asylum appropriations.[28]

Veteran pensions would be similarly spared much of the politics of retrenchment, though Redeemers in this case too eventually had to look to public land to escape new fiscal burdens. In Texas as elsewhere, pensions would become a very large exception to the tendency of nineteenth-century governments not to spend much on social welfare. During Reconstruction, pensions for veterans of the Texas Revolution and several subsequent military enterprises of the Republic of Texas had been established as an entitlement. The Reconstruction-era law, allowing all such veterans $250 annually ($500 to those wounded in service), quickly and apparently unexpectedly created a sizable public obligation. Governor Davis felt obliged to veto as too expensive the almost $225,000 in appropriations required to make good on them.[29] Democrats, however, apparently saw little political reward in attacking the costly pledges the Reconstruction legislature had made to the heroes of San Jacinto. The same platform that in 1873 attacked a bloated and extravagant Republican school system declared it "the imperative duty of the great State of Texas, in the plenitude of her wealth, to provide with a liberal hand for the battle-scarred veterans of the Texas revolution" (this emphasis on Texas' wealth, of course, was most unusual for Redeemers, who usually pleaded the state's poverty). If letters to the *Galveston Daily News* are any indication, many Texans seemed inclined to hold Democrats to the promises made by a Republican-dominated legislature, at least in this case.[30]

Hemmed in on one side by the political appeal of providing for veterans and on the other by the exigencies of retrenchment, Democratic lawmakers proved reluctant to pay the pensions in full or straightforwardly repudiate them. After much legislative back and forth, they eventually passed a law issuing bonds to meet obligations incurred under the pension act and limited future entitlements, pegged at $150 annually, to indigent and disabled veterans alone.[31] Still, even with such limitations, obligations piled up more rapidly than solons anticipated. Democrats had to repeal the 1874 law a year after its passage and in 1879 were forced to appropriate $190,000 to supplement the $40,000 budgeted, under the terms of an 1876 law, for a more restricted set of indigent veterans. Bonds totaling more than $1 million had been issued to veterans by that time, accounting for almost half of the increase in the state's funded debt since the passage of the 1874 laws and making for interest charges of over $500,000.[32]

It is little wonder then that Democratic lawmakers finally conceded that this public service also had to be supported by public land. The Sixteenth Legislature (1879) canceled the 1876 pension law and instead offered indigent veterans 640 acres of public land. The appeal of this policy to retrenchment-minded lawmakers—if not to aged and disabled veterans—was such that it was expanded upon two years later. In a spectacular, if tardy, example of Redeemer Democrats' generosity with the state's landed wealth, the legislature doubled the size of the veterans' land grants and made them available to the poor and disabled soldiers of the Confederacy as well as to the widows of Texans killed in the service of the Lost Cause.[33]

If generosity with the public domain served the interests of Democrats of all stripes, delegates to the Redeemer convention nevertheless had to face up to the issues that had divided them through the preceding years: How much and what kind of tax-based revenue—if any—would go toward public education? Who would actually establish schools and decide what was taught in them? As the convention opened, delegate W. P. Ballinger noted in his diary a "strong hostility to Common School system" among his fellow delegates.[34] But the divisions within the convention over these issues did not involve anything so simple as contention between two well-defined factions, one more and the other less friendly to public education.

The small Republican delegation stood at the generous end of the spectrum. These men tended to propose both the reservation of a generous portion of the annual revenue for the schools and some combination of local ad valorem taxes, corporate taxes, poll taxes, and even state ad valorem taxes specifically earmarked for education. Republican-drafted articles also vested a great deal of authority over school administration in the state government.[35]

A diverse lot of Democrats—and not an inconsiderable one, either in terms of their number or stature in the party—proved willing to travel some way toward the Republican position, particularly by supporting direct taxation in support of education. Many Texas Democrats, both before and after the Civil War, made a qualitative distinction between devoting some stipulated portion of general tax revenue to education and levies made specifically to support schools. The former seems not to have been as frequently regarded as robbing Peter to educate Paul's children. But at the convention Democrats as different as plantation county attorney George McCormick, German-born Cayton Erhard and Jacob Waelder, and the old frontier soldier "Rip" Ford spoke, at least in general terms, in favor of the less popular position of taxation specifically for education. When it came to the form and amount of such a levy, some among these Democrats, including Granger H. W. Wade of Hunt County, supported an unprecedented statewide ad valorem tax. In addition to or instead of a state property tax, some proposed a substantial poll tax to benefit schools. These included Galveston attorney W. P. Ballinger, an erstwhile Whig, and Granger and hard-shell Democratic editor Charles DeMorse. Some Democratic delegates, including DeMorse and E. L. Dohoney, even endorsed the sort of local taxation for education their party had fiercely denounced during Reconstruction.[36]

At the other end of the spectrum stood Democrats resisting the expenditure of any tax-generated revenue on schools. They included not only rural devotees of minimal government like Jonathan Russell of Wood County but also attorney George Flournoy of Galveston and Fletcher Stockdale, the South

Texas lawyer, politician, and railroadman. Some of them argued on principle against taxation's redistributive effects. "What is it," asked Williamson County farmer Richard Sansom, "to take the hard-earned dollars of a portion of the people and divide it among all of the people for educational purposes, if it be not agrarianism?" While some of these delegates allowed that the state might provide charity—seeing to it that children whose families lacked the means to pay tuition received a basic education—at other times they argued specifically against any provision for the offspring of "lazy" men. Some invoked the slippery slope. The one-tenth of the annual revenue reserved for schools by one proposal represented "a mere pittance," Russell admitted, "but if one-tenth can be taken all can be taken." Delegates also spoke up for patriarchy, contending that governments ought not usurp the right and responsibility of family heads to determine the form and extent of education their own children should receive.[37]

Some delegates, in resisting any public financing of education, argued less from principle than upon pragmatic grounds. They contended that Texas lacked the large and evenly distributed population necessary to sustain a state school system. Some stressed political imperatives, noting that citizens believed taxes to be too high and that levies could not therefore be maintained at the levels required for a comprehensive school system.[38]

A centrist aggregation of Democrats generally disapproved of taxation of property specifically for school purposes but would accept the reservation of a portion of the annual revenue for education. Some even endorsed a very modest capitation tax, its very regressiveness apparently weighing in its favor, for it would reach "every non-property holder."[39] This group of delegates, however, determined to keep such taxing and spending at more modest levels than others advocated. Most seemed to prefer the one-tenth prescribed by the Constitution of 1845 than the one-fourth stipulated by the Reconstruction document.[40] John Reagan may have been the most prominent of the more grudging members of this centrist group. In interviews before the convention, he had trotted out the familiar arguments against education taxes but said he could stomach the reservation of one-tenth of the state's annual revenue. During the proceedings, though, he managed to have the poll tax to be levied for schools cut by half.[41]

The fact that one must describe as centrists Democratic delegates who proposed to spend far less on education than had theretofore been required to support even the most basic school system suggests how much the spectrum shifted toward minimalism once the party was no longer hemmed in by the Reconstruction constitution (as did the fact that E. L. Dohoney, an architect of the 1873 school law, proved to be one of the convention's more liberal Democrats when it came to education).

Yet as in the case of economic development, if the convention's educational provisions ended up being so restrictive as to raise objections even among prominent Democrats, they were not as tightfisted as some delegates had wished them to be.[42] In fact the measures ultimately adopted were the products of a revolt within the convention against greater extremes of parsimony. A minority report of the Education Committee entirely rejected the use of tax revenue for schools, and the same committee's majority report reserved no more than one-tenth of the state's annual revenue for education plus whatever capitation tax the legislature might feel compelled to levy. A slim majority of Democrats joined with a solid Republican bloc to force the reconsideration of the issue by an entirely new and decidedly more generous committee. It was this select committee that produced what became, with some amendments, the constitution's Article VII. In addition to proceeds of the land reserve, it directed *up to* one-fourth of the general revenue to public schools (the Reconstruction constitution, by contrast, had *guaranteed* one-fourth) to be supplemented by a two-dollar poll tax (cut by the convention to one dollar). This regressive tax may have been insufficient to the state's needs, especially in light of the elimination of most local school taxes, but the choice being made was between an inadequate state tax and no school tax at all.[43]

The Redeemer convention thereby cautiously defied antebellum precedent and the politics of retrenchment by allowing (though not mandating) the reservation of annual revenue at the Reconstruction level of 25 percent and perpetuating the one-dollar direct tax for schools. But it had been Republicans' local school tax that had been the chief object of Democratic resistance, and the convention kept the party faith in this regard, turning back measures that, as a general rule, would permit communities to tax themselves to further local educational efforts.[44] This seemed destined to have a grave effect on school funding. Even under the more restrictive Democratic school laws, over three-quarters of counties reporting had felt compelled to levy local taxes to make up for shortfalls in education funds. All that the convention supplied in the place of this local money was the proceeds from school land earlier reserved for county use (during Reconstruction, these funds had been redirected to the general school fund).[45] The Redeemer convention did make an exception in the case of cities and towns whose charters allowed them to support "a public institution of learning." These could levy an ad valorem school tax, though only if two-thirds of the community's taxpayers approved (the 1876 law implementing this provision interpreted it to mean two-thirds of a municipality's *property* tax payers).[46]

If these severe restrictions on local finance honored antebellum precedent, they also served Redeemers' immediate political interests. They kept taxing authority firmly in the grip of a Democratic state government and out of the hands of African American majorities in old plantation counties that might be tempted to educate poor children by means of large levies on local propertyholders. In cities, where local school taxes could be levied, property qualifications likewise discouraged any radically redistributive efforts.

Honoring the antebellum prejudice against local taxation, the convention also upheld its discordant counterpart, the decentralization of initiative and authority in the establishment and administration of public schools. If a majority of delegates refused to drive retrenchment to the hilt when it came to school financing, most Democrats—even those inclined to relatively generous funding—were prepared to go to considerable lengths to honor their party's stated commitment to local self-government. The compromise education article the convention hammered out remained silent on most administrative issues, eliminating much of the apparatus and most of the state initiative provided for by the Reconstruction constitution. It established only an ex officio board of education, consisting of the governor, comptroller, and secretary of state, which would distribute school funds to the counties and perform such duties as the legislature might prescribe. In contrast to the Republican constitution, Redeemers established no minimum annual school term, did not define the age group entitled to free schooling, and included no language making education compulsory. The new constitution did not assign the state government any specific role in seeing that communities actually founded schools. In fact its only positive mandate with respect to school administration was that requiring racially segregated facilities.[47]

The thoroughly Democratic legislature that convened the following spring to write laws in conformance with the new constitution took the document's silence on all but matters of finance as license to resurrect the minimalism of the antebellum era. County officials, together with community trustees, gained complete authority over personnel and curriculum. By defining the school age as between eight and fourteen, the 1876 law entitled young Texans to only half as many years of public instruction as allowed under the Republicans. It made the actual establishment of schools the work not even of county officials but of interested parents—on an ad hoc, annual basis. Communities had to furnish half the funds necessary to build their school-houses, but this money could not be raised by local taxation except in cities and towns.[48] Several little-noted acts of the 1876 legislature did channel some local money to schools, directing fines paid for violations of locally imposed prohibition laws and the proceeds of a state tax on dogs to county treasuries for educational purposes. But the more lucrative of the two devices, the dog tax, was as regressive a device as lawmakers could have imposed—not simply because it required the same amount from dog owners rich and poor, but because dog ownership appears to have been associated in the public mind with the poor, especially African Americans, and the tax understood to burden them disproportionately.[49]

Decentralization, especially when combined with the requirement of segregation, would do particular damage to the cause of black education in Texas. As much as many white Texans may have doubted the utility or desirability of educating African Americans, and resented the use of their tax dollars to do so, it would have been difficult for Democrats to legislate in a direct manner against black opportunity. The terms of the state's readmission to the Union in 1870 prohibited official action discriminating against African American educational efforts, and federal lawmakers continued to cast a watchful eye on the state's actions with respect to schools.[50] In terms of finance African Americans remained entitled to the same pro rata portion of state school monies as white students. But the local officials charged with distributing state funds seem not to have always done so in the prescribed equitable manner. The ad hoc system allowed whites in black-majority areas to organize their own schools while not *requiring* that their black neighbors be similarly served. The requirement that classroom construction be, in part, privately funded by communities also disproportionately burdened the generally poorer African American population. In subsequent decades the construction of black schools continued to lag far behind that of white facilities.[51]

But white students seem also to have suffered by decentralization. A Grayson County judge lamented: "Under the present law, it is everybody's business to organize [school communities], and what is everybody's business becomes no one's."[52] Great disparities quickly emerged. In the 1876–77 school year, for example, the average public-school term ranged from 20 days in Mason and 30 days in Young to 130 days in Cameron and 160 days in McCulloch counties. The most pervasive of these disparities existed between rural and urban schools. Municipalities had far greater power to fund local educational efforts to the extent their residents thought appropriate. Lawmakers interpreted the constitution's provision exempting cities from the taxing ban rather liberally, allowing any incorporated municipality to vote to organize itself as a school district and tax itself to support education—for ten months a year rather than the four-month standard Democrats had earlier applied statewide (1879 laws, however, limited local school taxes to a maximum of 0.5 percent). Some city charters allowed portions of their general revenue to be devoted to education as well. By the end of the decade, the average length of the school year in municipal districts was more than twice the county average. Houston and San Antonio had established genuine educational systems, complete with secondary and graded primary schools. Austin and Galveston were building systems of relatively generous dimension, and even a number of smaller towns such as New Braunfels, Navasota, and Palestine managed eventually to keep public schools open ten months a year. The latitude the state granted cities and towns did most Texas schoolchildren little good, however, for in the early 1880s, only slightly more than 10 percent of them attended municipal schools.[53]

Examining the Redeemer convention's debates on education only deepens one's appreciation for the complexities of factionalism among Texas Democrats. In this realm too it is difficult to discern the dueling of any very cohesive "New South" and "agrarian" or "Bourbon" factions, such as historians have sometimes sought to identify in the politics of post-Reconstruction southern states. Nor does one find the bipartite contention between Grangers and lawyers, restrictive and liberal constitutionalists, or a protopopulist rank and file and a Democratic elite that some contemporaries and many scholars have perceived in the convention proceedings.[54] As we have seen, delegates representing "agrarian" constituencies differed with one another over crucial matters of suffrage and economic development. Democrats from overwhelmingly white and Democratic rural counties squared off against those from black-majority plantation counties on the poll tax. Grangers divided on the question of continuing corporate land grants. Such differences made perfect sense, for they mirrored Texas' frontier diversity. After the founding of its state organization in 1873, the Grange established lodges in many, very different parts of Texas—from former plantation counties in the northeast to the blackland prairie to more hardscrabble areas closer to western fringes of Anglo-American settlement.[55] Accordingly, delegates identified as Grangers ranged from development enthusiast John Reagan to E. S. C. Robertson, the anti-subsidy scion of one of Anglo Texas' first families, to the more rough-hewn Collin County farmer John "Rutabaga" Johnson. For their part, non-Grange Democrats ran the gamut from Populist-to-be Thomas Nugent to William Ballinger, the attorney of the Galveston elite, to Louis Cardis, a borderland political boss born in Italy.

One finds that delegates who stood together on issues of economic development might well be at odds on educational finance and administration. Reagan, Ballinger, Fletcher Stockdale, and Jacob Waelder all demonstrated their support for positive government action in pursuit of railroad development, population growth, and an adequate labor supply. But Reagan and Stockdale, in contrast to Waelder and Ballinger, sought strict limits on public spending for education.

Such divisions could certainly suggest that those embracing economic development represented multiple interest groups that stood to be variously served by an aggressive state effort in education. The Texas Democrats most supportive of public schools often viewed education as a counterpart to, or a component of, economic diversification. Ballinger and Waelder hailed from the state's most cosmopolitan cities (Galveston and San Antonio respectively), places that might look forward to building even more complex commercial and industrial economies with the aid of a skilled labor force. Ballinger plainly felt that Texas had prospects beyond "making cotton, wheat, and corn [and] raising stock" and would later deride the Redeemer constitution for not cultivating them.[56] The disproportionate Democratic vote against ratification of the constitution in urban counties might have been due in part to the perception that the document had not served cities' interest in education well enough.

Developmentally oriented Democrats less solicitous of public education—Reagan, Stockdale, and James Throckmorton, for example—in some instances came from smaller towns. Growth for them may have seemed more likely to take the form of improved transportation enhancing their regions' cotton or cattle trade, sectors that were not premised on the existence of an educated labor force.[57]

Yet even if one more carefully delineates possible divergences of interests among cities, smaller towns, and countryside, the effort to correlate them with distinct stances on public education at the 1875 convention can rather quickly be confounded. Joining Waelder and Ballinger in pressing a more thoroughgoing public effort were Democrats representing decidedly agrarian constituencies—such as J. R. Fleming of Comanche County and C. R. Smith of Milam County. Joseph Haynes of Caldwell County voted to ban railroad land grants and opposed a publicly supported immigration bureau, but he endorsed a state property tax for education and sought to raise the poll tax levied for the benefit of schools.[58] In contrast, Galveston attorney George Flournoy, surely no hayseed, denounced public funding of schools while embracing corporate land grants. Interestingly, a fellow delegate suspected

Flournoy's Catholicism might make him hostile to public education. As German resistance to the Radical school establishment had suggested, the state's unusual diversity could give the politics of public education an ethnocultural dimension, such as it had in the North.[59]

A number of the Democrats who managed to get elected to the convention from counties with large black populations, including George McCormick of Colorado County and W. L. Crawford of Marion, did not hew to modern historians' understanding that plantation-area whites opposed public education as neither necessary to getting their community's work done nor especially conducive to the continued political or social subordination of their black labor force.[60] They proved to be among the better friends of public education. McCormick even exhibited a specific, if paternalistic, solicitude for black education, attempting to guarantee proportional funding for a state college for African Americans—all while he endeavored by various expedients to diminish that population's political influence.[61] About ten delegates like McCormick supported suffrage restriction as well as more aggressive financing of public education (on occasion they proposed to establish a school tax and then make it a prerequisite for voting). If they identified with the argument that universal education would exercise a conservative influence upon the electorate, other restrictionists, including Stockdale, Reagan, and Robertson, apparently did not find that logic sufficiently compelling to support generous provisions for schools.

Nor can one find any very cohesive or predictable "agrarian" or "New South" alignments on education in the fourth estate. Many city newspapers did back more thoroughgoing educational provisions, but the *Austin Democratic Statesman*, which vehemently opposed a constitution it contended had been framed by country bumpkins and throttled development, consistently attacked public funding of mass education, referring to school taxes as confiscation of wealth. The editors seemed to doubt formal education fitted young people for professions especially useful to Texas, chiding those who believed "the youths of the country must be converted [into] shysters and pill-pedlers." The *Waco Examiner*, a paper identified with the Texas Grange, however, denounced the convention for its indifference to public education (and differed too with the convention majority in supporting the spending of public money to encourage immigration to Texas).[62] The *Navasota Tablet*, headquartered in black-majority Grimes County, adamantly supported suffrage restriction and the founding of a white man's party locally while calling upon white citizens to support African Americans' efforts to establish a high school in the community.[63]

The divisions over education that appeared among friends of economic development and supporters of suffrage restriction only emphasize the general failure of Texas Redeemers to maintain coherent factional groupings across the spectrum of issues their party had to address. At the constitutional convention, delegates built shifting coalitions rather than engage in bipartite factionalism. That does not mean delegates voted randomly, however. Distinct patterns appear in Democratic voting on economic-growth and social-welfare issues. But these patterns involved more than a simple split between those supporting government activism on the one hand and those opposing it on the other.

Instead, four fundamental orientations emerge. Among those believing the public interest would be most directly and immediately served by rapid commercial and agricultural development were many who thought that the state's role lay in nurturing private enterprise while otherwise minimizing the burdens government imposed upon citizens, particularly by reducing taxes and cutting spending for public services. Thus delegates Reagan, Stockdale, and Flournoy as well as Congressman Throckmorton and Lieutenant Governor Hubbard, all backed state promotion of railroad development while questioning the legitimacy of spending tax revenue for public education.[64] Others of those believing the commonweal would best be served by rapid economic development, however, at least implicitly felt that, in addition to promoting expansion under private auspices, government had a responsibility to cultivate Texas' human resources. The editors of the *Galveston Daily News* and, at the convention, Ballinger and Waelder, proved willing to qualify their party's commitment to retrenchment in the interests of a broader public investment in economic growth and a social well-being commensurate with what they believed to be the spirit of the age.[65] Thus they supported not only corporate land grants but also a more generous investment in common schools than did many of their fellow Democrats.

A third position seemed to attend more exclusively to the human side of Texas' development. At the convention Democrats like DeMorse and Joseph Haynes voted against corporate land grants but supported more liberal funding of education, defining a stance not unlike those of some earlier Reconstruction Republicans, particularly Edmund Davis, and later third-party dissidents. While they did not necessarily oppose economic modernization in the form of railroad building, they voted as if they believed that government's chief responsibility was not to aid private interests in developing their enterprises but to tend to things that private interests could not or would not accomplish on their own, such as educating the state's children. This attitude might coexist with a suspicion of corporate intentions, as suggested by DeMorse's reputation as an anti-monopoly man.[66]

This same suspicion of business interests could be found among a fourth group, which placed far more things beyond the scope of legitimate governmental action. Many Texans—represented perhaps most forcefully at the convention by Jonathan Russell of Wood County—seemed to feel that the populace would be better served the less it was burdened by government. Accordingly, such men not only opposed public support for railroad development or the promotion of immigration but (unlike DeMorse, Haynes, or later Greenbackers) also opposed any very extensive expenditure on social welfare, including funding schools. This minimalist position has often been associated with the Grange. But in fact at the convention, only a decided minority of Grange-affiliated delegates acted together in voting against railroad land grants, tax-supported education, an immigration bureau, and a poll-tax prerequisite on voting and for lower official salaries. What solidarity existed among these ten to fourteen Grangers hardly bears out the familiar image of an agrarian faction having its way with the constitution, particularly since when it came to a number of issues upon which they made common cause—banning railroad land grants, opposing the expenditure of tax revenue on schools, and further restricting the state's ability to contract debt—they did not carry the day but *lost*.[67]

These fundamental orientations clearly emerge only in retrospect rather than being a recognized basis of allegiance at the time. Even delegates described a convention in which one side had it out with another. One of them, identified in the press as a ringleader of agrarian delegates, crowed: "They had 'fit' the opposition carefully and beaten them. There were thirty-six lawyers in that body, but they had been superior to them. They had beaten the talent of the Convention all along the line."[68] Yet if the more complicated set of ideological affinities were often unstated and even unrecognized, identifying them nevertheless seems to shed more light on the Redeemer constitution than do more-familiar models of single pairs of contending interest groups, one of which prevailed and the other of which was routed. Thus, for example, support for railroad land grants came not from a single like-minded group. Instead those supporting state promotion of private development but not investment in public services and those supporting state activism in both realms combined to perpetuate the policy. Members of the first group, however, voted against those of the second, and with those seeking governmental retrenchment across the board, in support of parsimony in the realm of public education.

Whichever of these orientations they wittingly or unwittingly subscribed to, Texas Democrats in the 1870s could hardly have resisted making the state's landed endowment support a wide range of public purposes. By doing so they could meet both the ideological requirements of those objecting to the redistributive effect of taxation and the political requirements of those whose enthusiasm for state activism had to be reconciled to their party's stated goal of retrenchment. In contrast to their posture on railroads subsidies, however, Democrats did not look to the federal government to supply funds that political imperatives prevented them from raising from Texans. Unlike many southern Democrats, Texas Redeemers stubbornly refused to embrace direct federal funding for education, a very real possibility by the 1880s. Although some in the state press and the educational community expressed support for the Blair bill, which would have distributed a tariff-generated federal surplus to states in proportion to their illiterate population, most prominent Texas Democrats stood united against it. Senator Coke favored federal backing of railroad construction in the name of national defense and frontier settlement, but he could find no justification for congressional funding of education in the "general welfare" language of the Constitution. Like Coke, Senator Maxey and his successor, John Reagan, invariably voted against the several versions of the Blair bill. The House of Representatives never voted on the bill itself, but if an 1886 referral of it is indicative of congressmen's stance, every Texan who voted opposed the measure, including Throckmorton and David Culberson, both enthusiasts for federal and state railroad subsidies. The state Democratic party, saying it opposed further centralization of power in the federal government, denounced the Blair bill in its platforms of 1884 and 1886.[69]

Federal funding of education, it seems, raised questions of control that federal railroad subsidies did not. In opposing the Blair bill, Coke asserted that if Congress could justify spending revenue it raised from the citizenry on schools, there was little it could not claim the authority to do. Ceding to the federal government the power to fund education meant granting it the power to govern schools, with integrated classrooms being a logical consequence—a prospect that so horrified him that, when Congress had debated Charles Sumner's civil rights bill in 1874, he pledged to close every public school in Texas rather than permit their desegregation.[70] Coke's arguments suggest that as grave as the problem of school finance might be, the most powerful Texas Democrats refused to deal with it in ways that might conceivably imperil the authority they had consolidated through Redemption. There had been important things they would not sacrifice in the 1870s to extend their party's power—for example, universal manhood suffrage and local election of officeholders. But to safeguard their authority in the 1880s, they seem to have been prepared to see Texas schoolchildren do without.

Perhaps Texans could afford to be more hardnosed than other southern Democrats when it came to the Blair bill because their state's unique and bountiful school fund afforded it resources that other former Confederate states lacked. In 1880 Texas finished dead last in the percentage of total tax receipts directed to schools. Yet the state by that time tended to surpass its southern counterparts in per capita educational spending, avoiding, for example, the brutal penury visited upon neighboring Louisiana.[71]

Yet Texas could claim success for its land strategy only when compared to impoverished Dixie. The lazy reporting of school statistics by local authorities makes exact comparison of the relative condition of public education in Texas and other states impossible. But as far as can be determined, the Lone Star State ranked at or very near the bottom nationally in such areas as length of school term (outside cities) and the number of years children were entitled to free instruction. Texas appears to have trailed all, or at least most, non-southern states—and even western territories—in per capita spending on education.[72]

Clearly, public land had not spared Texans hard choices between levying upon citizens or doing without. With much of the school land situated in the sparsely settled western half of the state, demand in the 1870s was not such that acreage sold at high prices or in great quantity. From the time that Democrats put the land on the market in 1874 through 1879, the permanent school fund never netted more than $65,000 annually from this source (and after 1875 only the interest on such receipts actually became available to schools). Neither could county school lands be counted upon to provide a reliable and uniform basis for local funding. By the end of the 1870s, increasing numbers of counties reported that they were supplementing state school money with proceeds from the sale or lease of their reserved lands, but many realized little or nothing from this source. The money derived from state lands together with the interest on the bonds held by the permanent school fund continued to supply considerably less than half of the many hundreds of thousands of dollars required annually to meet even the diminished expectations enforced by Redeemers.[73]

Texas frontier lands thus produced limited returns. Yet its frontier population boom at the same time only increased demands upon the state. Democrats had cut by half the span of years during which youngsters were entitled to publicly funded education. But by the end of the 1870s, the number of school-age children had nearly reached Reconstruction-era proportions. Enrollment actually exceeded earlier levels. Texas legislatures in the years following ratification of the Redeemer constitution, therefore, continued to reserve the constitutional maximum of one-fourth of the annual state revenue for common schools—the same fraction provided for under the Reconstruction constitution.[74]

The clear failure by the end of the 1870s of public land to support a school system meeting Texas' needs, and its simultaneous failure to deliver citizens from the sort of spending Democrats had condemned in their crusade against Reconstruction, would be but a single element in a larger crisis in Redeemer political economy. This crisis would require Democrats, during Oran Roberts's two terms as governor (1879–83), to rethink some of their fundamental strategies of government and put Texas' exceptional status within the post-Reconstruction South to the test.

6

The Crisis of Redeemer Government, 1878–84

I think I see away down the corridors of time, this splendid territory teeming with millions. No more public lands; no more cheap homes—poverty and squalid want gathering fast and thick around the inhabitants; when some one of them will gather up the fragments of our history and read to the gazing and mind-famished multitude how this generation had in its power and keeping a fund that should have gathered like the snowball as time rolled on, and how, if we had been true to ourselves, to posterity, to them, they could have educated all their children, paid all their taxes, reared school houses, built roads and bridges—and then I see them turn with deep mutterings from the wicked folly that crazed our people from 1865 to 1882.

GOV. JOHN IRELAND,
INAUGURAL ADDRESS, 1883

Texas' frontier needs, its southern politics, and its unique bounty of public land had combined to forge a strategy for governing that set the state's Democrats apart from other Redeemers. They created a constitution that in terms of tax rates, tax exemptions, and immigration promotion was even more stinting than those of a number of other post-Reconstruction states. At the same time, though, they did not always have to choose the least generous alternative in addressing their growing state's outsized needs, such as ending developmental land subsidies or publicly funded education, as some party members advocated. But the Redeemers' governing strategy, premised on the state's landed wealth, quickly crumbled. Texans soon discovered that they too had to make choices between paying more or doing without.

Democrats found it far more difficult than they anticipated to retrench—and thus deliver on their party's central promise. Their constitution set low ceilings on tax rates and public debt, but in the years immediately following its ratification in 1876, some prominent Redeemers doubted that fundamental change in state finance had in fact occurred with the shift from Republican to Democratic rule. "Mismanagement and recklessness were inaugurated under the carpet bag government imposed by reconstruction," Ashbel Smith complained in 1879, "[and] the practice has been persisted in by the democratic administrations of the last four years and for its continuance the democratic party have made ourselves responsible."[1] Yet if Texans complained of the continuing cost of government, they also grumbled about the sorry state of the public schools, persistent lawlessness, and the absence of an immigration bureau.

Accordingly, by the late 1870s Democrats faced new political challenges and internal dissensions occasioned by their constituents' perception that taxpayers had yet to receive the rewards of retrenchment and at the same time were underserved by government. The state *asked* too much and *owed* too much but did not *do* enough, it seemed. Moreover, Texas was plainly running out of the land Democrats had counted on to accomplish public ends without burdening the citizenry. With their strategy for governing stalling on all fronts within ten years of assuming power, Redeemers had to abandon certain of their goals and find new (and less painless) ways of pursuing those to which they held fast.

When it came to the state debt, Democrats by the later 1870s had not simply failed to ease Texans' burdens but had not even managed to hold the line. The debt had climbed since Reconstruction from some $2.5 million to more than $5 million by the end of fiscal year 1877–78. Democrats could fairly argue that its growth was due not to their fiscal irresponsibility but precisely the opposite. Although they had engaged in deficit spending within the limits allowed by the new constitution, the ballooning debt was largely the product of their refusal to repudiate the state's existing obligations. While Democrats declined to spend current tax revenue to pay off state warrants issued under the Republican administration, neither would they simply refuse to honor obligations incurred before the transfer of power, as Redeemers in other states did. The legislature had sold bonds to cover the warrants, converting much of the Reconstruction-era floating debt into bonded debt, and to fund earlier bonds then coming due. As noted, they had also issued bonds to meet veterans' claims. As a consequence of such policies, Democrats could point to a decided improvement in the state's credit. Still, Texas staggered under interest payments of hundreds of thousands of dollars annually, debt service becoming one of the largest single items in the state budget.[2]

If retrenchment had had to yield to the distaste prominent Texas Democrats felt for repudiation, Redeemers at the same time would not defy the politics of retrenchment in order to reduce the debt. Too many party members had made too much noise about standing fast on taxes. So while Governor Coke suggested his willingness to use school money to pay interest charges on time, he would not countenance a special 0.15 percent surtax to meet those interest charges, though the new constitution empowered lawmakers to exceed the 0.5 percent cap on property taxation to pay down the debt.[3]

But if debt reduction had had to yield in turn to the goal of tax relief, neither had Democrats made appreciable progress toward the latter by the late 1870s. Democrats found it difficult to trim state spending. The appropriations of the first legislature to meet after the new constitution's fiscal ceilings were in place actually exceeded those of the immediately preceding years, and lawmakers subsequently had to appropriate nearly $500,000 more to provide for expenses inadequately funded by that session.[4]

Texas' position on Dixie's western frontier continued to impose substantial, and steadily increasing, costs. The rapid expansion of the population—both spatially and in sheer number—during the late 1870s required considerable spending if government was going to carry out its most basic duties through the length and breadth of the huge state. As native resistance wound down to scattered raiding and the ascension of Porfirio Diaz somewhat stabilized things along the Rio Grande, the state government had to bear less of the cost of Indian fighting and border patrol. But lawmakers still felt compelled to spend hundreds of thousands of dollars on defense and law enforcement: for the "protection of the frontier," for rewards and other expenses incurred in apprehending fugitives, and for maintaining the ranger forces of L. H. McNelly and John B. Jones. The Redeemer constitution had cut the number of district courts and the pay of judges, but the fees paid to judicial officers such as sheriffs, prosecutors, and clerks gobbled up tens of thousands of dollars annually. And as towns and counties became more thickly settled and citizens dispersed in greater numbers across a wider expanse of Texas, lawmakers had little choice but to create new judicial districts. Within five years of the constitution's ratification, the number of judges exceeded Reconstruction-era levels. The new constitution's smaller salaries had made for savings in various executive departments, but appropriations for others, such as the comptroller and the Land Office, had to remain near or even above earlier levels if the state were to distribute land to, and collect revenue from, its rapidly growing number of citizens.[5]

This population boom continued to impose costs on towns and counties too. Communities had no alternative but to spend money to construct, improve, or expand the infrastructure of civil government. As elsewhere in the post-Reconstruction South, the construction of public buildings could become the source of bitter local contention. Some saw new courthouses as essential symbols of their communities' commercial and political importance (or at least ambitions); others resisted them as expensive luxuries. But in many Texas counties, such expenditures were a practical necessity. Courthouses and jails had to be established where none had earlier existed and replacements built for the numerous structures destroyed in a spate of courthouse burnings during the 1870s.[6]

The costs imposed by demographic and spatial expansion could theoretically have been more than offset by the corresponding growth of the tax base. Tax receipts more than tripled during the 1870s, but persistent undervaluation of property and evasion of payment (aggravated by widespread absentee ownership) limited the return on growth.[7] The population boom served instead to vastly expand the ranks of school-aged children. As noted, land sales were not such that the schools' share of general revenue could be reduced. Since schools were already receiving the constitutional maximum of one-quarter of state income, taxes could not be cut without battering education.

As a consequence, Texas, unlike a number of other southern states, found itself unable to reduce the state ad valorem tax in the years following its Redemption.[8] The rate remained stuck at the legal maximum of 0.5 percent. This meant that for all the Democrats' howling about high taxes, from the seating of the first Redeemer legislature in 1873 through the end of the decade, the state ad valorem levy continued at the level imposed during Reconstruction.[9] Despite the curtailment of school and road levies, local taxes after 1875 were not uniformly reduced either. County taxation varied tremendously from place to place, but given the exemptions written into the Redeemer constitution, local rates might considerably exceed the state rate in places that had accrued large debts or had pressing infrastructure needs. While the local ad valorem rate in Bell County (in Central Texas) declined steadily after 1874, falling below the state rate and even below 0.25 percent before rising in the mid-1880s to accommodate courthouse and jail construction, local taxes in black-majority Harrison County were levied at more than twice the state rate even after white conservatives took power, due chiefly to the debt run up by railroad subsidies.[10]

The fact that the state and some local tax rates remained fixed at or near Reconstruction levels was more than simply an embarrassment to a party that had made retrenchment its watchword. If anything, state levies after 1875 bore more heavily on many Texans than they had during Reconstruction. Democrats presumed to speak for taxpayers at large, but property taxpayers had always been their chief object of concern. In 1876 lawmakers had actually doubled the state poll tax from one to two dollars (one dollar going to education, the other to general revenue). If this hike might have been more than offset for many propertyholders by the curtailment of local ad valorem school and road taxes, it unmistakably increased the tax liability of the poor and propertyless. But even property owners might find themselves harder pressed to pay their taxes in these years. Even if they owed less, the national economy's sluggishness in the years following the Panic of 1873 and especially the falling price of cotton made money hard to come by. As the leader of the Texas Grange observed in early 1879: "There is now more complaint of high taxes than when a few years ago [the people] were required for state & county purposes to pay double the present taxation. Then they were more able to pay because they received better wages and better prices for their products."[11]

A movement that emerged out of this economic distress demonstrates how apparent the shortcomings of Redeemer government had become to Texans little more than two years after the ratification of the new constitution. The Greenback Party, which appeared in Texas in 1877, emphasized a national solution to hard times, favoring government issuance of paper currency to raise crop prices and lower interest rates. But Texas Greenbackers also addressed the specific failings of the state's Redeemer regime. Their platforms during the gubernatorial campaigns of 1878 and 1880 demanded not only state and local tax cuts and an end to convict leasing but also an improved educational system, more efficient frontier protection and crime prevention, and veterans' pensions. In effect Greenbackers argued that retrenchment to date had not sufficiently eased the burdens the state imposed on the citizenry while Texans remained underserved in vital areas, particularly public education and law enforcement. They also challenged the centerpiece of Democratic developmental strategy by calling for distribution of public land to settlers only. By way of reconciling their discordant demands for lower taxes and more services, Greenbackers suggested a reduction in the interest paid on state bonds, even lower official salaries, and taxes on incomes over one thousand dollars.[12]

The Greenback agenda appealed to a diverse bunch of Texans: indebted farmers beset by deflation, urban working people contending with stagnant local economies, and even entrepreneurs, apparently suffering from the curtailment of credit in the post-panic years (the party leadership in Texas included a number of decidedly nonagrarian sorts, including William Hamman, B. J. Chambers, J. T. Brady, and E. M. Daggett, all of whom had commercial and railroad interests). In Cross Timbers districts the specifically Texan issue of state land seems to have animated Greenbackism. Local concerns that land, pasturage, and water were being engrossed by railroads and speculators dovetailed with the party's demand that the public domain be reserved for actual settlers.[13] The Greenback appeal drew white men out of the Democratic party and black ones out of the Republican. In 1880 Walker County, black majority and typically Republican, voted for Greenback presidential candidate James Weaver instead of James Garfield. The other Texas county to go for Weaver, Blanco—in the Hill Country—was overwhelmingly white and formerly Democratic.[14]

If soft money—and to fusion-minded Republicans, the prospect of building an anti-Democratic coalition—might have been the key elements in the Greenback appeal, the platforms of other political groups nevertheless suggest that the third party's critique of Redeemer government was striking responsive chords. "Straight-out" Republicans, who preferred in 1878 to run a gubernatorial candidate of their own rather than supporting the Greenbacker Hamman (as the dominant faction in their party did), attacked Democrats on similar grounds—the state had failed to reap the rewards of retrenchment but neither had it seen much benefit from its spending. These Republicans doubtlessly relished the opportunity to turn the politics of retrenchment against Democrats, complaining of the taxes "wrung" from the people and wasted in "extravagant and profligate expenditure" while decrying the impoverishment of the public education system.[15]

Democrats did little to respond to these critiques. They attacked Greenbackers' financial unorthodoxy by denouncing "fiat money" and insisted that their own party was the better equipped to secure an expanded money supply. They made much of the support the third party won from African Americans and Republicans.[16] But in 1878 Democrats would retreat from neither the promise of retrenchment nor that of adequate state services. Their own platform called for the "perfection of a common school system" while stoutly pledging "that no money shall be borrowed or bonds issued to meet the current expenses of the State government, the rate of taxation will not be increased, and the current expenses should be confined within the current revenue."[17]

Tellingly, the Democrats' standard bearer that year, Oran Milo Roberts, Texas' chief justice and the president of the 1861 secession convention, recognized his own party's promises as contradictory and "seemingly irreconcilable."[18] Roberts had been nominated as a compromise candidate after a convention deadlock that illustrated the degree to which personal rivalries and parochial allegiances prevailed in the party's internal struggles rather than any more coherent factionalism pitting Bourbons or agrarians against New South Democrats. The leading contenders for the gubernatorial nomination included incumbent Richard Hubbard (who had become governor after Coke was elevated to the U.S. Senate in 1876), Reps. James Throckmorton and John Reagan, and Grange leader W. W. Lang. All supported railroad development while being willing to spend less than many Democrats on public education. What seemingly separated them was sectional affiliation. North Texan Throckmorton vied against East Texans Hubbard and Reagan and a "West" Texan, T. J. Devine, their rivalry likely reinforced by Throckmorton's identification with the Texas and Pacific and Hubbard's, Reagan's, and Devine's past support for the International Railroad.[19]

If Roberts had been nominated as an acceptable second choice, "the Old Alcalde" possessed clearer ideas than many of his brethren as to how to dislodge the state from the fiscal impasse shadowing the 1878 campaign. Elected by a comfortable margin over his Greenback and straight-out Republican opponents, the stiff-necked judge would not continue to promise Texans both retrenchment and expanded state services. Instead he was determined to eliminate deficit spending and the floating debt (some $500,000 by the time he entered office in 1879) and to reduce the bonded debt, all while holding the line on, and eventually lowering, state property taxes. To this end Roberts would force his party to make unpleasant choices it had earlier shied away from, for he declared the greatest principle of government to be "that the ordinary expenses must be brought within the ordinary revenues, from year to year, so as to prevent an increase of public debt, and that no object of expense, however cherished, shall be exempt from diminution if it should be necessary to preserve that principle in practice."[20]

Not surprisingly, his plans stirred controversy within his party. The interests Roberts proposed to subject to "diminution" were ones to which Democratic colleagues had formally dedicated themselves. The choices Roberts made during his two terms as governor, and the stormy responses they brought, would together bring an end to the inaugural period of post-Reconstruction Democratic rule, when Redeemers had counted on land to reconcile the politics of retrenchment and the demands of development.

Oran Roberts would pursue several strategies to cut the Gordian knot that his party's commitments to retrenchment and development had twined. One was to trim spending to a greater degree than Redeemer lawmakers had ever attempted. The least controversial aspect of this strategy involved issuance of new bonds bearing 5 percent interest to retire or replace ones issued earlier at higher rates—first and foremost the 10 percent pension bonds. The conversion of those bonds alone appears to have saved Texas over $50,000 annually in interest payments.[21] Also, the state's small workforce had its salaries cut. Roberts also recommended lowering veterans' annuities from $150 to $100, but, as noted, the legislature chose instead to substitute land grants for further pensions.[22]

But to pare the state budget meaningfully, the governor had to address the core elements of public spending. Roberts insisted that the practice of giving education and debt service first claim on tax revenue inevitably produced deficits. Together just these two items would, in fiscal year 1879–80, require $900,000 of a projected $1,600,000 in tax receipts, leaving the balance to cover all other current expenses as well as existing deficiencies. The governor demanded instead that the actual running expenses and fixed costs of state government be paid in full, as well as that part of existing deficiencies in excess of the $200,000 that could be raised by a bond issue, and that schools and debt service receive only what was left. Putting government on a "pay as you go" basis to his mind trumped education, which would be provided for only "in a manner that would least discommode the accomplishment of the more important object."[23]

Accordingly, the governor in the spring of 1879 vetoed the school appropriations for 1879–80 and 1880–81, forcing the legislature to trim back educational funding from one-fourth to one-sixth of annual revenue. School expenditures fell by as much as $200,000 for the 1879–80 school year—even as the school-age population grew at its typically brisk pace. Declining spending per student led many districts to shorten already brief school terms and cut back, sometimes sharply, on teacher salaries.[24]

Roberts paired his school veto with a veto of the appropriation of $500,000 for debt service for each of the next two fiscal years. In doing so he suggested that he might be willing to qualify his party's strictures concerning repudiation in order to rein in deficit spending without increasing property taxes. "It is better," he opined, "that we should not have good credit, if it is to be made the reliance for increasing the debt, increasing the taxes, and increasing the prospect continually of ultimate bankruptcy to the State or impoverishment of its people." But in fact Roberts appears to have had no intention of compromising the state's credit, the chief object of his vetoes unmistakably being to dethrone the schools' fixed claim to a quarter of general revenue. While requiring the reduction of the schools' share of the revenue to one-sixth, Roberts eventually accepted an appropriation for debt service nearly as large as the one he had rejected.[25]

Not surprisingly, given the expectations that Redeemers had created that Texas could maintain or improve public education while reducing spending, Roberts's veto created widespread dismay both within his party and without. A significant number of Texans—not just rural landowners, more burdened by property taxes than concerned with education, but also prominent merchants, lawyers, bankers, and politicians—endorsed Roberts's remorseless ordering of the state's priorities. Even some Democrats who had earlier supported relatively expansive public efforts when it came to education—including the editors of the *Galveston Daily News*—proved willing to concede the more immediate importance of getting the state's fiscal house in order.[26] But others were less ready to see education do without. Many newspapers fiercely denounced the veto as betraying the state's promise. Some of those styled "progressive" or "young" Democrats, including Lt. Gov. Joseph Sayers, proved inclined even to challenge Roberts's renomination in 1880, partly because of the low priority accorded public schools.[27]

The governor's second strategy—*increasing* the revenue coming in to state coffers—was bounded of course by his and his party's conviction that certain sorts of taxes could not be raised but actually had to be cut. More funds would have to come "from sources that would not increase the burdens upon permanent property."[28] Texas had a long history of taxing certain non-agricultural and non-"mechanical" occupations in part to discourage such suspect or decidedly unwholesome activities as gaming, fortune telling, mesmerism, circuses, and bowling. But occupation taxes were also intended to reach people such as merchants, brokers, and professionals, who could handle relatively large amounts of money or inventory over the course of the year but might not have a great deal of assessable property on hand when tax time arrived, as well as those doing business without a fixed residence. Seeking to reach "property of a transient nature," the legislature, at the governor's inspiration, raised occupation taxes on large mercantile firms and imposed a hefty $200 per annum "drummers" tax on traveling salesmen.[29]

Lawmakers also imposed a series of corporate taxes. Insurance firms had already been made subject to occupation taxes, but except during Reconstruction, when railroad and telegraph companies had had to turn over a small percentage of their annual receipts to the state, corporations had otherwise simply paid the standard ad valorem rate on their propertyholdings in Texas. Roberts reasoned that they actually owed something more for the protection their enterprises received from the state. The legislature accordingly levied a 1 percent tax on the gross receipts of rail, stage, and steamboat companies for passenger travel in the state; taxed telegraph concerns at a penny per message; and made gas companies subject to occupation taxes. In addition, property- and occupation-tax obligations were tightened for out-of-state insurance and sleeping-car companies operating in Texas. In corporate taxation as with corporate regulation, then, state efforts seem to have focused on those sectors of the economy—such as transportation and insurance—dominated by firms owned outside of Texas.[30]

The most lucrative of the new levies Roberts saw enacted, though, was the "Bell Punch" tax on liquor dealers and alcohol sales. Under this 1879 law, those retailing alcohol in quantities of less than a quart had to pay $250 to the state annually ($25 if dealing only in malt liquors) and also pay two cents per drink sold (one-half cent if malt). Each glass of liquor or wine would be rung up on a state-furnished register, each mug of beer on a second register.[31]

For many Democrats, the Bell Punch law surely served that classic purpose of occupation taxes—to increase the expense of pursuits deemed undesirable. Given both the decided absence of consensus within the party on issues of temperance and the state's ethnic complexity, that antiliquor odor probably helped make it the most unpopular of Roberts's tax measures. The Bell Punch apparently raised the same sort of ethnocultural furies among Texas' unusually diverse population that prohibition evoked in the Gilded Age North: A Guadalupe County man told Roberts: "few of the Bell Punches is turned when the Liquor is drank Especially with the forigen Elements. The general clameor—That *Their rights* is taken from them by the Sunday Law & Bell Punch.... The Bell Punch Tax reach a set of people generally around the town that never paid one Dollar Tax before and it gos verry hard.... The Bell Punch can be enforced if ... the Sheriffs did not have to look to the people for their authorety. They will not inforce the law on that acct."[32] The German-language *Freie Presse* also denounced the measure as "a bold attack on the personal rights of the citizen."[33]

The Bell Punch law and the other new or increased occupation and corporate levies of 1879 tell us something important about Redeemer government. As noted, while Redeemers had denounced excessive taxation in general, their animus had always been directed specifically at property taxation, such that they could usher through these tax hikes, in addition to the doubling of the poll tax three years earlier, and apparently not, in the minds of many, betray first principles. The cumulative effect of Redeemer policies in Texas (as in a number of other southern states) was less to reduce the tax burden as to shift it away from property. Ad valorem levies fell from 71.7 percent of all taxes assessed in 1875 to 57.4 percent in 1880, while occupation taxes grew from 16.8 percent of the total to 22.9 percent. The poll tax's share increased from 11.5 percent to 19.5 percent.[34]

This shift favored specific classes of Texans. In the second half of the 1870s, the largest single category of property rendered for taxation was rural land, so any move away from ad valorem taxation bid fair to favor Texas' landowning farmers.[35] The direction of state tax policy certainly might suggest that Roberts, among Redeemer leaders, might be regarded as the most straightforwardly agrarian in orientation. Over the years and in a number of forums, he stated plainly his conviction that Texas had first to tend to its agricultural and stockraising interests before developing a manufacturing sector, his distrust of state railroad subsidies, and his anxiety over the "money power" and the advantages government had afforded "accumulated capital." He looked, Roberts declared, to Texas' farmers to sustain good government, "on the principle that the civilization capable of republican, local self-government begins and ends with the plow."[36]

But while the governor might invoke the needs of agriculturists in general, his tax strategies, in chiefly serving landowners, benefited a specific, *relatively* privileged, and in proportional terms, shrinking sector of the farm population.[37] The number of landless cultivators was increasing. By 1880 over one-third of the farms in Texas were operated by tenants. Even outside old plantation regions and among white farmers alone, the landless might constitute a substantial fraction of the agrarian population—more than one-third, for instance, in Milam County and greater than one-fourth in Palo Pinto.[38] Those tenants who owned their own livestock would enjoy some modicum of savings by falling ad valorem rates, but they might have stood to be better served by more immediate attention to the poll tax or by different land or school policies than the ones Roberts pursued in the name of retrenchment.

Another aspect of his strategy for increasing state revenue made for an even more significant and revealing episode in the political economy of Redemption. The controversy it generated illustrated in yet another way the conflict among "agrarian" interests in post-Reconstruction Texas, though it also cut to the heart of the Democrats' mode of governing. Redeemers had relied on the state's vast land holdings to accomplish a wide variety of purposes. Governor Roberts proved more prepared than others, however, to pick and choose among these good causes. He thereby forced Democrats to face up more squarely to the finitude of the public domain. Roberts insisted that state land be utilized first and foremost to serve his priorities of debt reduction and tax relief in the short term. In preference to giving away land in order to serve some more distant goal of development or yeoman settlement, or reserving it until it appreciated in value, the governor wished for more of the public domain to be sold quickly and the proceeds applied to the debt and to education—so that less tax money had to be spent.

The "Fifty Cents" law, passed in July 1879 in the wake of Roberts's school and debt vetoes, set aside unappropriated state land in the Texas Panhandle and western plains (as well as smaller scraps elsewhere) for sale in essentially unlimited quantity at fifty cents an acre. Half the proceeds would go toward the state debt and half toward the school fund. None of this territory would be available for railroad land grants. As for the acreage already reserved for the benefit of the school fund, Roberts, noting that sales under existing laws had been relatively slight, wished to increase demand by eliminating the requirement that it be offered only in farm-sized tracts. A second land law allowed the purchase of up to 640 acres of school land, if arable, and of up to 1,920 acres suitable for grazing purposes, instead of in plots of not more than 160 acres, as had formerly been the rule. Rather than favoring would-be settlers over those looking simply to speculate, the new law treated all potential purchasers alike, with the exception of those who had already settled on and improved the land they wished to purchase—they were granted first claim. To encourage sales, the minimum price of school land was also cut from $1.50 to $1 an acre.[39]

The 1879 land laws caused a stir within the Democratic party, just as that year's school veto had. When Redeemer lawmakers had first put school lands on the market five years before, some Democrats had complained that by favoring those settling small tracts rather than selling land in unlimited quantity or to the highest bidder, Redeemer legislators were shortchanging education.[40] The 1879 laws generated an opposite complaint. In seeking to maximize the short-term return on the land by selling larger tracts to non-settlers, the legislation undermined the state's interest in nurturing a population of small farmers. The measures did not end homesteading. The Redeemer constitution promised 160 acres of public land to every head of family without a homestead and 80 acres to single men over seventeen, provided claimants occupied their tracts for three years.[41] But if unappropriated state lands were also subject to sale, less would be available for homesteading. Editor and politician Charles DeMorse complained that the laws served the interests of speculators, corporations, "foreign" capitalists, and ultimately "landlordism." He insisted that the 1875 convention, in which he had played such a prominent role, had never intended that Texans "become tenants at will of foreign princes or nobility, and divested of that independence of character which has made the name of Texas representative of that indomitable courage which does not grow up at the firesides of a pauper peasantry, controlled by a rich land proprietary." Other Democrats worried that the school lands would be sold too quickly or on too easy terms, thereby squandering the schools' resources for short-term profit.[42]

Surely the most important critic of Roberts's land laws was a member of the executive branch elected in his own right—W. C. Walsh, the commissioner of the Texas General Land Office from 1878 until 1887. In retrospect he derided the Fifty Cents law as "almost criminal folly" that occasioned a "saturnalia of speculation," but even in his official reports, he characterized it as "a misfortune rather than a benefit." Walsh called the school-land provisions "*wrong in principle, and worse in . . . application.*" They sold state lands (especially timbered acreage) for less than they were worth—or at very least, less than they would eventually be worth—to provide short-term increments to the school fund, increments that in per capita terms would be almost immediately overwhelmed by population growth. But he seemed also to doubt if the state should so quickly transfer its public domain to private hands under any terms. Not only would Texas forgo the proceeds of any future appreciation in land values, it rendered itself powerless to prevent the subsequent growth of large landed monopolies and effectively ceded control over its future development. The state would say "in substance to toiling masses who are to follow us: 'If you want homes, you must purchase from the capitalists to whom I have sold.'" By retaining title and simply leasing school land, it could better enforce a socially optimal distribution of resources. For Walsh, this involved dividing the land into small tracts. "It is certainly better for the State to have five hundred families, representing one thousand dollars each, than to have one man, or syndicate, representing one million."[43]

For his part, Roberts by no means conceded that, by opening state land to purchase in larger plots by nonsettlers, he was sacrificing the interest of the yeomanry. Instead he countered one agrarian concern with another. Subtly playing on the specter of growing tenancy in Texas, he hinted that if the state stopped hoarding land in the interest of *prospective* settlers, it might keep *current* residents from losing their farms. As land revenue increased, and as the tax base expanded with the transfer of the public domain into private hands, ad valorem rates could fall, putting fewer homesteads at risk for nonpayment of taxes. The governor believed that the claims of potential settlers in any case would have to give way to the arid realities of the southern plains. Much of the remaining public domain, concentrated in the Panhandle and far western Texas, was not well suited for cultivation in compact plots. Roberts evidently felt that offering the public domain in large plots and at low prices would encourage ranchers to buy land that otherwise would remain uncultivated or be grazed upon with no return to the state (he went so far as to publicly encourage stockmen to acquire more school land than the law allowed any single individual by making purchases in the names of family members and friends).[44] But in fact some of the tracts offered were situated east of the Caprock Escarpment, where the ranching and farming frontiers overlapped. Railroads had surveyed tens of thousands of acres of school land in counties such as Eastland, Coleman, and Callahan that, if primarily devoted to stockraising, were by 1880 also being planted here and there in wheat and cotton. (Significantly, these areas became the center of the fence-cutting conflicts of the early 1880s that pitted farmers and stockraisers against one another.)[45] In encouraging competition for this land from stock interests and nonresident speculators, Roberts, in a more immediate fashion than he perhaps imagined, was indeed undermining the prospects of certain hardscrabble farmers.

Not surprisingly, the conflict over the public domain, like the school veto, became an issue when Roberts ran for reelection in 1880. Greenbackers of course challenged the land laws, but so did Roberts' fellow Democrats, notably the "progressives" led by Lieutenant Governor Sayers, who also deplored cuts in school spending. A proposed platform at the 1880 Democratic state convention insisted that Texas sell its land only to those who would settle and cultivate it in small plots while also demanding appropriation of the constitutional maximum for education (one-fourth of state revenue) and more vigorous promotion of immigration. The draft also called for the repeal of the Bell Punch law and officially deplored the imposition of taxes on any occupation "not pernicious in its tendencies or requiring police supervision." But a year into the operation of the land laws, the potential difficulties they created for settlers and the long-term well-being of the school fund seem not to have outweighed the promise of tax relief that Roberts held out to already established landowners. Roberts easily triumphed at the convention, which adopted another platform more attuned to his policies by a vote of 390–139. Texans rather decisively reelected the governor for a second two-year term over two challengers: William Hamman, again the Greenback candidate, and the old Radical thoroughbred Edmund J. Davis, given one more turn around the track by his party brethren.[46]

During his first term, Governor Roberts had forced Democrats to pick and choose among things they had once suggested Texans could have all at once—lower taxes, good schools, less debt, and yeoman settlement. In his second term, those hard choices bore fruit, helped along by circumstances that finally allowed the government to spend less on certain vital services.[47] With the frontier increasingly pacified, substantially less funding was needed for defense and suppressing lawlessness (a rather serious outbreak of Apache raiding, led by Victorio, reached southwestern Texas in 1879–80, but federal and Mexican troops did most of the work of squelching it).[48] The prison system generated income as the state profited from a new leasing arrangement contracted in 1878.[49]

Redeemers at last could keep their promises. Texas' population boom seemed finally to be paying off in the increase of taxable property. Lawmakers cut the state property-tax rate from its constitutional maximum of 0.5 percent to 0.4 percent in 1881 and 0.3 percent in 1882. Yet by 1884, ad valorem taxes were bringing more into state coffers than ever before. More tardily, Democrats extended tax relief to the propertyless, reducing the poll tax by 25 percent in 1882. Lawmakers also saw their way clear to scale back some of the more controversial of the 1879 measures by which the tax burden had been shifted. Condemned by Republicans, Greenbackers, and the "progressive" minority at the 1880 Democratic convention, and generally conceded to be a failure, the Bell Punch law was repealed in 1881. The legislature slashed the "drummers" tax and reduced levies upon merchants. Corporate taxes were trimmed a bit in 1882.[50]

But if Roberts had delivered on the central promise of his administration, he seems to have been somewhat chastened by the controversy he had stirred. In his second inaugural message, Roberts spoke in warmer terms of public education, and during his second term he allowed school appropriations to edge back up to one-fourth of annual revenue. Accordingly, local reports showed longer school terms and more generous teachers' salaries in many counties—though progress was far from universal or uniform.[51] Lawmakers also modified the controversial laws applying to school lands, apparently with an eye to meeting the objection that the state's resources were being squandered. The original legislation had done little to classify these acres according to their widely varying value, beyond distinguishing between those suitable for cultivation and for grazing. Laws passed in 1881 and 1882 graded school

The Crisis of Redeemer Government

land more carefully, raising the minimum price of tracts blessed with fresh water and timber. The land commissioner was authorized to reject prices that he felt had been set too low by local officials and to correct inaccurate classifications. Commissioner Walsh would employ this authority to impede the operation of laws he plainly disliked.[52]

Although progress occurred on several fronts, Roberts's second term also saw Democrats forced to surrender certain of the essentials of Redeemer government. The governor's land policies had shown that Democrats might have to choose between the treasured goals of retrenchment and yeoman settlement. At the same time, the public domain's simple finitude upended their cherished expectation that land could promote economic development and social welfare at little cost to taxpayers. Even in 1879—as Roberts argued that sales be given priority in the disposition of state land—lawmakers continued to give away large tracts to meet assorted public purposes. They made good on the constitutional mandate to set aside three million acres to finance construction of a new capitol building. As noted, Democrats also looked to the public domain to solve the problem of skyrocketing pension costs, offering veterans land grants instead of bonds or cash payments. Still in a generous mood two years later, the state increased the acreage granted to veterans and offered similar bounties to indigent and disabled Confederate veterans and to soldiers' widows.[53]

Such giveaways, however, were becoming increasingly problematic. With railroad construction picking up after its post-Panic slump, railway companies by the late 1870s found it increasingly difficult to locate the acreage to which their land certificates entitled them. The land sales and grants provided for in 1879 and 1881 accelerated the drain upon the public domain. Confederate soldiers and widows quickly claimed more than two million acres; veterans of the Texas Revolution more than one million. Between 1880 and 1882 the state issued to private parties certificates for thirteen million acres of land. Under the constitutional formula, much of this had to be matched by new reservations for the school fund, so that between 1878 and 1882, the area of the unappropriated public land declined by a staggering four-fifths—from more than forty million acres to slightly less than eight million. By the end of 1881, Commissioner Walsh was reporting that the land certificates awarded to railroads for construction entitled them to more acreage than was actually available for such purposes. By the next year, the total acreage due on outstanding certificates exceeded the acreage open to location by more than six million.[54]

The state had finally promised more than it could deliver. Having very nearly exhausted what many had long seen as the key resource by which the public's work would be done, Democrats had to make fundamental changes in policy. Governor Roberts, who had already convinced himself that it was better to sell land for revenue than give it away, called for an end to railroad land grants. The legislature in 1882 complied, doing away with what theretofore had been the state's chief developmental strategy.[55]

By that time Texas had turned over more than thirty-two million acres to a relatively small number of railroad companies and granted four to five million acres more for other internal improvements, including canals and dredged waterways. Had it all been contiguous, the land given to railroads would have occupied an area larger than Indiana. Many of these grants were in the western half of the state and, given the contemporary market, not in great demand. Sales were often slow and prices low. Still, they represented an enormous transfer of public wealth into private hands. According to federal estimates, railroads ultimately netted at least $37 million on sales of granted land in Texas. The discovery of oil under some of this acreage decades later meant the amount of wealth actually ceded by the state was far greater.[56]

The end of developmental land grants, it should be stressed, did not mean the government entirely abdicated its role in shaping economic growth. Texas continued to make convict labor available for railroad construction, though this bit of promotion actually made the state money. Through agencies established in subsequent decades—a railroad commission, fish and game commissions, agricultural experiment stations, and levee and drainage boards—Texas leaders hoped to more carefully manage the exploitation of natural resources, encourage new levels of sophistication in commercial agriculture and extractive industry, and ensure that local businesses won their share of the benefits of growth. Early in the twentieth century, lawmakers established a system of state-chartered banks and deposit insurance, thus expanding in-state sources of capital and credit. By the 1920s state employment offices helped recruit Mexican labor to supply the needs of Texas cotton planters. But these various public agencies and initiatives did not involve direct outlays to private parties nor were they funded so as to make any great demands on taxpayers. When Texas did initiate a major development project—building state highways in the 1920s—it was funded by a regressive gasoline tax.[57]

At the same time as Redeemer Democrats gave up on corporate land grants, lawmakers had to surrender their hope that the public domain might bear another important burden. In 1883, admitting that little land remained available for such purposes, they ended land grants for Confederate veterans. Land grants for Texas Revolution veterans survived, but only until 1887.[58]

If Texans had had to decisively lower their expectations when it came to what the public domain could do for their state, Oran Roberts had much to show as he completed his four years in office. The state had moved beyond the fiscal deadlock of the immediate post-Reconstruction years. Total receipts from public lands had grown from $172,036 to $2,505,487 between 1879 and 1882. The size of the permanent school fund had more than tripled to more than $5,000,000. Tax receipts had climbed from $2,048,850 to $2,632,547 even as the state ad valorem tax rate was cut by 40 percent and the poll tax by 25 percent. The state debt fell by $1,500,000; interest payments lightened accordingly.[59]

As much as Roberts made good on his promises, though, many Texans seemed unwilling to continue to take his medicine at its prescribed dosage. Some appeared to doubt that he had been doctoring the most worrisome maladies. Roberts had succeeded on his own terms, yet by the end of his tenure in office, his party faced its greatest challenge since returning to power in 1873–74: the independent gubernatorial candidacy of George Washington "Wash" Jones of Bastrop. Jones, as the Greenback candidate from the Fifth Congressional District, had been elected to the House in 1878, though the party's gubernatorial candidate won only 23 percent. He seemed to have something to offer just about everyone. An opponent of secession, he had fought in the Confederate Army. He had served as lieutenant governor after the Civil War and been removed from office by Gen. Philip Sheridan as an "impediment to reconstruction," but by the 1870s Jones proved more than willing to solicit Republican and African American votes. His sheer likeability seemed to increase his reach among discontented Democrats. The Greenback and Republican parties both endorsed his 1882 run for governor. Jones spoke up for soft money on the campaign trail, but where the Greenback and Republican platforms coincided were in condemning the inadequacy of public education in Texas, the convict lease system, occupation taxes, and Democrats' prodigality with public land. Greenbackers denounced the land laws as "a system of class legislation in favor of the rich," while Republicans embraced the demand for sales of school lands to "*bona fide* settlers" only.[60]

Public land continued to be an issue to be reckoned with. Corporate land grants had been eliminated, but the 1881–82 amendments had represented no real change in direction when it came to the interests that land *sales* would serve. Acreage could still be sold to nonsettlers in large tracts and on easy terms. In fact lawmakers in 1881 had halved down payments on school land and raised the amount of grazing land that individuals could buy.[61] While Roberts may have persuaded his fellow party members that serving one state interest by means of the public domain could inevitably require that other worthy ends be slighted, many of them were prepared to make different choices than he. The platform constructed for John Ireland—old "Oxcart John," the man the party nominated in 1882 to oppose Jones and succeed Roberts—called for the transfer of public land reserved under Roberts for debt service to the state university endowment. The party apparently felt compelled to tack away from the governor, its platform seeming obliquely to criticize the "waste and sacrifice" of the school lands and pledging to secure a return on them "commensurate with [their] real value."[62]

Both major candidates in 1882, then, spurned Roberts's land policies and also called for a more generously endowed school system. Ireland won the 1882 election, but Democrats had their closest call since the 1860s, Jones securing some 40 percent of the vote.[63] Soon afterward lawmakers set to work revising the land laws that the new governor, in his inaugural address, essentially derided as folly and madness. Among the first measures passed in 1883 was one ending sales on Roberts's terms. Thereafter, public land would serve first and foremost the state's interests in public education and yeoman settlement rather than being employed to reduce the state debt. As the Democratic platform had demanded, the legislature placed up to one million acres of the land reserved to pay the debt in 1879 to the service of higher education instead. It likewise reserved up to one million additional acres of this land for the benefit of the common-school fund.[64]

Texans had made a choice. They largely gave up on actually paying down the principal of the state debt. In 1887 legislators once again directed a portion of the proceeds of unappropriated land sales to debt service—probably because two years earlier their predecessors had departed from Roberts's "pay as you go" doctrine and added the constitutional maximum of $200,000 to the bonded debt. This effort, however, yielded relatively little, bringing in only about $70,000 over the lifetime of the law. Thus while not actually increasing in the following decades, the debt principal did not appreciably decrease either. Interest costs continued to run to several hundred thousand dollars annually, though constituting a declining proportion of total state spending. The wealth of public land did allow management of the debt in a roundabout way, though. The constitution required that the proceeds of state land sales directed to the permanent school, university, and asylum funds be invested in government bonds. By 1890 these trust funds had thereby taken control of over two-thirds of the state's bonded debt; by 1911 they held all of it. This allowed bonds to be re-funded at lower interest rates, with interest payments applied to public purposes.[65]

If lawmakers had given up on using land revenue to pay off the debt, at the same time they accorded yeoman settlement more importance in selling school land. Arable and timbered land would be sold to actual settlers exclusively and in tracts no larger than 640 acres (pastureland could continue to be purchased in larger plots). The legislature raised the price of school land, but Texans could pay for their tracts over thirty years and at low interest rates. To further increase the school fund's income while reserving its land for future settlement, lawmakers instituted the sort of lease system that Commissioner Walsh had been pressing. Pasture could be rented for up to ten years at a minimum price of four cents per acre per annum, though in most cases it remaincd liable for sale to settlers even while leased.[66]

These changes in 1882–83 by no means meant that the disposition of the public domain ceased to be a contested matter. Quite the opposite—the new leasing system raised hackles across the state. Some believed it favored stockraising interests over those of cultivators, while stockmen and timber interests complained that the state withheld certain tracts from market and pegged leasing rates considerably above the minimum set by statute. Stockraisers refused to lease on these terms, some of them wishing to rent for longer periods at far lower prices. Others wanted to continue to run their cattle on public land free of charge.[67]

Still, whatever the controversy, there had been a fundamental reorientation of the role of public land in Redeemer political economy. Having been the keystone of post-Reconstruction fiscal, developmental, and social policy, public land would thenceforth be dedicated to two causes alone: public education and the promotion of small-scale settlement by farmers and ranchers. This narrowing of the uses to which land would be put was accompanied by the recognition that, to serve certain public purposes, the state would simply have to pay more. The first year of Governor Ireland's administration saw lawmakers reverse the judgment of 1879 that land alone was sufficient to support Texas' old soldiers and subsequently restore cash pensions to indigent veterans of the Texas Revolution. The state thereby committed itself to spending tens of thousands of dollars annually on the aged and infirm (in 1899, cash pensions were extended to disabled and indigent Confederate veterans and widows). In 1883 Democrats also resumed state management of the Texas prison system, consequently having to increase appropriations for its support.[68]

This increasing willingness to accept new public burdens led to another reorientation of government during Roberts's second term and Ireland's first, which if anything was more fundamental and enduring in its consequences than the reworking of land policy. While Roberts had allowed funding for public education to rise during his second term, the continued sorry state of so many Texas schools appears to have inspired a decisive number of Democrats to a basic reconsideration of educational finance and administration. By the early 1880s they were ready to implement reforms that, when they did not directly repudiate Roberts's priorities, went considerably beyond anything the governor was willing to embrace. Orlando N. Hollingsworth, who had become secretary to the Texas Board of Education upon the abolition of the superintendency in 1876, led the way. Hollingsworth used the reports of the board to call for reforms distinctly at odds with the policies of the board's ex officio members, particularly the governor. While Roberts looked back wistfully toward the antebellum practice of the state simply providing tuition support for indigent children, Hollingsworth's reports recommended a stronger state and county role in administering schools and expanded ad valorem tax support.[69]

In terms of administration Hollingsworth called for something far more like the old Republican school establishment than most Redeemers had earlier been willing to contemplate: a state superintendent, county officers to carry out the school laws locally, and a stronger state board. Apparently agreeing that their party's commitment to decentralization had yielded extremes of incoherence, Democratic lawmakers began as early as 1879 to strengthen state oversight. That year they made statutory revisions to allow the state education board to issue binding interpretations of school policy rather than merely to counsel and advise local officials. By the early 1880s, reports of county judges—the officers charged with administering the school laws—showed widespread support for the creation of the offices of county and state superintendent and the establishment of permanent school districts rather than leaving the formation and maintenance of school communities and the provision of school facilities to concerned parents. A few even called for the resurrection of two features of the Reconstruction school system that Democrats had most frequently condemned as "militaristic"—compulsory education and state oversight of curriculum. Several of these administrative reforms quickly came to pass. By 1883 the requisite two-thirds of the state legislature and a majority of the electorate embraced a constitutional amendment that authorized the legislature to provide for the creation of permanent school districts in any or all counties. The following year saw the resurrection, by statute, of a statewide hierarchy in educational administration. An elected state official would exercise "a general superintendency" of school business, including curriculum, and enjoy the final word, over subordinate school officers, in interpreting education laws. Most importantly, the 1884 law made children eligible for free instruction for eight years (ages eight to sixteen) instead of the six years provided in 1876.[70]

The rethinking of school finance proved even more dramatic in shedding certain of the verities of Redemption. Even before Roberts accelerated land sales so that the tax revenue going to schools could be cut or even eliminated, Hollingsworth had argued that the expectation that the public domain could be the cornerstone of educational funding was "visionary and fallacious." Given the state's population boom, even the sale of *all* school lands at two dollars an acre would not yield a sufficient interest income to support the education of children for four months a year. "The time is not, *nor ever will be,* when this department of our state government can be efficiently maintained without taxation," he declared. Population growth so outstripped the growth of the school fund, in fact, that the state, merely to maintain existing standards, would have to do more than reserve portions of the general revenue and tax at the maximum levels allowable under the existing constitution. It would have to develop new sources of funds.[71]

At the 1875 convention, friends of public education had been able to secure direct school taxation only in its most modest and regressive form, a one-dollar poll tax. By the 1880s more Texans seemed ready to submit to an unprecedented state property tax for education. A number of county judges, in submitting local school statistics, indicated their support for such a levy. Under the existing system, Smith County's judge lamented, "The money is entirely insufficient."[72] In 1882, in the same platform that distanced the party from Roberts's land policies, Democrats officially embraced a constitutional amendment providing for a school tax. The following year an overwhelming majority of legislators and some 60 percent of the electorate ratified a separate statewide property tax of 0.2 percent for school purposes—or as much thereof as would, together with other state funds, provide for six months of schooling annually. While the portion of the poll tax collected for general revenue had been halved, the one dollar devoted to education remained in place. This new provision did not swell school coffers as much as it might have, however, for in establishing a separate school tax, Democrats had wanted more than to increase educational funding. They also sought to separate such funding from general revenue so that they might cut the general tax rate without shrinking the educational budget. Rather than simply adding the revenue generated by a 0.2 percent school tax to that derived from existing sources, they reduced the schools' claim on general tax revenue from one-fourth of the annual total to one-fourth of the revenue derived from occupation taxes alone. The legislature, furthermore, chose the next year to impose a school tax rate of only 0.125 percent, considerably below the maximum allowable.[73] Still, this school levy would amount to one-third or more of total state ad valorem taxation. When it came to school taxes then, lawmakers defied the overall trend toward sharply decreased property taxation.

A more striking aspect of the reorganization of educational finance in the 1880s would be its localization. The opposition to county and municipal taxation for schools had been among the firmest of Democratic doctrines both before the war and during Reconstruction. Yet the need for funds—and probably the obvious logic of making school finance subject to the same principle of local control as Democrats had enforced in the realm of administration— eventually carried the day. Even Governor Roberts, who clearly distrusted his fellow Democrats' plans for an expansion of state authority over educational administration and imposition of a state property tax for schools, had seemed to support expanded local funding of education. Lawmakers in 1881 permitted any village with two hundred or more inhabitants to impose a tax of up to 0.5 percent to support its schools. The 1883 constitutional amendment went further, allowing other districts to levy an ad valorem tax of up to 0.2 percent. Yet if Democrats had dispensed with certain of the cardinal principles of Redemption, they had not forgotten the lessons of Reconstruction as well as of urbanization: universal suffrage might permit the propertyless to impress wealth to whatever ends they chose. As with the exemptions granted cities and towns in the 1876 school law, the measures providing for local taxation mandated that a district's property-tax payers alone could decide whether it would be imposed, then only by a two-thirds majority.[74]

By 1884 then, Redeemers had altered crucial patterns in educational finance and administration first established in the antebellum era and reaffirmed in the dismantling of Reconstruction. The imposition of an ad valorem school tax, local levies, and a more centralized administration suggest that the imperatives of anti-Reconstruction politics had faded in the face of more immediate exigencies. Yet the legacy of these reforms proved decidedly mixed, for certain of them codified and even intensified existing disparities among communities. The legislature did not make universal the new system of educational administration and finance. Initially, it exempted over fifty counties from the requirement that permanent districts be established, leaving the old ad-hoc system in place. In 1885 it expanded the exemptions to cover nearly all of eastern Texas as well as much of South Texas and all but one of the state's black-majority counties—places where large African American or Latino populations, owning little taxable property, might have been expected to be the chief beneficiaries of more aggressive educational efforts.[75]

But even where permanent districting and local taxation had been provided for, considerable disparities in the extent and quality of public instruction naturally emerged between more wealthy and less wealthy districts. The most immediately apparent imbalance existed between rural and urban districts, the latter being able to levy local taxes of up to 0.5 percent rather than only 0.2 percent. Municipal districts continued in subsequent decades to far outdistance rural ones in terms of expenditures per pupil, length of school term, teacher salaries, value of school property, and availability of secondary education. But the inequality in educational opportunity did not result from differences in districts' tax rates or their taxable wealth alone. The requirement that local taxation be approved by a two-thirds vote of property-tax payers could mean that a relatively small number of residents might ultimately determine what opportunities a district's citizens enjoyed. Whatever a community's absolute wealth, and no matter how much value its residents might attach to common schools (African Americans' interest in education, for instance, is well documented), where landlessness was prevalent, an adequate level of funding could very easily be blocked. Landlords, it seems, often proved unwilling to subsidize the education or their tenants and sharecroppers' children. In the late 1880s only a fraction of the state's districts actually levied a school tax.[76]

Whatever its shortcomings and unfortunate consequences, the reorientation of educational finance and administration in 1883 and 1884, together with the changes made in the land laws in 1882 and 1883, represent a decisive turning point in the political economy of post-Reconstruction Texas. No longer would the public domain be the keystone of fiscal, developmental, and social policy. The abundance of land at the disposal of the state had encouraged Texans to believe that they could retrench but not do without. By the early months of John Ireland's administration, Democrats had acknowledged at least tacitly that this was not the case. Direct subsidy of economic development had ended, payment of the state debt lagged, and Texans resigned themselves to paying more out of pocket for certain services, including education and veterans' care. In the three decades after 1880, the money the state spent on schools, charities, prisons, veterans' homes, and pensions grew at more than twice the rate of total net expenditures. The larger part of the money in the available school fund was raised through taxation.[77]

By the late 1880s, in other words, their state's exceptional landed wealth no longer allowed Texans to defer the sorts of decisions other, less well-endowed states had long faced. They had either to impose burdens on the citizenry or concede that the need in question would go unmet. Not surprisingly, Lone Star conservatives most often made choices similar to those made in southern states lacking Texas' frontier resources. Other southern Democrats in the 1880s also admitted the need to spend more on such things as public education and soldiers' pensions.[78] But spending more did not necessarily mean spending much, Texans and their Dixie counterparts preferring limited services to pressing more aggressively the redistributive work of taxation. Even as the state's western reaches became more thickly settled in the later 1880s and 1890s, Texas, in terms of political economy, became more—not less—southern.

Significantly, this watershed in Texas government occurred in the same years as decisive shifts in state politics. Lawrence Sullivan Ross, serving between 1887 and 1891, would be the last governor of that Redeemer generation that had forged its politics in the fires of sectional crisis, secession, and civil war.[79] His successor, James Stephen Hogg, born in 1851, personified in a most ample way the emergence of a new and younger cohort of Democratic leaders. Other of the internal dynamics of the party had changed by the late 1880s. Redeemers had always argued among themselves, and prohibition had been one of the issues they contested. But the local-option mechanism established by the Redeemer constitution had limited the damage alcohol could do to the party by confining contention to individual communities. By the 1880s, however, alcohol had become so central a public concern as to occasion a statewide referendum in 1887. The party divided in two, the most prominent Redeemers turning up on both sides of the issue—Richard Coke, Oran Roberts, and James Throckmorton opposing a prohibition amendment, and John Reagan and Samuel Bell Maxey supporting it. Never before in the postbellum era had Democrats so directly or comprehensively organized and campaigned against one another. Walter Buenger and Alwyn Barr have suggested the degree to which the referendum weakened party bonds, initiating, Buenger says, "a process of creative destruction" that "eventually restructured Texas politics." Weakening party loyalty would be very much in evidence by 1892, when Governor Hogg had to run for reelection against another Democrat—Richard Coke's erstwhile chum, George Clark.[80]

But Hogg faced another formidable opponent that year, Populist Thomas Nugent, the erstwhile Redeemer who had voted for a poll tax and against railroad land grants at the 1875 constitutional convention. The third-party politics that the Greenbackers had launched in 1878 had become a more widespread and deeply rooted phenomenon over the course of the 1880s. The emergence in Texas of local antimonopoly parties, the cooperative endeavors of the Farmers Alliance, and the Knights of Labor's successes in organizing workers on the state's railroads suggest that even as Redeemers trimmed their ambitions to more conventionally southern proportions, an increasing number of Texans were beginning to push beyond the old Democratic verities, experimenting with new organizations and new ways of understanding their situations, and contemplating measures once unthinkable, such as federal intervention in credit and market relations and even federal control of the nation's transportation and communications infrastructure.[81] Oran Roberts emphasized the novelty of such proposals, referring grimly to their "socialistic features of government ownership."[82] The demand for a federal "subtreasury" system proved so alarming as to prompt some Alliancemen's excommunication from the Texas Democratic party.

Thus the emergence of Populism not only moved party competition in Texas farther away from the Democrat-versus-Republican paradigm established during Reconstruction but also, at least for a time, shifted the focus of politics. Redeemers had looked to the federal government for frontier and border defense, for river and harbor improvements, and for subsidizing railroad construction so that Texans would not have to. At the same time, they had always been on their guard against threats that federal authority might pose to their power. But Texas politics had remained chiefly concerned with what *state* and *local* government "ought and ought not to do," could demand and must not demand of citizens. Much more than Greenbackers, Populists rewrote the terms of debate by calling for the most fundamental federal action to reshape the daily experience and livelihoods of farmers and urban laborers. When Texas Democrats and Populists argued, they did so chiefly over what the federal government ought to do, not simply with respect to Texas but to the United States at large. Texas Populists, in their platforms, did give considerable attention to issues long debated in state politics, for example demanding, as had Greenbackers and many Democrats before them, the reservation of the public domain for actual settlers and enhanced educational efforts. But interestingly, Democrats chose to prominently feature in their platforms of 1892 and 1894 lengthy expositions of matters state government had little to do with, such as the tariff and the coinage of silver.[83] An era in Texas politics had ended.

Redemption's Final Act

The odor from oil refineries settles over the cotton fields and makes scarcely perceptible the magnolia scent of the Old South.

V. O. KEY (1949)

I f a distinct period in the political history of Texas had closed by the end of the 1880s, Redeemer Democrats left behind unfinished business and enduring patterns of government. Over the next century, the state's fundamentally southern politics would continue to be shaped by resources and populations that set it apart from much of Dixie.

Corporate regulation was one of the state's more conspicuous bits of unfinished business when Governor Hogg clambered into office in 1891. The widespread enthusiasm for public oversight of railroads had been obvious in the first years of Redemption. But for fifteen years thereafter, Democrats argued over how and when the government should exercise the powers the Redeemer constitution gave it to regulate rates and prevent discrimination. Should it allow railroads to expand farther before wielding those powers too aggressively? Could the legislature delegate its regulatory powers to a commission? The old antagonists James Throckmorton and John Ireland both supported the establishment of a state railroad commission (Throckmorton, the longtime Texas & Pacific ally, had by the late 1870s voiced a concern that "the corporations are becoming masters of the people and the government"). Gov. Sul Ross, though, doubted the constitutionality and utility of such an agency and preferred regulation by statute. The state experimented in the late 1870s and early 1880s with general laws setting maximum rates and restricting long-haul/short-haul discrimination and with the appointment of a state engineer to oversee railroad operations.[1]

Regulatory sentiment grew more insistent as the ownership of Texas railroads became increasingly consolidated. Despite Redeemers' eagerness to cultivate homegrown lines, the management of the state's most important routes fell into the hands of two decidedly remote tycoons, Jay Gould and Collis Huntington, who came to agreements between themselves on rates and traffic. In the latter half of the 1880s, Hogg, then Texas attorney general, began to litigate against various corporate abuses, such as pooling and failure to maintain offices in the state, and helped draft a state antitrust law that passed in 1889. At the same time, domestic business interests, including merchants and lumbermen, joined with the burgeoning Farmers Alliance in seeking expanded and more routine oversight. Texans voted to amend the constitution to provide explicitly for the establishment of a railroad commission in 1890, the same year they elected Hogg governor. This hardly put the issue of regulation to rest, though. Hogg and members of the Farmers Alliance fell to fighting over whether commission members should be elected or appointed by the governor. Democrats more solicitous of railroad interests worried that Hogg's brand of energetic regulation might drive capital from the state. This squabbling contributed to the three-man gubernatorial race of 1892, which pitted Hogg against a fellow Democrat and the Populist Nugent.[2]

Despite its creation during the seedtime of Texas Populism, the Texas Railroad Commission would in subsequent decades regulate in the manner and to the ends envisioned by developmentally oriented Redeemers in the 1870s. In overseeing transportation and eventually the oil industry, the commission's policies seem to have focused more on protecting indigenous business interests and rationalizing commerce than on easing any burdens on farmers and consumers. The commission's early rate policies favored shipping through the ports of Galveston and Houston rather than to out-of-state entrepôts. For four decades after the opening of the East Texas oil fields at the beginning of the 1930s, the commission limited oil production in the state to prevent gluts and keep prices from collapsing. David Prindle has pointed out that with this system, Texas—popularly imagined to be a citadel of laissez-faire—departed more aggressively from free-market economics than a number of other important oil-producing states. Commission policies also routinely favored Texas-based independents and landowners over major petroleum concerns dominated by out-of-state capital. In both symbolic and practical terms then, it was surely significant that the commission's first chairman was John H. Reagan, that ardent advocate of railroad regulation and equally ardent promoter of economic development.[3]

Among Redeemers, Reagan had also been an early and ardent advocate of suffrage restriction. For some Democrats, that remained a second bit of unfinished business as a new generation took the helm. Urban elites had secured devices by which they might pacify city politics. Black-majority counties in many cases had been redeemed by extraparliamentary means. But only with the dawn of the new century did restrictionists reach that promised land they had sought since Reconstruction—a Texas in which local political threats could be contained by the de jure exclusion of many citizens from the electorate. In 1901 the Texas legislature voted by large margins to amend the constitution to stipulate that any citizen subject to pay a poll tax "shall have paid said tax before he offers to vote at any election."[4] The minority of the electorate who turned out to vote on the measure ratified it by a margin of nearly two to one. (J. Morgan Kousser, however, makes a plausible case that African American votes were fraudulently cast or counted in support of the poll tax.)[5]

Appropriately enough, the election law passed in the next legislature to put this poll tax into effect, as well as various emendations made in subsequent sessions, were written by and named for the man who had led the fight for disfranchisement in Texas for a quarter-century—Alexander W. Terrell. The Terrell laws enforced a poll tax due far in advance of election day and applying to primaries as well as general elections. They also promoted the more general exclusion of African Americans from local Democratic primaries by allowing county party committees to establish the criteria for participation. In mandating a secret ballot, the legislation extended to the state at large a device previously applied only in cities. But at the same time, it perpetuated the tradition of imposing more stringent conditions on voters in cities of 10,000 or more than on Texans at large, requiring city dwellers to pay their poll taxes in person while prospective voters elsewhere might delegate others to pay their tax (a concession won by South Texas machine politicians).[6] And as was the case with disfranchisement measures across the South, the Terrell laws did a particularly thorough job of decimating the ranks of urban voters, both black and white. By one estimate Houston's electorate shrank from 76 percent to 32 percent of the adult male population between 1900 and 1904 alone. In Galveston only about one of every eight adult black males could pay his poll tax, while in Fort Worth, a local newspaper reported, "much of the irresponsible white vote was banned by the tax restrictions."[7]

But why, after twenty-five years of shrugging off comprehensive disfranchisement measures and after most of the opposition strongholds in black-majority counties had been reduced by fraud and force, had the legislature and the electorate shifted so decisively toward formal suffrage restriction?

The answer lies in a combination of factors—regional, national, and peculiarly Texan. The old restrictionist constituencies presumably remained in place. Democrats in black-majority areas surely still yearned for the poll tax, for it would relieve them of much of the hard, expensive, and technically illegal work of fraud and intimidation. Although the national trend toward containing the power of the transient and propertyless in urban politics had already manifested itself in the array of restrictive devices applied to Texas cities, outright disfranchisement must still have carried some appeal to urban conservatives. Accordingly, urban counties and black-majority counties where de facto disfranchisement had already been accomplished tended to vote heavily for the poll-tax amendment. But restrictionists seem also to have gained new allies.[8]

Texas' western-style population boom, underwritten largely by white migration from the Southeast, had hindered the cause of suffrage restriction in the 1870s by peopling large portions of the state with an overwhelmingly white citizenry. Yet the progress of politics since Redemption had, ironically, rendered Texas less securely Democratic. In 1894 twenty-two Populists had been elected to the state house of representatives, two to the state senate. Many more won local office. Two years later Populist candidate Jerome Kearby won 44 percent of the gubernatorial vote, the highest proportion for any non-Democratic aspirant since 1869.[9]

Populism made the dangers to be apprehended from universal manhood suffrage more immediate to a broader range of Texans. One could still argue, as delegates to the 1875 constitutional convention had, that the poll tax would burden not only African Americans but also hardscrabble white cultivators. But one could no longer assume that this white rural population was not a likely source of challenge to Democratic authority. With the era's chronically depressed cotton prices and the rapid increase of white tenancy, farmers had become far from inevitably Democratic. The most extreme examples of this phenomenon were seen in a number of counties—including Comanche, Erath, Hamilton, and Palo Pinto in West Central Texas and Sabine in the east—which when the constitution had been framed in the 1870s were overwhelmingly Democrat, recording few (or even no) opposition votes. All voted Populist in 1892, 1894, and 1896 gubernatorial balloting.[10] And if Populism seemed all but dead by 1901, Democrats could not simply assume that discontented rural whites would return to the fold, or if they did, would placidly acquiesce in conservative domination of the party. The conditions that had helped breed political turbulence had not entirely disappeared with the nineteenth century. The proportion of landless farmers, for instance, continued to increase after 1900.[11] The potential of this development to make trouble for Democrats would be illustrated in coming decades by the successes—even with a poll tax in place—of Socialist organizing in certain rural districts and of James "Pa" Ferguson's appeals to tenants in his fights within the party for the governorship.[12] As many in the rural population grew more closely to resemble those propertyless, politically unreliable whites that restrictionists had long included among their targets, many Democrats may have reconsidered their opposition to the poll tax.

The Populist threats to Democratic hegemony likely accelerated disfranchisement in another way—by enhancing the power of Republican and black voters even where they were in a decided minority. With the emergence of the Greenbackers in the late 1870s, divisions within the traditionally Democratic electorate occasionally had allowed a Republican minority to tip the scales toward the faction of their choice or even, through alliances with third parties, to elect local officeholders more sympathetic to demands for fair elections and better schools. In the late 1870s and early 1880s, such circumstances had permitted the election of black legislators from white-majority counties like Bastrop, Robertson, and Brazos. Populism made for divisions within the white electorate across a broader expanse of Texas, increasing opportunities for an outnumbered black electorate to affect the balance of power. The campaigns by black Populists like John Rayner to bring African Americans directly into third parties must have illustrated even more pointedly the threat politically cohesive minority populations posed even in white-majority regions.[13]

But Populism seems to have expanded the constituency for disfranchisement in yet another way. Some insurgents crawled from the wreckage of their movement convinced that certain Texans, particularly black Texans, should no longer be allowed to vote. Their party, they believed, had been robbed of local and even statewide victories because Democratic opponents had bribed, coerced, and defrauded black voters. And many seemed to decide that the easiest and most thoroughgoing response to such villainy would be to disfranchise the object of manipulation, the African American electorate—a logic also indulged by some Democratic devotees of "good government." The poll tax, they could argue, might serve as a de facto system of voter registration, discouraging the corrupt practices that sustained conservative political machines, whether in old plantation counties, South Texas ranching regions, or towns and cities. By the first years of the twentieth century, "progressive" Democrats, identified with the figure and legacy of former governor Hogg, were offering up the poll tax as one of a number of "reforms" with which they hoped to rally quondam Populists and secure their faction's preeminence in a rejuvenated Democratic party. The poll tax's image as a reform measure was doubtlessly burnished by the fact that some of suffrage restriction's longtime advocates, including Terrell and Reagan, had also long been among the state's important crusaders for corporate regulation. This reform impulse seems to have played a consequential role in furthering disfranchisement. A regression analysis of the 1902 poll-tax referendum performed by historians Gregg Cantrell and D. Scott Barton suggests that almost 30 percent of the votes for the measure came from former Populists and not their old Democratic foes.[14]

But in addition to the longstanding concerns of Democrats in black-majority areas and cities and the new circumstances bred by Populism, other factors brought Texas to de jure disfranchisement. The politics of prohibition—which the state's unusually large German and Latino populations had long made particularly piquant—intensified interest in disfranchising African Americans and footloose whites in places where the Republican party or even Populism had not necessarily made much of an impression. Black voters, like German and Latino ones, seem by all accounts to have gone overwhelmingly wet in the 1887 referendum.[15] In subsequent years African Americans continued to be a factor in local-option elections (from which they could not be excluded by the mechanism of a white primary), and prohibitionists often blamed them when the dry vote came up short—not entirely without reason. John Rayner, for one, had turned from mobilizing black voters in the interest of Populism to turning them out at the behest of brewing and liquor interests. Those for whom prohibition had become a central public concern could see the disfranchisement of black men as a means of advancing temperance. Wets clearly made the same calculation, brewers and liquor dealers being prominent in their opposition to the poll tax amendment.[16]

But something that set Texas apart from the rest of the South—borderland politics—also moved the state toward the quintessentially southern device of de jure disfranchisement. As noted, South Texas Democrats had long resisted suffrage restriction. Their power rested in part on the carefully orchestrated mobilization of a Latino electorate that was in many cases too poor, not sufficiently fluent in English, or too recently arrived in the United States to meet the most common sorts of voting qualifications. Accordingly, South Texas political bosses like Jim Wells became some of the Terrell laws' most noted opponents—and also among their chief targets. If some pursued disfranchisement in the name of good government, what needed cleaning up more than the often flamboyantly corrupt machine politics along the Rio Grande?

Terrell explicitly named Mexicans as among the populations he would like to see disfranchised. But by the early twentieth century, a constituency for suffrage restriction had emerged *within* South Texas as well. The Anglo (in many cases midwestern) immigrants who surged into the area during these years to farm the Rio Grande Valley ran up against existing ranching elites who had little interest in ceding their control over county government or local development. As a practical matter these new arrivals had to loosen corrupt and often conservative machines' grip on the Latino electorate if they were going to secure what they saw as their fair share of power and resources. But suffrage restriction was more than a means to that end. Many doubtlessly saw Latinos as a nonwhite agricultural workforce whose claims upon civil society were every bit as tenuous as African American sharecroppers' were in the eyes of Central and East Texas landowners. In counties controlled by this new class of farmers, as well as in cities and towns with significant Hispanic populations, Anglos employed the whole array of Redeemer restrictive de- vices—the poll tax, the white primary, and at-large representation—to curtail the electoral power of Latinos and reduce or eliminate Tejano officeholding. Democrats also circumscribed the Latino electorate by eliminating voting by aliens, who earlier could cast ballots if they had declared the intention to become citizens—though in this, Texas was following a national anti- immigrant trend more than simply a southern path to disfranchisement.[17] Its southern politics thus intruded into its borderlands, showing yet again how regional histories overlapped in the Lone Star State.

For all its varied sources, though, disfranchisement did not bring peace to Texas politics. In not being cumulative over the years, Texas' poll tax proved less onerous than some others in the South. The now all-important Demo- cratic primaries remained lively affairs, with enough cantankerous whites participating to ensure that victory did not inevitably go to the party's most conservative factions.[18] Repeatedly in the one-party era, Democrats would divide over substantive issues—whether prohibition, the power of the Ku Klux Klan in the party, or the New Deal. But the violence the poll tax did to democracy in Texas must not be understated. It brutally shrank the electorate. By 1910, Kousser reports, little more than half the state's adult males paid their poll taxes. That meant that at very most only 64 percent of eligible whites could or would pay for the right to vote. As political scientist V. O. Key noted long ago, voter turnout in Texas had begun to fall well before the passage of the Terrell laws, whether due to the extraparliamentary manipulation of the electorate or Populists' frustration in the wake of their losses. But the poll tax, by giving disfranchisement the force of law, assured that turnout did not rebound. Indeed, participation by potential voters in gubernatorial elections, even in the most contested Democratic primaries, remained substantially below 50 percent through the following four decades. The state's population grew by more than three-quarters of a million people in each of the first two decades of the twentieth century, but until the enfranchisement of women, *fewer* people voted for governor in general elections than had in the 1890s. Only on occasion did the number of voters in the more decisive Democratic primaries match the 1890s figures.[19]

The poll tax showed how Texas Democrats, for all that set their state apart, had by early in the twentieth century firmly committed themselves to strategies that proved regrettably unexceptional in southern terms—fraud, political violence, formal disfranchisement, and Jim Crow (in 1891, early in the Hogg administration, the legislature had passed a separate-coach law). Texas had also answered the questions of land, labor, and credit raised by emancipation and the intensification of commercial cotton culture in manners similar to other former Confederate states. These included the development of the crop-lien as the prime mechanism of rural credit and the growing dispossession of white cotton cultivators. The transformations in Texas' post-emancipation arrangements of race and class in the twentieth century—the out-migration of large numbers of black people, the mechanization and westward migration of cotton cultivation and the dispersal of the tenantry, and a second reconstruction spearheaded by local activists and ultimately carried through by federal authority—likewise followed broader southern patterns.

But Texas' specifically southwestern circumstances made for significant variations on these southern themes, including the relatively early emergence of a seasonal Latino labor force in certain agricultural areas, introduced in addition to—or eventually in lieu of—black croppers and white tenants.[20] At the same time, disfranchisement and segregation as applied to Tejanos was never as far reaching or uniform as it was in the case of African Americans. In some counties the survival of paternalistic ranching enterprises and Tejano landownership tempered discrimination and exclusion. Latinos continued to cast ballots in large number and hold public office in significant number in these places, as well as where surviving machines paid their poll taxes to produce a bloc vote. Latinos found themselves confined to Jim Crow facilities in many places, but segregation remained a de facto rather than a de jure phenomenon, Tejanos being considered "white" for many official purposes (if not in the minds of many Anglos). In some places Tejano children attended white schools. By the 1940s Texas Democratic leaders seem to have been hardly as adamant about preserving what disfranchisement and segregation had been visited upon Latinos as defending the Jim Crow imposed on black Texans (in part because the Mexican government threatened to cut off guest-worker programs in response to the discrimination heaped on immigrants and Tejanos). Tejanos returned to the state legislature and even began being elected to Congress some years before the renaissance of African American officeholding.[21]

Its borderland aspects alone did not make Texas' southern history distinctive in the twentieth century—so did its natural wealth. The state's public land and frontier population boom had given a peculiar cast to its experience of Reconstruction and Redemption. That anomalous place within the New South had faded in the 1880s, however, as Texas began to exhaust its public domain. In 1898 the state's supreme court brought down a final curtain on the political economy of Redemption. The court found in *Hogue v. Baker* that because legislators had not always been careful to set aside corresponding amounts of acreage when they made certain large grants of state land, such as to veterans, the school fund had not yet received the one-half of the public domain promised by the Redeemer constitution. To make good on that pledge, all the unappropriated public land that remained became reserved for sale or lease to benefit schools. The purposes to which public land could be put had thus been whittled down to one. The state's interest in providing homesteads to humble settlers had given way to its interest in generating nontax revenue for public education.[22]

Yet within three years of this declaration that the state's landed wealth had been spoken for, rich oil deposits were discovered at Spindletop in southeastern Texas. Other strikes would follow in northern, western, and then eastern Texas over the next three decades. A new sort of natural wealth again made the state atypical within the South—though its distinctiveness in this case had to do with the sheer scale of its holdings rather than an unusually extensive authority over its disposition. (One estimate is that Texas sold or granted 91.4 percent of its land without reserving claim to the mineral resources they harbored.) Oil contributed mightily to an economic buoyancy that through much of the twentieth century widened an existing gap between per capita income in Texas and in the rest of the old Confederacy.[23] With oil came jobs in drilling, refining, and a host of associated industries as well as revenue generated by severance taxes. The state's industries, big cities, and millionaires set it apart from much of the South not only in image but also in fact.

It seems likely that this boom economy premised on petroleum and petrochemicals, aviation and defense industries, and construction and eventually electronics—and not simply its relatively small proportion of black people—helped ensure that resistance to the civil rights revolution was not quite as savage in Texas as in the less dynamic parts of the Deep South. Hatefulness and footdragging, particularly in terms of school and housing desegregation, were certainly very much in evidence. But after 1957 few statewide politicians trafficked in massive resistance in the same way that their brethren in Arkansas, Mississippi, Alabama, or Georgia did. With their fortunes tied far less exclusively to the traditional southern pursuits of agriculture and milling, the state's business elites and certain of its leading national politicians, most notably Lyndon Johnson, may have seen a certain logic in accommodating the new demands, or at least not making war on the federal government. As much as many in the Texas business community resented federal intrusion when it came to promoting civil rights, union representation, or social welfare, they at the same time profited off federal dollars in the form of defense and construction contracts.[24]

In considering politics and government, though, the extent to which oil and prosperity set Texas on a different course from other southern states may be less significant than that prosperity resurrected painful ironies of the postbellum period. Again it was booming as compared to Dixie, but again Texas was not serving its citizens very much better than the other former rebel states. Oil steered Texas back toward Redeemer habits of government. Petroleum through much of the twentieth century seemed to promise what land had in the 1870s—that prosperity and well-being could be achieved without undue demands on the public purse. Texas government had never been inert. Even in the 1870s many Democrats had supported government activism in pursuit of economic growth, provided they did not have to pay taxes to support it. But neither Redeemers nor twentieth-century lawmakers would build a regime of taxing and public spending sufficiently comprehensive to spread the benefits of the state's undeniable wealth more evenly across the length and breadth of Texas. Severance taxes on oil and gas were complemented only by a patchwork of franchise taxes, license and excise taxes (such as on motor fuel and cigarettes), property taxes, and beginning in the 1960s, a general sales tax. Conspicuously and insistently absent was a state income tax, yielding, even in the 1990s, one of the most regressive tax systems in the nation.[25] Not surprisingly, Texas continued to lag behind a great many states in what it invested in its citizenry. It stood in the top half of states in per capita personal income as its oil economy peaked, but like more obviously bereft southern states, it ranked near the bottom in various indices of its citizens' well-being, including percentage of families below the poverty line and rates of illiteracy and incarceration.[26]

As had been the case in the 1870s, the contrast between economic dynamism and southern standards of welfare was particularly conspicuous in public education. Much changed for the better through the course of the twentieth century—an expansion of funding with the discovery of oil under state school and university lands; more comprehensive tax support; the growth of state and local administrative bodies; and vast improvement of rural schools. But both inequality of opportunity and relatively low educational achievement persisted. Even during the oil boom years of the later 1970s, Texans were considerably worse off than the national average in terms of graduation rates and teacher salaries. In 1979 the state ranked twenty-first in the nation in per capita personal income but thirty-fifth in current expenditure per pupil in average daily attendance.[27]

The poor state of public education in the boom years might be traced back in part to the expectation Redeemer Democrats had done so much to instill, that natural wealth would allow Texas to defer a more intrusive marshaling of its powers to tax and spend. But another legacy of Redemption also hobbled the state's schools: the system of local financing that Democrats had instituted as their initial post-Reconstruction strategies collapsed in the early 1880s. One hundred years later, local taxation supplied approximately half of all school funds in Texas. This perpetuated enormous inequity, given that wealth per student ranged from $20,000 in the poorest district to 700 times that amount in the richest. Accordingly, though poorer school districts often taxed themselves at higher rates than wealthier ones, spending per student ranged from $2,112 to $19,333 within the state.[28] Yet so ingrained had the Democrats' 1880s expedient of local financing become that a statewide pro rata distribution of educational funds of the sort they had *initially* tried to enforce seemed almost collectivist to many modern lawmakers. More ironically still, the state supreme court, which in 1989 forced Texans to act on the issue by voiding the existing school finance system, cast its *Edgewood* decision in the language of the Redeemer constitution. The great disparities among districts in funding and facilities, Justice Oscar Mauzy wrote, betrayed the constitutional guarantee of an "efficient" school system providing for a "general diffusion of knowledge" across the state. Acknowledging that it had to consider the original intent of the Democrats who had made that constitution, the court gamely argued that even if the framers desired an inexpensive school establishment, they "never contemplated the possibility that such gross inequalities could exist within an 'efficient' system."[29] If the court thereby struck a blow for an equality of opportunity commensurate with the Lone Star State's material wealth and the richness of its human resources, it dealt too generously with Redeemers, whose actions with respect to education had been animated less by concern for equity than by the imperatives of anti-Reconstruction politics.

In the 1990s Texas moved slowly to reconstruct its educational system. After slumps in the oil industry and real estate in the 1980s, the state's economy diversified further, for instance, with greater investment in high tech. Texas again prospered, but even then it continued to compare poorly with other states in vital aspects of the common good. Twenty-two states had lower per capita incomes in 2003. Only six had higher poverty rates in 2000–2002. *No* state had a smaller proportion of its population covered by health insurance or holding a high school diploma. Texas remained in the bottom half of states in the amount it spent per student.[30] But a system of school funding that sought to equalize educational opportunity by redistributing locally raised money across the state was widely derided as a "Robin Hood" plan that "robbed" the rich rather than being understood by citizens as a mechanism for uplifting their fellow Texans. These conditions and this rhetoric might lead some to wonder if the state, even in the twenty-first century, had entirely escaped its post-Reconstruction past. In other words, was Texas truly beyond Redemption?

Notes

INTRODUCTION: SOUTH BY SOUTHWEST

1. Haley, *Buffalo War*.
2. Rather than identifying a specific faction of the party, "Redeemer" in this work denotes a generation of Democrats that had come of age by 1861, engineered Reconstruction's collapse during the 1870s, and continued to dominate Texas politics until the election of James S. Hogg as governor in 1890.
3. Thompson, *Juan Cortina*, 71–73, 91–93; Leiker, *Racial Borders*, 35–36, 58–63.
4. The exceptions include Foley, *White Scourge*; Leiker, *Racial Borders*; and Carrigan, *Making of a Lynching Culture*.
5. *Galveston Daily News* [hereafter *GDN*], Oct. 13, 22, 1874.
6. Census Office, Ninth Census, *Statistics of the Wealth and Industry*, 251, 255; *GDN*, Aug. 28, 1873.
7. Lowe and Campbell, *Planters and Plain Folk*, 12–13; Jordan, "Imprint of the Upper and Lower South," 677–85.
8. McMath, "Sandy Land and Hogs," 205–29; Francaviglia, *Cast Iron Forest*.
9. Brammer, *Gay Place*, 3.
10. Day and Winfrey, *Texas Indian Papers*, 307–30, 373–92; *GDN*, July 18, 20, 27, Nov. 21, 22, 1873; Nunn, *Texas under the Carpetbaggers*, 177–223.
11. Gammel, *Laws of Texas* [hereafter *LT*], 6:179–82, 219–20; *Journal of the Constitutional Convention . . . , 1875* [hereafter *1875 Convention Journal*], 261.
12. *GDN*, Oct. 25, 1873; Campbell, *Grass-Roots Reconstruction*, 49, 94–95, 160, 190, 218; E. T. Miller, *Financial History of Texas*, 165–67; Moneyhon, *Texas after the Civil War*, 173–76.
13. See the complaints of an 1871 "Taxpayers' Convention" in Winkler, *Platforms*, 136–39.
14. Census Office, Eleventh Census, *Compendium . . . , Part 1*, 2, 473; Kerr, "Migration into Texas," 184–216.
15. Winkler, *Journal of the Secession Convention*, 14, 20–22. Of James Alex Baggett's sample of Texas Redeemers, 76 percent had held local office and 22 percent state or federal office before the Civil War. Baggett, *Scalawags*, 277.
16. Campbell, "Population Persistence and Social Change," 185–204.
17. Perman, *Struggle for Mastery*, 6.
18. Foley, *White Scourge*, 27–35, 225–26n; Sanders, *Farm Ownership and Tenancy*; McMath, *American Populism*, 38–39; Martin, *People's Party in Texas*, 60–65.
19. Kousser, *Shaping of Southern Politics*, 197; Woodward, *Origins of the New South*, 21, 79, 327–29; Key, *Southern Politics*, 5–9, 260.

20. The term "Anglo" is itself a product of Texans' difficulties in fitting Latinos into a binary black-white racial system. It denotes not simply those of English background but anyone of European descent who is not Hispanic. The term thus sets Latinos apart without insisting they are not white.

21. Davis to Messrs. Powers and Maxan, Oct. 27, 1874, and Davis to Stephen Powers, Feb. 10 [quotation], Mar. 14, Apr. 19, 1876, Wells Papers; Campbell, *Grass-Roots Reconstruction,* 193–219; Crews, "Reconstruction in Brownsville."

22. De León and Stewart, *Tejanos and the Numbers Game,* 17; Bureau of the Census, *Negro Population,* 789–92.

23. A. J. Fountain to E. J. Davis, May 31, 1873, Correspondence, Davis Records; *State of Texas against Hon. S. B. Newcomb,* 39, 86.

24. Foley, *White Scourge,* 13, 24.

25. *San Antonio Daily Herald,* Feb. 4, 1876 [hereafter *SADH*]; De León, *They Called Them Greasers,* 57.

26. *Journal of the Senate of the State of Texas; . . . Thirteenth Legislature,* 89, 166, 233–35, 344–49, 816 [hereafter *Senate Journal, 13th Leg.*]; *Journal of the House of Representatives of the State of Texas; . . . Thirteenth Legislature,* 275 [hereafter *House Journal, 13th Leg.*].

27. Barr, *Reconstruction to Reform,* 203; Anders, *Boss Rule,* 90–91.

28. De León, *Tejano Community,* 45–49; Anders, *Boss Rule,* 3–25, 281; Kearney and Knopp, *Boom and Bust,* 176–79; García, *Desert Immigrants,* 157–64.

29. *SADH,* Dec. 24, 29, 1875, Feb. 4–5, 19, 1876; De León, *Tejano Community,* 28–45; R. B. Debrow to Ashbel Smith, Jan. 15, 1879, Smith Papers.

30. Leiker, *Racial Borders,* esp. 54–56.

31. E. O. C. Ord to Richard Coke, May 15, 1875 [first quotation], Correspondence, Coke Records; Richard Coke to Ord, May 24, 1875 [third quotation], and Coke to W. W. Belknap, Secretary of War, June 8, 1875 [second quotation], Letterpress, ibid.

32. Leiker, *Racial Borders,* 14, 34–35, 37–39, 52.

33. *Congressional Record,* 45th Cong., 3rd sess. (1879), 950.

34. Montejano, *Anglos and Mexicans,* 6–7, 34–37, 76–85.

35. Census Office, Tenth Census, *Compendium . . . , Part 1,* 332; Census Office, Eleventh Census, *Compendium . . . , Part 3,* 10.

36. Campbell, *Gone to Texas,* ix, 290; Jordan, *German Seed in Texas Soil.* On ethnic politics among German Texans, see, for example, *GDN,* Feb. 20, 23, July 27, Aug. 8–9, Sept. 24, 1873; and Winkler, *Platforms,* 151–54.

37. Barr, *Reconstruction to Reform,* 22; Ayers, *Promise of the New South,* 35, 50; Perman, *Road to Redemption,* 263, 277.

38. See, for example, Darden, *Annual Report of the Comptroller . . . 1874,* 67.

39. Perman, *Road to Redemption,* 221–63.

40. See, for example, Schwartz, *Radical Protest and Social Structure,* 11–13; and Going, *Bourbon Democracy in Alabama,* 45–49.

41. Darden, *Annual Report of the Comptroller . . . 1874,* 46–52.

42. Ira Evans to Ashbel Smith, Apr. 27, 1876, and Johns & Spence to Smith, Sept. 27, 1879, Smith Papers; Silverthorne, *Ashbel Smith,* 173, 177, 179–80.

43. Brockman, "Railroads, Radicals, and Democrats," 166n48, 312; *GDN,* Apr. 10, 1873, Aug. 13, 1875, Mar. 12, 1876; W. P. Ballinger Diary, July 21, 24, 28, 1875, Ballinger

Papers; R. Tyler et al., *New Handbook of Texas,* 2:878–79, 3:712; M. Turner, *Richard Bennett Hubbard,* 34–37, 45, 47, 94–95.

44. *GDN,* June 13, 1873, June 6, 1874; *North Texas Enterprise,* Aug. 28, Oct. 30, 1874.

45. James W. Throckmorton to Benjamin Epperson, Apr. 1, 1872, Epperson Papers; Ballinger Diary, Jan. 28, 1874, Ballinger Papers; John Hancock to Edward Burleson Jr., Dec. 28, 1875, Burleson Papers; *Austin Daily Democratic Statesman,* July 21, 1875 [hereafter *ADDS*].

46. D. M. Short to Oran Roberts, July 29, 1873, Roberts Papers; John Ireland to Samuel Bell Maxey, Dec. 14, 1873, Maxey Papers; *GDN,* Jan. 29, 1874, Aug. 13, 1875; *Paris [Tex.] Press,* Sept. 3, 1875; Ed. P. Marshall to Hon. O. M. Roberts, Dec. 2, 1878, Correspondence, Roberts Records.

1. REDEEMING STATE GOVERNMENT

1. *GDN,* Jan. 16, 1874.

2. *Journal of the Senate of Texas; . . . Second Session of the Fourteenth Legislature,* 8 [hereafter *Senate Journal, 14th Leg., 2nd sess.*].

3. As canvassed by the legislature, the results were Coke, 85,549 votes; Davis, 42,633. *Journal of the House of Representatives of the State of Texas; Being the Session of the Fourteenth Legislature,* 9–10 [hereafter *House Journal, 14th Leg., 1st sess.*].

4. *GDN,* Jan. 14–16, 1874.

5. Ibid., Jan. 4, 7, 14, 1874; E. J. Davis to Messrs. E. J. Brown, J. K. Williams, J. R. Ford, L. J. Gallant, and M. T. Hoskins, Jan. 9, 1874, Letterbook, Davis Records.

6. *San Antonio Express,* Jan. 12, 1913 [quotation], clipping in Coke Scrapbook; Ford, *Rip Ford's Texas,* 417, 424.

7. Statement of William P. Hardeman, Memoirs [typescript], 7:1272 [quotation], Ford Papers; Roberts, "Political, Legislative, and Judicial History," 208; T. B. Wheeler, "Reminiscences of Reconstruction," 56–63.

8. *GDN,* Jan. 20, 22, 25, 1874; Ford, *Rip Ford's Texas,* 428.

9. See, for instance, Ramsdell, *Reconstruction in Texas,* 317.

10. *GDN,* Jan. 16, 1873.

11. Moneyhon, *Republicanism in Reconstruction Texas,* 104–67; Carrier, "Political History of Texas during Reconstruction," 327–404, 469–75; Baum, *Shattering of Texas Unionism,* 180–228.

12. Local studies have suggested the support of foreign-born, Northern-born, and Mexican American voters for the Republican party was more conditional than that of African Americans. Campbell, *Grass-Roots Reconstruction,* 208; Nieman, "Black Political Power and Criminal Justice," 394–95.

13. Bureau of the Census, *Negro Population,* 51.

14. *American Annual Cyclopædia, 1871,* 735–36; Moneyhon, *Republicanism in Reconstruction Texas,* 163–66; Smallwood, *Time of Hope,* 154–55; Carrier "Political History of Texas during Reconstruction," 493–94, 497.

15. Barker, *Directory of the Members of the Thirteenth Legislature; Members of the Texas Legislature,* 57–77; Carrier, "Political History of Texas during the Reconstruction," 497–507; Marten, *Texas Divided,* 139–48; Baggett, "Rise and Fall of the Texas

Radicals," 175–76, 186–87, 190; Campbell, *Grass-Roots Reconstruction*, 47, 49–50; Casdorph, *Republican Party in Texas*, 249.

16. *LT*, 6:185–90, 193–95, 972–74.

17. Webb, *Texas Rangers*, 226.

18. Hardin, *Life of John Wesley Hardin;* Crouch and Brice, *Cullen Montgomery Baker.*

19. Baenziger, "Texas State Police," 471–73, 476–77; Crouch, "Spirit of Lawlessness," 217–32; Smallwood, *Time of Hope*, 32–35, 141–46, 149–51; Cantrell, "Racial Violence and Reconstruction Politics," 333–55.

20. Winkler, *Platforms*, 125–26, 131–33, 159.

21. *Senate Journal, 13th Leg.*, 351–55; *House Journal, 13th Leg.*, 596.

22. *GDN*, May 1 [quoting *Palestine Advocate*], Oct. 31 [Hubbard], 1873; Baenziger, "Texas State Police," 474, 486, 490–91.

23. *Senate Journal, 13th Leg.*, 56, 91, 479–80, 497–98, 568; *House Journal, 13th Leg.*, 11, 67–68, 466, 701–5; *LT*, 7:493.

24. *Senate Journal, 13th Leg.*, 53, 84–85, 118–19, 152, 298–99; *House Journal, 13th Leg.*, 45, 112, 115–17, 266, 310–11; *GDN*, Jan. 30, 1873; *LT*, 7:468–70.

25. *GDN*, May 17, 25 [first quotation], 1873; Merrick Trammel and Giles Trammel to E. J. Davis, June 23, 1873 [second quotation], B. F. Barkley to Davis, Apr. 21, 1873, and B. F. Barkley to Davis, May 3, 1873, Correspondence, Davis Records; E. J. Davis to A. J. Evans, Apr. 24, 1873, and Davis to M. J. Nelly, Aug. 15, 1873 [third quotation], Letterbook, ibid.; Baenziger, "Texas State Police," 488–89.

26. U.S. House, *Use of the Army in Certain of the Southern States*, H. Exec. Doc. 30, 44th Cong., 2d sess. (1876–77), 134–35 [quotation, 135], 137–39, 166–68.

27. *SADH*, Feb. 15, 1876; *GDN*, Jan. 13, 1875; *Report of the Adjutant General of the State of Texas*, 3 [second quotation]; Coke to S. J. Sturgis, Apr. 17, 1874, and Coke to T. B. Rankin, May 27, 1874, Letterbook, Davis Records. Sufficiently committed to retrenchment that he would not purchase fresh office supplies when he became governor, Coke continued to use Davis's letterbook. As a result, much of the outgoing correspondence of Coke's early months as governor is housed with his predecessor's papers.

28. *GDN*, May 29, June 5, July 1, 1874; *SADH*, Jan. 28, Feb. 15, 1876.

29. Webb, *Texas Rangers*, 233–38, 288–91; Utley, *Lone Star Justice*, 152–59; *LT*, 8:891–92.

30. Texas Constitution of 1869, art. 9; *LT*, 6:287–92, 959–62, 7:50–52; U.S. House, *Report of the Commissioner of Education* (1880–81), 308.

31. Moneyhon, "Public Education," 404–5; *GDN*, Aug. 21, 1873.

32. Moneyhon, "Public Education," 398–400; *GDN*, May 11 [second quotation], Oct. 31 [first quotation], 1873; *House Journal, 13th Leg.*, 798; Johnson, "Frugal and Sparing," 39–40.

33. Texas spent approximately $1,225,000 on public education during both the 1871–72 and the 1872–73 school years. U.S. House, *Report of the Commissioner of Education* (1880–81), 308.

34. Moneyhon, "Public Education," 402–3; Winkler, *Platforms*, 133–34; *House Journal, 13th Leg.*, 798–805.

35. C. C. Lee to E. J. Davis, Apr. 12, 1873, Correspondence, Davis Records; *D. P. Kinney v. G. B. Zimpelman*, 36 Texas Reports (1871–72), 554–92; *A. B. Hall v. Houston and*

Texas Central Railway Co., 39 Texas Reports (1873–74), 286–92; *John L. Peay v. E. W. Talbot & Bro.*, ibid., 335–47; King, *Great South*, 134–35; *GDN*, Apr. 17, 1873.

36. *House Journal, 13th Leg.*, 63–65, 194–95, 535, 681–85, 687–95, 699–701, 812–13, 1116–17; *Senate Journal, 13th Leg.*, 498–503, 647–48, 720–24; *LT*, 7:536–47, 8:211–15.

37. *GDN*, Sept. 12, 21, 24, Oct. 16, 30, Nov. 4, 1873; Moneyhon, "Public Education," 414; U.S. House, *Report of the Commissioner of Education . . . 1873*, 384–85; U.S. House, *Report of the Commissioner of Education* (1880–81), 308–9; Hollingsworth, *Fourth Annual Report of the Superintendent of Public Instruction*, 69–70; Hollingsworth, *Fifth Annual Report of the Superintendent of Public Instruction*, 5–6; Eby, *Development of Education in Texas*, 168.

38. Republican fractiousness as well as Democratic solidarity allowed these critical objects of Redemption to be achieved. Had several Republican senators not voted to override Davis's vetoes, the abolition of the state police and the Reconstruction school system might have been prevented. Dohoney, *Average American*, 155–57; *Senate Journal, 13th Leg.*, 568, 898.

39. *Report of the Special Joint Committee of the Thirteenth Legislature; House Journal, 13th Leg.*, 11–12, 49–50; *Senate Journal, 13th Leg.*, 76; *GDN*, Feb. 18, 1874.

40. *House Journal, 13th Leg.*, 240–43, 369–70, 427–32, 519–20, 663–73, 948–60, 1153–69, 1190, 1372–73, 1379; *Senate Journal, 13th Leg.*, 581–84, 726–32, 743–46, 756, 777–78, 1042–43, 1130, 1146, 1167–76; *GDN*, June 1, 4, 1873; *State of Texas against Judge John G. Scott*, 14–155.

41. Moneyhon, *Republicanism in Reconstruction Texas*, 207–11.

42. *LT*, 6:191–92; Merseburger, "Political History of Houston," 101, 120–22; Johnson, "Frugal and Sparing," 42; Crews, "Reconstruction in Brownsville," 69, 73, 76.

43. *LT*, 7:454.

44. *State of Texas against Hon. S. B. Newcomb*, 58–63, 71–72.

45. *LT*, 7:472–82, 506–10. The 1873 law provided that the presiding election officer in each precinct appoint judges and clerks from the opposite party "if demanded, so far as practicable, and there be present a sufficient number of the party making the demand, and willing to serve." Votes would be counted in the presence of at least one voter from the opposite party "if convenient to get." But such provisions seem often to have been defied. W. R. Miller, "Harrison County Methods," 119.

46. S. A. Hackworth to J. P. Newcomb, Aug. 3, 1873, Newcomb Papers; *GDN*, Sept. 17, 1873.

47. *LT*, 7:481–82.

48. *GDN*, May 9, 14, 28, 1873; *Senate Journal, 13th Leg.*, 586, 589–91, 746–48, 751–53, 896–97, 918, 927–28; *House Journal, 13th Leg.*, 921–23, 1127–28.

49. Texas Constitution of 1869, art. 3, secs. 39–40. In reapportioning the state's congressional districts, Democrats dealt with this Republican cluster of counties in another manner. Having to create only six districts rather than thirty, they could parcel out the Republican counties among districts with large numbers of friendlier counties. Thus the Brazos and Colorado river counties were divided between two narrow districts that stretched westward and northward to heavily Democratic areas of West and North Central Texas. Dispersing Republican voters could create problems of its own, however, such as when black Republicans in Texas'

most elongated congressional district combined with dissident white Democrats in 1878 to elect a Greenbacker. *LT,* 8:219–20.

50. *LT,* 7:495–99; Census Office, Ninth Census, *Compendium,* 92–96.

51. Dohoney, *Average American,* 156. Dohoney remembers Flanagan as being able to retain his old district. In fact a district more favorable to his prospects was created.

52. *GDN,* Apr. 30, 1873.

53. Ibid., July 17 [quoting *Henderson Times*], Sept. 5, 1874.

54. *Senate Journal, 13th Leg.,* 544, 733–34; *House Journal, 13th Leg.,* 742–43.

55. Moneyhon, *Republicanism in Reconstruction Texas,* 107–8, 145–46, 152–54, 176–77; Carrier, "Political History of Texas during Reconstruction," 488; Perman, *Road to Redemption,* 10–11, 77, 124, 151, 155; *GDN,* June 18–21, 1872, July 5, 11, 19, Aug. 14, 1873; Bailey, "Life and Public Career of O. M. Roberts," 204; John Reagan to B. Epperson, Apr. 23, 1872, Epperson Papers.

56. *GDN,* July 11, Aug. 16, 19, 30, 1873.

57. D. M. Short to Oran Roberts, July 29, 1873, Roberts Papers; *GDN,* Aug. 2, 1873.

58. *GDN,* June 11, 28, July 11, 16, 17 [quoting *Victoria Advocate*], 24, Aug. 6, 17, 19, 21, 28, 1873.

59. *Minutes of the Democratic State Convention . . . , 1873,* 30 [quotations], 33–34.

60. Samuel Bell Maxey to Marilda Maxey, Sept. 7, 1873, Maxey Papers; *GDN,* June 26 [Coke quotation], Aug. 15 [second quotation], 1873.

61. *House Journal, 13th Leg.,* 173, 224–25, 300, 357, 419, 435, 508, 981–82; *Senate Journal, 13th Leg.,* 166, 198, 233, 846; *GDN,* Jan. 31, Feb. 7, 11, Mar. 30, Apr. 3, 10, May 16, June 5, 8, 19, 29, July 2, 11, 18, 24, 31, Sept. 9, 19, 25, Oct. 7, 23, Nov. 8, 22, 1873, Mar. 25, Apr. 1, 1874; *North Texas Enterprise,* May 17, June 7, Aug. 2, 1873.

62. *Senate Journal, 13th Leg.,* 999, 1073; Dohoney, *Average American,* 160–61; *GDN,* Aug. 9, 1873; Winkler, *Platforms,* 153.

63. Winkler, *Platforms,* 161 [first quotation]; *North Texas Enterprise,* June 21, Nov. 1 [second quotation], 8, 1873, Nov. 20, 1874; *GDN,* July 2, Sept. 18, Oct. 23, 1873, Oct. 21, 1874.

64. Dohoney, *Average American,* 168–69; *Journal of the Constitutional Convention of the State of Texas . . . , 1875,* 80, 776–77 [hereafter *1875 Convention Journal*]; *Constitution of the State of Texas* [1876], art. 16, sec. 20; *LT,* 8:862–64; Ivy, *No Saloon in the Valley;* Barr, *Reconstruction to Reform,* 85–92.

65. Campbell, *Grass-Roots Reconstruction,* 29, 50 [first quotation]; *GDN,* Sept. 6, 19, 23, Oct. 19 [second quotation], 25, 31, Nov. 14, 30, 1873; Winkler, *Platforms,* 125, 160–61.

66. *GDN,* Aug. 6, 24, Oct. 26, 1873; Winkler, *Platforms,* 161 [quotation].

67. *GDN,* Oct. 18, 1873; E. J. Davis to Columbus Delano, Apr. 28, 1873, and Davis to W. C. Clayton et al., Aug. 8, 1873, Letterbook, Davis Records; *North Texas Enterprise,* May 3, 1873.

68. *House Journal, 13th Leg.,* 521–22.

69. Columbus Delano to E. J. Davis, Mar. 22, 1873, and C. C. Augur to Davis, May 29, 1873, Correspondence, Davis Records; *GDN,* May 13, July 10, Oct. 11, 18, 1873.

70. Pate, "Indians on Trial," 67; Cashion, *Texas Frontier,* 110.

71. Moneyhon, *Republicanism in Reconstruction Texas,* 122–28.

72. *GDN,* July 12, 18, Oct. 11, 1873; Nunn, *Texas under the Carpetbaggers,* 189–90.

73. *GDN,* Oct. 26 [second quotation], Nov. 6, 8, 15 [first quotation], 27, 1873; Gray, "Edmund J. Davis," 335.

74. *GDN*, Oct. 17, 31, Nov. 13, 15, 1873; Moneyhon, *Texas after the Civil War*, 197.

75. *GDN*, Nov. 16, 19, 28, 1873, July 7, 1874.

76. William Pitt Ballinger Diary, Sept. 11, 1873, Ballinger Papers; *State Journal*, Nov. 13, 1873 [quotation]; *GDN*, Nov. 16, 30, Dec. 2, 1873; J. W. Barnes to "Ed. Journal," Oct. 28, 1873, Newcomb Papers; *SADH*, Mar. 10, 12, 1875.

77. *GDN*, June 13, July 6, Sept. 17, Nov. 1, 14, 1873; *Brownsville Daily Ranchero and Republican*, Oct. 19, 1873 [first quotation], clipping in Newcomb Papers; Winkler, *Platforms*, 156–57 [second quotation].

78. Henderson, *Directory . . . of the Fourteenth Legislature*.

79. *GDN*, Dec. 12–13, 19, 1873.

80. Ibid., Dec. 9, 20, 23–24, 28, 30–31, 1873, Jan. 1, 1874; *Ex parte Rodriguez*, 39 Texas Reports (1873–74), 706–76.

81. Cooper, "'A Slobbering Lame Thing'?" 321–39.

82. *GDN*, Dec. 25, 1873, Jan. 10, 1874; Ballinger Diary, Dec. 23, 27–28, 1873; S. B. Maxey to Marilda Maxey, Jan. 6, 1874, Maxey Papers; E. J. Davis to Hon. B. H. Epperson "and other gentlemen of the committee," Jan. 13, 1874, and E. J. Davis to Hon. Richard Coke, Jan. 17, 1874, Letterbook, Davis Records; Moneyhon, "Edmund J. Davis in the Coke-Davis Election Dispute," 136–46.

83. *GDN*, Jan. 11, 14, 20, 22–23, Feb. 27, 1874; Brockman, "Railroads, Radicals, and Democrats," 156–61.

84. *GDN*, Jan. 16, Oct. 25, 1873; King, *Great South*, 99.

2. REDEMPTION'S SECOND ACT

1. *LT*, 8:239; *GDN*, Oct. 28, 1873 [second quotation].

2. *GDN*, Nov. 28, Dec. 2, 18, 27, 1873.

3. *Senate Journal, 13th Leg.*, 1146; *House Journal, 13th Leg.*, 558, 1339–40; *GDN*, Apr. 4, June 3, Dec. 4, 1873; Merseburger, "Political History of Houston" 165–237; Platt, *City Building in the New South*, 19–43; Platt, "Stillbirth of Urban Politics," 55–74.

4. *LT*, 8:237–38, 270–88; *House Journal, 14th Leg., 1st sess.*, 22–24, 28–29, 33–34; *GDN*, Jan. 21–22, 24, 27 [quotation], 1874; Merseburger, "Political History of Houston," 237.

5. *GDN*, Jan. 29, 31, Feb. 3, 5, 7, 13, 20, 25–28, Mar. 4, 11, 1874, July 22, 1875, Aug. 3, 1875, Feb. 16, 22, 1876; Platt, *City Building in the New South*, 53.

6. Census Office, Eleventh Census, *Report on the Population of the United States . . . : 1890; Part 1*, 430–32; Campbell, *Grass-Roots Reconstruction*, 55–58, 126–30; L. Rice, *Negro in Texas*, 93–95; Hahn, *Nation under Our Feet*, 394–99.

7. Ayers, *Promise of the New South*, 8.

8. Foner, *Reconstruction*, 355–56; Keller, *Affairs of State*, 343, 354–55.

9. Texas Constitution of 1869, art. 5, sec. 7.

10. Ibid., art. 5, secs. 9, 18; *LT*, 6:378–80, 398–99; *Ex parte T. E. Hogg*, 36 Texas Reports (1871–72), 14–16.

11. *In the Matter of Charges against Judge M. Priest*, 33–35.

12. Mauer, "Poll Tax," 153–54.

13. Citizens of Washington County to E. J. Davis, Mar. 13, 1873, Correspondence, Davis Records.

14. King, *Great South*, 142.

15. *GDN*, Oct. 21, 1873, Jan. 22, Feb. 21 [quotation], 1874.

16. William Pitt Ballinger Diary, Nov. 14, 1873, Ballinger Papers; *GDN,* Jan. 18, Feb. 20, 1874; *LT,* 8:236.

17. *GDN,* Jan. 28, 1874; E. D. Linn and A. L. Kessler to Coke, Jan. 24, 1874, Correspondence, Coke Records.

18. R. Tyler et al., *New Handbook of Texas,* 2:613, 3:258, 294–95, 4:819, 5:508, 611–12; Campbell, "District Judges of Texas," 361, 372–73, 375–76; Winkler, *Journal of the Secession Convention,* 20–22.

19. *GDN,* Oct. 3, 1873.

20. Campbell, "Scalawag District Judges," 87–88.

21. I have counted as judges proceeded against all those who had charges filed against them in the legislature in 1873 or 1874—even if those charges, ultimately, were not acted upon. They are John G. Scott, William Chambers, Tilson Barden, Henry Maney, Mijamin Priest, Simon B. Newcomb, J. B. Williamson, Leroy W. Cooper, James R. Burnett, John Osterhout, James J. Thornton, Martin W. Wheeler, and William H. Andrews.

22. Thomas Paschal to J. P. Newcomb, Mar. 13, 1876 [quotation], Newcomb Papers; Nunn, *Texas under the Carpetbaggers,* 126; *State of Texas against Judge John G. Scott,* 148.

23. Crews, "Reconstruction in Brownsville," 89–90; E. J. Davis to Stephen Powers, Oct. 1, 1874, Wells Papers; *GDN,* Aug. 29, 1874.

24. *GDN,* Nov. 21, 1873; *Minutes of the Democratic State Convention . . . , 1873,* 9; Speer and Brown, *Encyclopedia of the New West,* 192.

25. *GDN,* Jan. 16, Nov. 15, Dec. 24, 1873, Jan. 15, 1876; Ballinger Diary, Dec. 24, 1873; Kittrell, *Governors Who Have Been,* 82, 251–52.

26. Campbell, "Scalawag District Judges," 87; McCaslin, *Tainted Breeze,* 163, 169–70.

27. Curiously, the constitution failed to suggest what would be sufficient grounds for impeachment. Texas Constitution of 1869, art. 5, sec. 10; art. 8.

28. *GDN,* Feb. 21, 1874 [quotation]; *Journal of the Senate of the State of Texas; Being the Session of the Fourteenth Legislature,* 177 [hereafter *Senate Journal, 14th Leg., 1st sess.*].

29. With a two-thirds vote to remove unlikely, Democrats in 1873 had adjourned the proceedings against Scott until the next year. The state constitution suspended judges against whom articles of impeachment had been preferred from exercise of their duties. *Senate Journal, 13th Leg.,* 777–78, 780–89; Opinion of Atty. Gen. William Alexander, June 10, 1873, Correspondence, Davis Records.

30. *House Journal, 14th Leg., 1st sess.,* 203, 208, 225, 279–80, 399; *Senate Journal, 14th Leg., 1st sess.,* 169–70, 180, 189, 227, 256, 365; ADDS, Mar. 15, 1874.

31. *GDN,* Mar. 19, 1874.

32. Ibid., Mar. 27, 1874 [quotations]; ADDS, Mar. 27, 1874.

33. *State of Texas against William Chambers,* 8–9, 34–35; *State of Texas against Hon. L. W. Cooper,* 5, 10.

34. *House Journal, 14th Leg., 1st sess.,* 64, 99–100 [quotation].

35. *In the Matter of the Charges against Hon. J. B. Williamson,* i; *State of Texas against Hon. S. B. Newcomb,* 3; *Evidence Taken before the Joint Committee of the Thirteenth Legislature, Investigating . . . Judge T. C. Barden,* 3; *State of Texas against Hon. L. W. Cooper,* 3; *In the Matter of Charges against Judge M. Priest,* 2.

36. *State of Texas against Hon. L. W. Cooper,* 6–7, 11, 19; *Senate Journal, 14th Leg., 1st sess.,* 370.

37. *In the Matter of the Charges against Hon. J. B. Williamson,* 25.

38. *GDN,* Feb. 20, 1874; *House Journal, 14th Leg., 1st sess.,* 399; *Senate Journal, 14th Leg. 1st sess.,* 180; *In the Matter of Charges against Judge M. Priest,* 62–63; *State of Texas against Hon. S. B. Newcomb,* 80, 83, 91–94, 101.

39. *Ex parte Wm. Rust et al., Ex parte Ireland et al.,* and *Ex parte Henry Maney,* 38 Texas Reports (1872–73), 344–72; J. L. Haynes to James P. Newcomb, Apr. 21, 1874, Newcomb Papers; *House Journal, 14th Leg., 1st sess.,* 279–280; *Senate Journal, 14th Leg., 1st sess.,* 256.

40. *State of Texas against Hon. L. W. Cooper,* 28–29, 43–45, 50–52, 62–65, 75–77, 81–83; *Evidence Taken before the Joint Committee of the Thirteenth Legislature, Investigating . . . Judge T. C. Barden,* 44, 61, 64, 67–68, 74–75; *State of Texas against Hon. James R. Burnett,* 34–36, 41–42, 56–59; Memorials from Grimes County citizens protesting removal of Judge Burnett, Apr. 28, 29, 1874, to 14th Legislature, 1st sess., Records of the Legislature.

41. *State of Texas against Hon. James R. Burnett,* 6, 14–23; *State of Texas against William Chambers,* 32–54, 78–82, 85–94.

42. Winkler, *Platforms,* 115, 141, 155, 157.

43. *State of Texas against Hon. L. W. Cooper,* 190 [quotation]; *In the Matter of Charges against Judge M. Priest,* 24–32; T. C. Barden to E. J. Davis, Dec. 22, 1872, Correspondence, Davis Records; S. B. Newcomb to James P. Newcomb, June 24, 1873, Newcomb Papers; *In the Matter of the Charges against Hon. J. B. Williamson,* iii–iv, 77–81.

44. *In the Matter of the Address against Judge Henry Maney,* 10–12, 41.

45. Subsequent Coke appointees to the district bench like Charles Howard and James Ware would not hesitate to involve themselves in local party politics, Howard to the point of killing and being killed. Howard's politicking, however, earned him condemnation, and unflattering comparisons to Davis appointees, from other Democrats in his badly factionalized borderland district. See *SADH,* July 10, 12, 26, 1875; and *GDN,* July 7, 1875.

46. *In the Matter of Charges against Judge M. Priest,* 1–10; *State of Texas against Hon. S. B. Newcomb,* 9; *State of Texas against Hon. L. W. Cooper,* 3–4; *In the Matter of the Charges against Hon. J. B. Williamson,* iii–vi; *Evidence Taken before the Joint Committee of the Thirteenth Legislature, Investigating . . . Judge T. C. Barden,* 3–4, 7–9.

47. Dobbs, "Defying Davis," 39–40.

48. Campbell, *Southern Community in Crisis,* 309–13.

49. *ADDS,* Feb. 26, 1876.

50. Sonnichsen, *Pass of the North,* 168–98; Gibson, *Life and Death of Colonel Albert Jennings Fountain,* chaps. 4–6; Mills, *Forty Years at El Paso,* 111–18, 138–41.

51. *In the Matter of Charges against Judge M. Priest,* 9 [second quotation], 28 [first quotation]; Baum, *Shattering of Texas Unionism,* 217–19.

52. *House Journal, 13th Leg.,* 1225–26; *House Journal, 14th Leg., 1st sess.,* 208, 225; *Senate Journal, 14th Leg., 1st sess.,* 227; Barker, *Directory of the Members of the Thirteenth Legislature;* Henderson, *Directory of the . . . Fourteenth Legislature.*

53. *LT,* 8:84–86.

54. *GDN*, Mar. 18, 1873, Jan. 31, Feb. 13, 21, 1874; S.B. 307, 13th Leg., Original Bill File, Records of the Legislature; *House Journal, 14th Leg. 1st sess.*, 80.

55. Opinion of Atty. Gen. George Clark, Mar. 23, 1874, Manuscript Journal [House], 14th Leg., 1st sess., Records of the Legislature; *GDN*, Mar. 22, 1874.

56. McCaslin, *Tainted Breeze*, 183–85; Campbell, *Grass-Roots Reconstruction*, 89–90, 183–85; *GDN*, Feb. 20, Mar. 11, May 6, 1873, Feb. 26, 1874; R. Coke to Hardin Hart, Jan. 29, 1874, and R. Coke to John Cocke, Mar. 6, 1874, Letterbook, Davis Records; A. J. Hood, J. N. Roach, et al. to Hon. Chas. Soward, Mar. 1, 1873 [copy], James Milliken to E. J. Davis, Mar. 7, 1873, and Charles Soward to Davis, Mar. 20, 1873, Correspondence, ibid.

57. *Senate Journal, 13th Leg.*, 192, 923; W. H. Andrews, Hardin Hart, and Lucas F. Smith to Davis, Mar. 4, 1873, Charles L. Martin to Davis, Mar. 28, 1873, L. W. Williams to Davis, Dec. 23, 1873, Wm. Phillips to Davis, Feb. 12, 1873, and F. A. Vaughan to Davis, Feb. 28, 1873, Correspondence, Davis Records.

58. *Daily State Journal*, Mar. 4, 1874, quoted in Horton, *Samuel Bell Maxey*, 56. See also ibid., 50–51; and *Senate Journal, 13th Leg.*, 223.

59. Winkler, *Platforms*, 50, 58, 65, 77, 78, 93, 147; Campbell, "District Judges of Texas," 361, 370–71, 373–75; Lynch, *Bench and Bar of Texas*, 328–32; Campbell, *Grass-Roots Reconstruction*, 93.

60. *GDN*, Jan. 13, 1875.

61. Ibid., Jan. 16, 23 [quotation], 1874.

62. Ibid., Feb. 28, 1873 [quotation].

63. Ibid., Jan. 28, 1876.

64. *ADDS*, July 29, 1875.

65. Woodward, *Origins of the New South*, 54–55; Hair, *Bourbonism and Agrarian Protest*, 118–19.

66. *1875 Convention Journal*, 819; *GDN*, Apr. 29, 1874.

67. *GDN*, Oct. 21, 1873; Guy Bryan to John Reagan, Oct. 17, 1875, Reagan Papers.

68. *GDN*, Jan. 28, 1876.

69. *LT*, 3:474; Texas Constitution of 1866, art. 4, secs. 2, 5.

70. *Senate Journal, 14th Leg.*, 1st sess., 461; *GDN*, Apr. 26, May 1, 1874; *LT*, 8:568.

71. Ballinger Diary, Jan. 5, 1875.

72. Alexander W. Terrell to O. M. Roberts, Sept. 10, 1875, Roberts Papers.

73. *1875 Convention Journal*, 32, 117, 406–22, 543–52.

74. McKay, *Debates*, 430 [quotation]; *1875 Convention Journal*, 651.

75. Hyman, *Anti-Redeemers*, 87–97.

76. *Senate Journal, 14th Leg. 1st sess.*, 462.

77. Quoted in *SADH*, Sept. 25, 1875.

78. *1875 Convention Journal*, 563–64; R. Tyler et al., *New Handbook of Texas*, 6:945.

79. McKay, *Debates*, 386 [Stockdale], 387, 424 [Whitfield].

80. Ibid., 97; Campbell, *Grass-Roots Reconstruction*, 45–46, 52–53; Barker, *Directory of the Members of the Thirteenth Legislature*; Henderson, *Directory . . . of the Fourteenth Legislature*.

81. McKay, *Debates*, 97–98.

82. *1875 Convention Journal*, 642.

83. Ibid., 470 [first quotation]; McKay, *Debates*, 98 [Brown].

84. *1875 Convention Journal*, 470–77, 727–29; *Constitution of the State of Texas* [1876], 65–75; L. Rice, *Negro in Texas*, 26–29; Barr, "Impact of Race in Shaping Judicial Districts," 429–31.

85. Mauer, "Poll Tax," 154–55n [quotation]; *1875 Convention Journal*, 479–85.

86. Bentley and Pilgrim, *Texas Legal Directory for 1876–77*, 14–17; Cardwell, *Sketches of Legislators;* Winkler, *Platforms*, 84, 124, 202.

87. *Constitution of the State of Texas* [1876], art. 15, sec. 6.

88. Ibid., art. 5, sec. 24; *GDN*, Mar. 12, 1875 [quotation]; *LT*, 8:541–42.

89. *LT*, 7:519–21, 8:906–8; *James S. Rogers v. A. H. Johns*, 42 Texas Reports (1875), 339–42.

90. Campbell, *Southern Community in Crisis*, 343–55; *J. B. Williamson v. George Lane*, 52 Texas Reports (1879), 335–47.

91. *In the Matter of Charges against Judge M. Priest*, 4–5, 17–21; *GDN*, Oct. 25, 1873; Campbell, *Grass-Roots Reconstruction*, 51; Hahn, *Nation under Our Feet*, 256–59.

92. W. Coleman to R. Coke, Feb. 16, 1875, Correspondence, Coke Records.

93. *LT*, 8:6–7, 95–96, 100–102, 464–66, 890, 968–69.

94. L. Rice, *Negro in Texas*, 88–89.

95. *GDN*, Feb. 4, 12 [third quotation], Feb. 26 [second quotation], Mar. 12, 23, 1876; *Navasota Weekly Tablet*, July 5, 1878 [first quotation].

96. L. Rice, *Negro in Texas*, 121–26.

97. *GDN*, Feb. 8 [quoting *Guadalupe Times*], 11 [quoting *Rockport (Tex.) Transcript*], 1876.

3. BALLOT BOX AND THE JURY BOX

1. Perman, *Struggle for Mastery*, 9–36.

2. Texas Constitution of 1869, art. 6.

3. Mauer, "Poll Tax," 35n, 43–48; *Senate Journal, 14th Leg., 1st sess.*, 194.

4. *GDN*, Feb. 25 [first quotation], Mar. 17 [Coke quotation], July 17 [second quotation], 1874.

5. Smallwood, *Time of Hope*, 43 67; Barr, *Black Texans*, 52–60, 88–98.

6. McKay, *Debates*, 169 [first quotation]; *ADDS*, Feb. 11, 1876 [second quotation].

7. *Navasota Weekly Tablet*, June 28, 1878.

8. Reagan to W. G. Webb, Mar. 9, 1869, Reagan Papers; *Houston Telegraph* quoted in McKay, *Making the Texas Constitution*, 98; *SADH*, Sept. 22, Oct. 22, 1875; Kousser, *Shaping of Southern Politics*, 202 [Terrell quotation].

9. *GDN*, Oct.19, 1875; McKay, *Debates*, 177 [second quotation], 188 [first quotation]; A. W. Terrell to Oran Roberts, Nov. 11, 1878 [third quotation; emphasis in the original], Roberts Papers.

10. *GDN*, Jan. 8, 1876.

11. Ibid., Oct. 8 [Reagan quotation], 19, 1875; *ADDS*, July 29, Aug. 1 [second quotation], 6 [fourth quotation], 1875, Feb. 1, 1876 [third quotation].

12. Beckert, "Democracy and Its Discontents"; McGerr, *Decline of Popular Politics*, 45–52; Sproat, *The Best Men*, 253–56; Foner, *Reconstruction*, 492–93; Katz, *From Appomattox to Montmartre*, 92, 119–20, 166–68.

13. Foley, *White Scourge*, 13, 24.

14. *SADH*, Oct. 22, 1875.

15. *GDN*, Jan. 26, Feb. 9, Oct. 24, 1873, June 17, 1874.

16. Ibid., Feb. 28, Mar. 2, 1875.

17. Doyle, *New Men, New Cities, New South*, 9–10; C. Miller and Johnson, "Rise of Urban Texas," 6, 8.

18. Census Office, Eighth Census, *Manufactures of the United States*, 583–85, 592–93; Census Office, Ninth Census, *Statistics of the Wealth and Industry*, 572–73, 735–36.

19. Fayman and Reilly, *Galveston City Directory for 1875–6*; Butterfield and Rundlett, *Directory of the City of Dallas . . . for the Year 1875*.

20. Census Office, Ninth Census, *Statistics of the Wealth and Industry*, 815; Census Office, Tenth Census, *Compendium . . .*, Part 2, 1383.

21. *ADDS*, July 29, 1875; Webb and Carroll, *Handbook of Texas*, 2:92.

22. *GDN*, Apr. 8, 1873.

23. Dallas and Harris County tax rolls are at the Texas State Library, Austin.

24. American courts defined "householder" variously, but the requirement does not seem necessarily to have disfranchised all propertyless men, for one could qualify as a householder without owning one's dwelling. But this classification did exclude many single men, the term being understood to apply only to those who headed a family or otherwise managed a household.

25. Platt, "Stillbirth of Urban Politics," 60; K. Wheeler, *To Wear a City's Crown*, 74; *LT*, 1:1298–99, 1380, 2:442, 705, 1000, 1006, 4:553, 5:550, 721, 1387–88, 1532, 6:570, 763, 766, 1484–85.

26. Fayman and Reilly, *Galveston City Directory for 1875–6*; *GDN*, Mar. 2, 1875.

27. Zeigler, "Houston Worker," 41.

28. Reese, "Early History of Labor Organizations in Texas," 16–18.

29. *GDN*, Oct. 29, Nov. 4, 7, 18, 1873, Jan. 23, June 3, 1874.

30. Ibid., June 24, 1875.

31. Ibid., Aug. 20 [quotations], Sept. 9, 1874.

32. *Navasota Weekly Tablet*, Nov. 9, 1877 [quotation].

33. *GDN*, Feb. 25, 26 [quotations], 1875.

34. Ibid., Mar. 15 [first quotation], 1873, Feb. 23, 1875, Feb. 20 [second quotation], 1876.

35. The Strand delegates, though, were drawn more exclusively from the mercantile elite—cotton factors or brokers, commission merchants, and bankers. See *GDN*, Jan. 30, 1876; Heller, *Galveston City Directory 1876–7*; Fayman and Reilly, *Galveston City Directory for 1875–6*.

36. *GDN*, Jan. 29, Feb. 9 [first quotation], Mar. 16, 1873, Feb.13, 1875 [second quotation].

37. Ibid., Mar. 11, 27, Aug. 2, 1874, Jan.16, 20, Feb. 25, 1875.

38. Rodriquez, "Urban Populism," 30–31, 36–40, 47–51, 59–61, 66–76; Platt, *City Building in the New South*, 96–101, 138–40, 151–52, 157–60; Johnson, "Frugal and Sparing," 33–57.

39. *House Journal, 14th Leg., 1st sess.*, 671 [quotation]; *GDN*, Apr.17, 1874.

40. *ADDS*, July 30, 1875.

41. *GDN*, Apr. 26, 1873.

42. Texas Constitution of 1869, art. 12, sec. 45; *LT*, 7:62–63.

43. Ben Thomas et al. to E. J. Davis, Aug. 30, 1873, Correspondence, Davis Records.

44. *GDN*, July 23, Oct. 10, 1873, Mar. 6, 1874; Campbell, *Grass-Roots Reconstruction*, 161;

State of Texas against Hon. S. B. Newcomb, 86; William Pitt Ballinger Diary, May 12, 27, 1875, Ballinger Papers.

45. *GDN,* Nov. 24, 1872, Oct. 21, 1873, May 23 [quotation], 26, 1874.

46. Ibid., May 20, 1873 [first quotation], July 7, 1875 [second quotation]; *ADDS,* July 30, 1875 [third quotation].

47. Reagan to W. G. Webb, Mar. 9, 1869, Reagan Papers.

48. *GDN,* May 22, 24, 1873; *Senate Journal, 13th Leg.,* 881–82; *LT,* 7:533–35.

49. *GDN,* Apr. 17, 1874.

50. *1875 Convention Journal,* 29, 142, 238 [quotation].

51. Ibid., 304–10, 328–30, 405–6, 697–98, 785.

52. McKay, *Debates,* 172 [second quotation], 174–76 [Martin quotation, 174], 180; Mauer, "Poll Tax," 3–4.

53. *1875 Convention Journal,* 320–22, 808–14; McKay, *Debates,* 190–91, 203–11; McKay, *Making the Texas Constitution,* 131–37.

54. McKay, *Making the Texas Constitution,* 97–98; Kousser, *Shaping of Southern Politics,* 200; Barr, *Reconstruction to Reform,* 204; Baum and Calvert, "Texas Patrons of Husbandry," 49; Calvert, De León, and Cantrell, *History of Texas,* 170; Mauer, "State Constitutions in a Time of Crisis," 1644.

55. For Grange delegates, see *Walsh & Pilgrim's Directory of the Officers and Members of the Constitutional Convention.* Two delegates not listed as Grangers there, F. J. Lynch and W. D. S. Cook, identified themselves as such during debate. McKay, *Debates,* 190, 207.

56. I have regarded the twenty-seven Democrats who voted against tabling W. D. S. Cook's amendment allowing the legislature to impose a poll-tax qualification as the core group of restrictionists at the convention. *1875 Convention Journal,* 308–9. George McCormick of Colorado County also spoke for the poll tax but did not participate in any of the roll calls.

57. In 1873 gubernatorial balloting, the Republican median was about 22 percent in Grange-represented counties and approximately 33 percent in counties represented by non-Grange Democrats.

58. McKay, *Debates,* 176 [quotation], 184.

59. Baum and Calvert, "Texas Patrons of Husbandry," 38–41, 45–49; Spratt, *Road to Spindletop,* 5–8, 45–46, 51–52, 64–66.

60. McKay, *Debates,* 171–72; Kousser, *Shaping of Southern Politics,* 64–65.

61. At the convention Ballinger, for instance, spoke against a state poll tax but seconded John Reagan's desire that something be done "to protect towns and cities from the floating population not interested in the welfare of the community [and] used often to fasten upon it burdensome measures." *GDN,* Oct. 8, 1875 [quotation]; Moretta, *William Pitt Ballinger,* 216.

62. *1875 Convention Journal,* 139, 238, 311–12, 315–16; *GDN,* Oct. 8, 1875. Democrats had to be careful about measures disfranchising those who had not paid all taxes due. In earlier years supporters had resisted certain taxes levied by Republican authorities, and cities like Houston experienced chronic problems collecting the taxes they imposed to fund local development.

63. Legislative acts implementing this provision interpreted "tax-payers" as payers of property taxes alone and not also propertyless payers of capitation taxes. See *1875*

Convention Journal, 695, 790–91; *Constitution of the State of Texas* [1876], art. 11, sec. 10; and *LT*, 8:1045.

64. Platt, *City Building in the New South*, 19–64; Rodriquez, "Urban Populism," 36–37; Johnson, "Frugal and Sparing."

65. *1875 Convention Journal*, 62, 135, 348, 360, 699–700.

66. On Terrell, see Gould, *Alexander Watkins Terrell*; Kousser, *Shaping of Southern Politics*, 201–8, 247; Perman, *Struggle for Mastery*, 272–73; and Barr, *Reconstruction to Reform*, 204, 206, 235–36.

67. *LT*, 8:914–20 [quotations, 915].

68. Census Office, Tenth Census, *Compendium . . . , Part 2*, 1649, 1653.

69. Nieman, "Black Political Power and Criminal Justice," 398–408.

70. L. Rice, *Negro in Texas*, 256–57.

71. See *Seth Carter, Plff. in Err., v. the State of Texas*, 20 Supreme Court Reporter (1899–1900), 687–90; *Robert Smith v. the State*, 58 Southwestern Reporter (1900), 97–98; *Ralph Whitney v. the State*, 59 Southwestern Reporter (1900–1901), 895–96; *Starks Collins v. the State*, 60 Southwestern Reporter (1901), 42–43; *Cal Leach v. the State*, ibid., 422; and *Earnest Thompson v. the State*, 74 Southwestern Reporter (1903), 914–15.

72. Winkler, *Platforms*, 213, 230; Cantrell and Barton, "Texas Populists," 666–67; Barr, "Impact of Race in Shaping Judicial Districts," 433.

73. Census Office, Ninth Census, *Statistics of the Population of the United States*, 1:429–31.

74. The state court of appeals had ruled that renters qualified for jury service but in 1890 modified that judgment, insisting that the term "householder" "means something more than the mere occupant of a room or house," and required that one be "the head or master of a family." See *Louis Robles v. the State*, 5 Texas Court of Appeals (1878–79), 357; and *Lane v. the State*, 15 Southwestern Reporter (1890), 829.

75. *P. S. Nolen v. the State*, 9 Texas Court of Appeals (1880), 419–26; *James Wright v. the State*, 12 Texas Court of Appeals (1882), 163–69; *Apolinario Garcia v. the State*, ibid., 335–41 [quotation, 338].

76. *GDN*, Jan. 8, 1876.

77. McKay, *Making the Texas Constitution*, 182–83; *GDN*, Jan. 7, 30, Feb. 9, 11, 1876; Coke to O. M. Roberts, Nov. 8, 1875, and Coke to Roberts, Nov. 26, 1875, Roberts Papers; *ADDS*, Feb. 3, 9, 1876.

78. Election Returns, Secretary of State Records. It seems safe to assume that Republicans who voted against the constitution also cast ballots for governor (turnout in Republican as well as Democratic counties being generally higher in the gubernatorial race) and that a county's vote for Chambers reflects fairly accurately the maximum number of Republican votes against ratification.

79. *GDN*, Jan. 8 [first quotation], 28, Feb. 1, 17, 1876; *ADDS*, Feb. 5, 19 [second quotation], 1876.

80. *LT*, 8:1420; Kousser, *Shaping of Southern Politics*, 201–4; Barr, *Reconstruction to Reform*, 196; L. Rice, *Negro in Texas*, 116, 132.

81. For fusion arrangements in one Texas county, see *Navasota Weekly Tablet*, May 24, 1878. More generally, see Ayers, *Promise of the New South*, 41–43; and Hahn, *Nation under Our Feet*, 385–87.

82. L. Rice, *Negro in Texas,* 41–42, 98.

83. U.S. Congress, Senate, *Testimony on the Alleged Election Outrages in Texas,* 518 [quotation]; Barr, *Reconstruction to Reform,* 201.

84. A. D. Lister to Oran Roberts, July 25, 1878, Roberts Papers.

85. Campbell, *Southern Community in Crisis,* 338, 358–63, 364 [quotation]; W. R. Miller, "Harrison County Methods," 112–16; L. Rice, *Negro in Texas,* 114–18.

86. L. Rice, *Negro in Texas,* 113–27; Barr, *Reconstruction to Reform,* 194–201.

87. Kousser, *Shaping of Southern Politics,* 81–82.

88. U.S. Senate, *Testimony on the Alleged Election Outrages in Texas,* 233; Nieman, "Black Political Power and Criminal Justice," 395n; Pitre, *Through Many Dangers, Toils, and Snares,* 148–49; Shook, "Texas 'Election Outrage' of 1886," 20–30; Moseley, "Citizens White Primary of Marion County," 524–31; Buenger, *Path to a Modern South,* 77–79.

89. Goodwyn, "Populist Dreams and Negro Rights," 1435–56; Hine, *Black Victory,* 34; W. R. Miller, "Harrison County Methods," 125; L. Rice, *Negro in Texas,* 121–26.

90. *GDN,* Oct. 13, 15, 18, 21, 24, 1874, June 13, 1875; Ballinger Diary, May 18–22, 1875, May 1, 1876; *Navasota Weekly Tablet,* Dec. 20, 27, 1878, Jan. 17, 1879.

91. Goldman, *"Free Ballot and a Fair Count,"* 56, 58, 111–13, 135–38; Campbell, *Southern Community in Crisis,* 355–56, 362–63; R. Tyler et al., *New Handbook of Texas,* 2:979.

92. *Navasota Weekly Tablet,* Nov. 9, 1877.

93. Platt, *City Building in the New South,* 75–103; Hales, *Southern Family in Black and White,* 28–33.

94. Barr, *Reconstruction to Reform,* 44, 48–49, 56; *GDN,* Apr. 29, 1879; Zeigler, "Houston Worker," 47; J. T. Dennis to S. B. Maxey, [Aug. 1, 1879], Maxey Papers; Kellam, "Shadow of Itself," 173–75, 193–95; Martin, *People's Party in Texas,* 32.

95. Rodriquez, "Disfranchisement in Dallas," 43–64.

96. Rodriquez, "Urban Populism," 91; *LT,* 8:1262, 9:501, 1324; Census Office, Eleventh Census, *Report on Farms and Homes: . . . 1890,* 30, 366–70.

97. Rodriquez, "Disfranchisement in Dallas," 48–51; *LT,* 10:49.

98. *1875 Convention Journal,* 314–15; McKay, *Debates,* 191–93 [quotation, 193].

99. Barr, *Reconstruction to Reform,* 202–3; Kousser, *Shaping of Southern Politics,* 203; Rodriquez, "Disfranchisement in Dallas," 51, 53–55.

100. *LT,* 10:377–83; Kousser, *Shaping of Southern Politics,* 203–4; Census Office, Eleventh Census, *Report on the Population of the United States . . . : 1890; Part I,* 328–41, 482.

101. Census Office, Eleventh Census, *Compendium . . . : 1890, Part 1,* 848–49.

102. Kousser, *Shaping of Southern Politics,* 47–56; Graves, "Negro Disfranchisement in Arkansas," 211–14.

103. Baum and Miller, "Ethnic Conflict and Machine Politics," 66; Rodriquez, "Urban Populism," 233, 255–57, 307, 310.

104. B. Rice, *Progressive Cities,* 4–6, 77 [quotation]; Hales, *Southern Family in Black and White,* 30–31; E. Turner, *Women, Culture, and Community,* 11–12, 195–96; Zeigler, "Houston Worker," 44; *LT,* 9:773, 10:289, 738–39, 965, 981.

105. B. Rice, *Progressive Cities,* 3–33, 86; Platt, *City Building in the New South,* 181–208; "Texas Idea," 839–43; R. Miller, "Fort Worth and the Progressive Era," 89–121.

1. *LT*, 2:861–62, 996–97, 5:982, 6:276–78.
2. *GDN*, Nov. 14, 1873.
3. *LT*, 8:57–61; H.B. 113, 13th Leg., Original Bill File, Records of the Legislature; *Senate Journal, 13th Leg.*, 828–29, 860, 1147; *House Journal, 13th Leg.*, 1351–53; *GDN*, Feb. 12, 1874, Feb. 25, 1875; *ADDS*, Feb. 12, 26, 1874; *North Texas Enterprise*, Nov. 1, 1873.
4. Sanders, *Farm Ownership and Tenancy*, 1–5; Evans, "Texas Agriculture," 311, 318–19.
5. Hyman, *Anti-Redeemers*, 37–44; Moses Austin Bryan to Guy Bryan, Oct. 25, 1874, Bryan Papers.
6. *GDN*, Dec. 19, 1873, Mar. 5, 1874; *North Texas Enterprise*, Nov. 27, 1874, Jan. 15, 1875.
7. *LT*, 8:569, 1063–64; *1875 Convention Journal*, 685–87; *Constitution of the State of Texas* [1876], art. 16, sec. 11.
8. *LT*, 2:353–54, 7:11–12, 493–94, 528–31, 8:203–4, 986–88; *1875 Convention Journal*, 700–701.
9. Holt, "Introduction of Barbed Wire into Texas," 72–88; Gard, "Fence-Cutters," 1–15; McMath, "Sandy Land and Hogs," 216–18.
10. Hahn, "Hunting, Fishing, and Foraging," 37–64; Foner, *Nothing but Freedom*, 61–67.
11. Citizens of Washington County, re. stock law, Apr. 5, 1873 [first quotation], Fence Law, Petitions from Numerous Counties, 1878–81, Memorials and Petitions, Records of the Legislature; J. L. Dickson to E. J. Davis, Apr. 21, 1873 [second quotation], and Citizens of Grimes Co. to E. J. Davis, Apr. 21, 26, 1873, Correspondence, Davis Records; *GDN*, Mar. 26, Apr. 4 [third quotation], 20, 1873.
12. Walker, *Penology for Profit*, 52, 66, 157–61; A. G. Malloy to E. J. Davis, Jan. 9, 1873, Correspondence, Davis Records; *House Journal, 13th Leg.*, 712–17; *GDN*, Aug. 25, 29, 1874, Jan. 13, 1875, Feb. 6, 1876.
13. E. T. Miller, *Financial History of Texas*, 106–14, 133.
14. Quoted in *GDN*, Nov. 15, 1873.
15. E. T. Miller, *Financial History of Texas*, 413; Thornton, "Fiscal Policy and the Failure of Radical Reconstruction," 351.
16. Darden, *Annual Report of the Comptroller . . . 1874*, 41; Darden, *Annual Report of the Comptroller . . . 1875*, 28, 35; *LT*, 8:228.
17. *LT*, 7:611–12, 666, 8:227, 529, 555–56.
18. Ibid., 7:522–24, 656, 659, 8:536–37, 899–906; Winkler, *Platforms*, 167 [quotation]; *Constitution of the State of Texas* [1876], art. 16, sec. 24.
19. Lowe and Campbell, *Planters and Plain Folk*, 12–13; Reed, *Texas Railroads*, 26–30, 41–45; Williams, "Development of a Market Economy in Texas," 175–77.
20. T. W. Peirce to Hon. Richard Coke, Sept. 25, 1875, copy in Ballinger Papers; *GDN*, June 23, 1872, May 14, 1873; Summers, *Railroads, Reconstruction, and the Gospel of Prosperity*, 35–36; Williams, "Development of Market Economy in Texas," 214, 421–22.
21. Reed, *Texas Railroads*, 48–53; Van Zant, "State Promotion of Railroad Construction," 57–59, 62–75.
22. Brockman, "Railroads, Radicals, and Democrats," 88–89, 92–98, 103–5; Summers, *Railroads, Reconstruction, and the Gospel of Prosperity*, 82–83.

23. Vernon, *American Railroad Manual* [1873], 371–76; Vernon, *American Railroad Manual* [1874], 401–7.

24. Brockman, "Railroads, Radicals, and Democrats," 116–22, 126, 141–42; *GDN*, Apr. 15, 1873.

25. McKay, *Debates*, 321 [quotation]; *GDN*, June 5, 1874, Dec. 21, 1886, Jan. 2, 1887; Reagan et al. to J. S. Barnes, Feb. 26, 1871, Reagan Papers; Procter, *Not without Honor*, 196–198; D. M. Short to O. M. Roberts, July 29, 1873, Roberts Papers; *ADDS*, Aug. 10, 1875.

26. *Houston Age*, Jan. 28, 1874, quoted in Horton, *Samuel Bell Maxey*, 55; *House Journal, 14th. Leg, 1st sess.*, 51–52, 54; *Senate Journal, 14th Leg., 1st sess.*, 45, 48; *GDN*, June 18, 1872, Jan. 27–28, June 16, 1874; *Sherman [Tex.] Register*, May 31, 1876; J. L. Camp to O. M. Roberts, Jan. 21, 1874, Roberts Papers; Elliott, *Leathercoat*, 218–32, 257–58; Spaw, *Texas Senate, Vol. II*, 206–7.

27. *GDN*, June 16, Oct. 31, 1872, July 18, Sept. 5, 1874; Winkler, *Platforms*, 142, 146 [quotation].

28. *LT*, 6:931–34, 8:120–21.

29. Reed, *Texas Railroads*, 131–34.

30. Campbell, *Southern Community in Crisis*, 323–28, 357–58; *GDN*, Mar. 25, Aug. 1, Sept. 30, Nov. 19, 1874; W. S. Wilkinson to Oran Roberts [Mar. 1879], Correspondence, Roberts Records; *LT*, 8:1010–11, 1460–61.

31. *GDN*, Mar. 29, 1874, Feb. 17, 1875 [quotation].

32. Ibid., Feb. 11, 1875.

33. *North Texas Enterprise*, Aug. 7, 21, 28, Oct. 30 ,1874; J. Q. Chenoweth to Coke, Aug. 1, 1874, Correspondence, Coke Records.

34. Brockman, "Railroads, Radicals, and Democrats," 126–28; Alexander, *Report of the Attorney General . . . 1872*, 3–6, 15–22.

35. *GDN*, July 31, 1873, Mar. 17, 1874 [quotation].

36. Ibid., Mar. 15, 1874, Jan. 7, Feb. 17 [quotation], 1875.

37. *House Journal, 13th Leg.*, 255–61; *Senate Journal, 13th Leg.*, 912–14; *GDN*, Apr. 19, June 26, 1873, Feb. 13, 1875.

38. *GDN*, May 23, 1873; Ira Evans to Ashbel Smith, Apr. 8, 1873, and James W. Barnes to Smith, May 24, 29, 1873, Smith Papers.

39. *GDN*, Feb. 21 [quotation], 26, July 23, 1873, Feb. 23, 1875; *North Texas Enterprise*, Aug. 21, 1874; Citizens of Marion County, re: compromise between International Railroad Co. and State, May 7, 1873, Memorials and Petitions, Records of the Legislature.

40. Ratchford, *American State Debts*, 183–96, 218; E. T. Miller, *Financial History of Texas*, 191–94, 229–39, 355–60.

41. *GDN*, Mar. 22, May 12, 1874.

42. Ibid., June 1, 1873, Aug. 8 [quotation], 1874, Feb. 20, 1875.

43. *SADH*, Jan. 15 [first quotation], 19, Mar. 5–6, 8–9, July 14, 20, Nov. 10, Dec. 20, 29 [second quotation], 1875, Feb. 10, 15, 1876; William Pitt Ballinger Diary, Dec. 30, 1874, Ballinger Papers; *GDN*, Mar. 10, 1875.

44. *GDN*, May 8, Aug. 3, 1873; *SADH*, Jan. 21, 1875.

45. *GDN*, July 24, 1873.

46. King, *Great South*, 148, 160.

47. *House Journal, 13th Leg.,* 245, 999–1002, 1056–58, 1203–6; *Senate Journal, 13th Leg.,* 963–66, 975–77, 1069–71; *GDN,* June 10, 1873. Support for the bond subsidy came chiefly from Republican holdovers in the thirty-man state senate; a handful of Democrats, several of whose districts would be served by the road; and three others remembered by a colleague to be subject to railroad influence. Dohoney, *Average American,* 154.

48. *LT,* 8:315–17, 341–42; *GDN,* Feb. 13, Mar. 13, 17, 21–22, 29, Apr. 11, 21, 23–24, Sept. 3, 1874. The near elimination of the Republican party from the legislature made voting patterns on the International issue less partisan and more sectional. Legislators from west of the Colorado River voted more uniformly in support of compromise, while those from Northeast Texas districts along the Red River (many already served by the T&P) more uniformly against.

49. *A. Bledsoe v. The International Railroad Company,* 40 Texas Reports (1874), 537–600.

50. Coke to W. L. Moody, Feb. 9, 1875, Letterpress, Coke Records.

51. James W. Barnes to Edward Burleson Jr., Jan. 6, 1875, Burleson Papers; Ballinger Diary, Mar. 18, 1875; *GDN,* Jan. 28, 30–31, Feb. 2–3, 14, 18, 26–28, Mar. 2, 1875.

52. Coke to W. L. Moody, July 15, 1874, and Coke to James C. Holmes, July 18, 1874, Letterpress, Davis Records; Coke to Moody, Sept. 2, Dec. 17, 1874, Letterpress, Coke Records; *GDN,* May 8, June 18 [quoting *Advocate*], Aug. 5, 1874, Jan. 13, 1875.

53. Coke to Oran Roberts, Jan. 24, 1875 [first quotation], Roberts Papers; *Governors' Messages,* 71; Barr, *Reconstruction to Reform,* 19.

54. Kittrell, *Governors Who Have Been,* 62.

55. *Senate Journal, 14th Leg., 2nd sess.,* 487–504 [quotation, 496].

56. Ibid., 518; *Journal of the House of Representatives of Texas; . . . Second Session of the Fourteenth Legislature,* 534 [hereafter *House Journal, 14th Leg., 2nd sess.*]; *LT,* 8:659–63.

57. *Senate Journal, 14th Leg., 2nd sess.,* 503 [quotation]; *GDN,* Mar. 30, 1875.

58. *GDN,* Mar. 10–11, 24, 26, 1875; *House Journal, 14th Leg., 2nd sess.,* 589–91.

59. Gates, *Public Land Law Development,* 804–5; Hibbard, *Public Land Policies,* 171–97, 228–42, 264, 269–88, 309–46.

60. Lang, *Financial History of the Public Lands,* 202–3; McKitrick, *Public Land System of Texas,* 7–9.

61. Wallenstein, *Slave South to New South,* 23–31, 210, 222–23n; Gunn, *Decline of Authority,* 138–41; Goodrich, *Government Promotion of American Canals and Railroads,* 275–76.

62. T. L. Miller, *Public Lands of Texas,* 27–44, 59–67, 69–74, 107–25, 191–211.

63. *LT,* 3:1455–60; Van Zant, "State Promotion of Railroad Construction," 114–16.

64. Texas Constitution of 1869, art. 10, sec. 6; Brockman, "Railroads, Radicals, and Democrats," 42–43; *GDN,* Apr. 11, 1873 [quotation]; Gray, "Edmund J. Davis," 123.

65. *LT,* 6:1062.

66. *GDN,* Feb. 23, 1873.

67. *LT,* 6:1623–28, 7:202–6, 1018–27; *House Journal, 13th Leg.,* 748–52, 762–64, 988–89; *Senate Journal, 13th Leg.,* 654–56, 670–72, 796; J. W. Throckmorton to Ashbel Smith, Jan. 19, 1879, Smith Papers.

68. *LT,* 7:886–91, 1027–29, 1033–40, 1051–54, 1067–72, 1081–84, 1106–9, 1133–35, 1250–57, 1262–71, 1273–82, 1295–98, 1302–7, 1328–37, 1344–46, 1375–78, 1380–89, 1395–1401,

1403–9, 1411–13, 1428–30; *House Journal, 13th Leg.,* 520, 571, 579–80, 674–77, 820–23, 850–54, 869–73, 889–93, 906–11, 923–24, 926–27, 992–95, 1007–10, 1019–24, 1065, 1100–1101, 1118–19, 1178–82, 1210–12, 1244–45, 1265; *Senate Journal, 13th Leg.,* 661–62, 688, 693–95, 702–3, 749–51, 760–61, 877, 916–17, 919, 930–32, 959–60, 1009, 1011, 1019, 1030, 1036–38, 1077, 1141.

69. *LT,* 8:304–9, 312–14, 317–28, 336–41, 344–47, 349–51, 354–56, 359–64, 596–99, 606–11, 619–20, 629, 636–42, 645–47, 650–56, 664–67, 672–81, 694–98, 700–708, 711–17, 729–33, 738–40.

70. *Official Returns of a General Election Held in the State of Texas,* 19–23.

71. *GDN,* Jan. 31, 1873.

72. Ibid., Feb. 14, Mar. 6, May 8, 1873; *House Journal, 13th Leg.,* 425, 533–34; *LT,* 7:1255–57.

73. *Senate Journal, 13th Leg.,* 201–10; *LT,* 7:467–68; *GDN,* Mar. 15, Apr. 11, 1873.

74. *LT,* 8:249–50; *GDN,* July 30, 1874, Jan. 18, 1876.

75. U.S. House, *Texas and Pacific Railroad.*

76. *Congressional Record,* 45th Cong., 2nd sess. (1877–78), 1470, 3253, 3349; 45th Cong., 3rd sess. (1878–79), 154, 949–53.

77. S. B. Maxey to Coke, Oct. 23, 1875, Correspondence, Coke Records; A. W. Terrell to Ashbel Smith, Nov. 29, 1877, Smith Papers.

78. Perman, *Road to Redemption,* 219–20, 257–58.

79. *LT,* 7:42.

80. *GDN,* Mar. 11, 1873, Oct. 3, 1874, Feb. 2, 1875; *ADDS,* Apr. 9, 1874; *Governors' Messages,* 348.

81. *Senate Journal, 13th Leg.,* 963; *GDN,* Jan. 28, Feb. 2, 1875.

82. *House Journal, 14th Leg., 2nd sess.,* 235–36.

83. See, for instance, *GDN,* Apr. 23, 1873, Mar. 4, Aug. 14, 1874; and Kinsey, "Immigrant in Texas Agriculture," 125–141.

84. *GDN,* Feb. 8, July 27, 1873, Jan. 13, 1875; *House Journal, 14th Leg., 1st sess.,* 41; Citizens of Karnes County to E. J. Davis, Jan. 15, 1873, Correspondence, Davis Records.

85. Texas Constitution of 1869, art. 11; *LT,* 6:1029–30.

86. *GDN,* Mar. 26, Apr. 18, 1873; W. H. Parsons to Davis, Apr. 25, 1873, Correspondence, Davis Records; Moneyhon, *Republicanism in Reconstruction Texas,* 133.

87. *Governors' Messages,* 49; *House Journal, 13th Leg.,* 519; *GDN,* Apr. 28–30, May 2, 1874, Mar. 5, 13, 1875; *LT,* 7:612–13, 666, 8:229, 231–32, 531.

88. *GDN,* Oct. 12, 1875; McKay, *Debates,* 239, 274–75, 281–86.

89. *LT,* 3:1339–45, 1538–39, 4:897–901; Reed, *Texas Railroads,* 31, 56, 117–22; T. W. Peirce to Hon. Richard Coke, Sept. 25, 1875, copy in Ballinger Papers.

90. *GDN,* Jan. 17, 1873; *House Journal, 14th Leg., 1st sess.,* 41 [quotation].

91. *House Journal, 13th Leg.,* 502–3, 820–23, 889–93, 898, 969–70, 1007–10, 1021–24, 1178–80, 1192–93, 1201, 1230–31, 1244–45; *GDN,* May 30, 1873, Apr. 17, 18, 1874.

92. Barr, *Reconstruction to Reform,* 113–14, 116–17; Peterson, "State Regulation of Railroads in Texas," 89–92.

93. *GDN,* Jan. 23, 1873, Apr. 16, June 26, 1874; Ballinger Diary, Sept. 2, 1873; *Senate Journal, 13th Leg.,* 306; Alexander, *Report of the Attorney General . . . 1872,* 6–7.

94. *GDN,* Jan. 24, July 24, Sept.17, Dec. 25, 1873 [first quotation], Jan. 28, Feb. 25 [second and third quotations], 1874.

95. Ibid., June 19, 1872.

96. Ibid., Jan. 31, Feb. 11, 25, Mar. 3, 6, 10 [quotation], 1874.

97. *ADDS*, July 25, 1875, Feb. 23, 1876; G. W. Kidd to Ashbel Smith, Feb. 8, 1879, Smith Papers.

98. *House Journal, 14th Leg., 1st sess.*, 43 [quotation]; *LT*, 8:199–202, 403–16, 1055–62; *GDN*, Feb. 15, 1874, Feb. 17, 1875.

99. Frank Bond to Epperson, June 2, 1875, Epperson Papers.

100. McKay, *Making the Texas Constitution*, 97–98, 185; R. Smith, "Grange Movement in Texas," 310; Spratt, *Road to Spindletop*, 12–13; Mauer, "State Constitutions in a Time of Crisis," 1623, 1640.

101. Perman, *Road to Redemption*, 204–5; R. Tyler et al., *New Handbook of Texas*, 2:290.

102. George Clark to Oran Roberts, Sept. 15, 1875, Roberts Papers; Samuel Bell Maxey to [Marilda Maxey], Sept. 26, 1875, Maxey Papers.

103. *Constitution of the State of Texas* [1876], art. 3, secs. 5, 24, 49; art. 4, secs. 4–5, 21–23; art. 5, secs. 2, 5, 7; art. 8, sec. 9; art. 11, secs. 4–6.

104. McKay, *Debates*, 152–55, 162–66, 425–30; Richard Coke to Oran Roberts, Nov. 8, 1875 [quotation], Roberts Papers; *GDN*, Oct. 19, 1875; McKay, *Making the Texas Constitution*, 85–87.

105. *1875 Convention Journal*, 378–83, 422–24, 451, 454–55, 530–31, 536, 693–95, 723–26.

106. The convention eventually required assessment and collection in the county where property was located but authorized the legislature by a two-thirds vote to allow nonresidents to pay their taxes directly to the state comptroller. Cockrell, "Making of the Constitution of 1875," 118; *1875 Convention Journal*, 404–5, 489, 492, 497–98, 532–33, 536, 721–22; McKay, *Debates*, 312–15, 374–76.

107. McKay, *Debates*, 114–16, 264–67; *1875 Convention Journal*, 164, 225–27, 388–89.

108. Accounts that emphasize Granger solidarity include Baum and Calvert, "Texas Patrons of Husbandry," 49, 51; and R. Tyler et al., *New Handbook of Texas*, 2:289, 3:279.

109. *1875 Convention Journal*, 226–27, 286–87, 464–67, 492, 495, 497–98, 532–33, 536, 653–55, 721–23.

110. *Constitution of the State of Texas* [1876], art. 10; art. 3, secs. 50–52; art. 8, sec. 4; art. 14, sec. 3; art 16, secs. 25, 56.

111. McKay, *Debates*, 392; *1875 Convention Journal*, 796–97.

112. *1875 Convention Journal*, 164.

113. Ibid., 240–41, 275, 288–90, 300–302, 353–54, 356–57, 401–3, 510; McKay, *Debates*, 239–42, 272–86.

114. *1875 Convention Journal*, 342–44 [third quotation, 342], 446–49; McKay, *Debates*, 269–71, 408–15 [second quotation, 410; first quotation, 412]; *SADH*, Nov. 15, 1875.

115. McKay, *Debates*, 126–29.

116. *1875 Convention Journal*, 264–65, 344–46, 620–24; McKay, *Debates*, 117–25, 400–408.

117. *Constitution of the State of Texas* [1876], art. 14, sec. 3; *LT*, 8:989–90.

118. *GDN*, Apr. 16, July 4 [quoting *Dallas Herald*], 1874; *LT*, 8:179–80, 558–60; Brockman, "Railroads, Radicals, and Democrats," 176–78.

119. *1875 Convention Journal*, 633–34, 684–85, 695–96, 735–39; McKay, *Debates*, 419–21, 436–40, 442–45, 448–50.

120. McKay, *Debates*, 116, 268, 317.

121. *Constitution of the State of Texas* [1876], art 10; *1875 Convention Journal*, 89–90,

376–78, 425–27, 431, 607, 716, 796–97; McKay, *Debates*, 389–92 [quotation, 390], 456–57; Poor, *Manual of the Railroads of the United States*, 717; *SADH*, Oct. 15, 1875.
122. R. Smith, "Grange Movement in Texas," 310.
123. Baum and Calvert, "Texas Patrons of Husbandry," 38–41.
124. *Paris [Tex.] Press*, Sept. 3, 1875.
125. "To the Voters of North-West, West and Eastern Texas," Galveston, 1876, Broadside Collection [quotation]; *ADDS*, Jan. 29, Feb. 11, 1876; *SADH*, Nov. 12, 1875, Jan. 19, 1876.
126. For example, Terrell, *Speech*, 31–35; and Winkler, *Platforms*, 181, 188, 207.
127. William Neal Ramey to Oran Roberts, Jan. 20, 1876, Roberts Papers.
128. *ADDS*, Feb. 12–13, 25 [quotation], 1876; *GDN*, Feb. 12, 1876; Winkler, *Platforms*, 177; Ashbel Smith to Horace Cone, Nov. 15, 1875, James Ware to Ashbel Smith, Dec. 31, 1875, Smith Papers.
129. *Constitution of the State of Arkansas . . . 1874*, art. 10, sec. 3; art 14, sec. 3; art. 16, secs. 8–9; Moneyhon, *Arkansas and the New South*, 19, 23–25; Going, *Bourbon Democracy in Alabama*, 83; Hair, *Bourbonism and Agrarian Protest*, 100–101.
130. *SADH*, Oct. 23, 28 [quoting *Sentinel*], 1875.

5. REDEEMER DEMOCRATS AND THE POLITICS OF SOCIAL WELFARE

1. Hollingsworth, *Fourth Annual Report of the Superintendent of Public Instruction*, 22; Kousser, "Progressivism—For Middle-Class Whites Only," 173.
2. *GDN*, Aug. 23, 1873, Feb. 18, 1874 [second quotation], Jan. 13, Mar. 4, Oct. 20, 1875; Hollingsworth, *Fourth Annual Report of the Superintendent of Public Instruction*, 30, 48–59 [first quotation, 57]; *SADH*, Oct. 28, 1875.
3. Winkler, *Platforms*, 146–47, 160; *GDN*, Oct. 29, Dec. 3, 1873; *North Texas Enterprise*, Nov. 22, 1873.
4. *LT*, 2:134–36, 320–22; Eby, *Development of Education in Texas*, 79–88.
5. *LT*, 3:1461–65, 4:449–55, 474–76, 478–79, 494, 1020–23, 1065–68. The legislature also passed laws allowing railroad companies to borrow from the school fund to support construction. Eby, *Development of Education in Texas*, 112–20.
6. Lang, *Financial History of the Public Lands*, 168–69.
7. Texas Constitution of 1845, art. 10, sec. 2; *LT*, 3:1461–65, 4:525–30, 996–99.
8. *LT*, 3:1461–65, 4:525–30; Eby, *Development of Education in Texas*, 89–94, 121.
9. Eby, *Development of Education in Texas*, 89–94, 104–9, 120–23; E. T. Miller, *Financial History of Texas*, 96–97.
10. Texas Constitution of 1866, art. 10 [sec. 2 quoted]; *LT*, 5:1009–10, 1086, 1088–92, 1113–14, 1126–27; Eby, *Development of Education in Texas*, 154–56.
11. Texas Constitution of 1869, art. 9; *LT*, 6:959–62, 7:50–52.
12. *LT*, 7:536–47.
13. *GDN*, May 4, June 29, 1873, Apr. 28, Oct. 3, 1874; *North Texas Enterprise*, Jan. 11, May 10, June 21, Aug. 9, 1873; Ashbel Smith to O. N. Hollingsworth, [Mar. 1874], Smith Papers.
14. Hollingsworth, *Fourth Annual Report of the Superintendent of Public Instruction*, 10–12, 15, 22–32, 38–39, 73; *GDN*, Aug. 12, 1875.

15. *GDN*, Jan. 13, 1875.

16. *House Journal, 13th Leg.*, 1221; *GDN*, June 24, 1875.

17. *ADDS*, July 21 [first quotation], Aug. 13 [second quotation] 1875; King, *Great South*, 134.

18. *House Journal, 14th Leg., 1st sess.*, 42.

19. *GDN*, Mar. 28, July 26, Aug. 21, 1873; *North Texas Enterprise*, Dec. 21, 1872; Hollingsworth, *Fourth Annual Report of the Superintendent of Public Instruction*, 9, 15.

20. *GDN*, Feb. 25, 1874.

21. *LT*, 7:467–68, 545, 8:74–80, 144–48, 376–79, 476–77.

22. *Constitution of the State of Texas* [1876], art. 7, secs. 2, 4–6, 11, 15. Texans subsequently disagreed over whether the Redeemer constitution proposed to reserve half of the public domain *plus* the alternate sections of internal-improvement land grants or whether it intended that the alternate sections be counted as part of the one-half reserved, also whether it proposed to reserve half of all public land existing at the time of ratification or only one-half of that which remained after other constitutional mandates, such as grants of one million acres to the university and three million acres to support construction of a capitol building, were provided. In 1889 the Texas Supreme Court opted for the less generous interpretations. See *Galveston, H. & S. A. Ry. Co. v. State*, 12 Southwestern Reporter (1889), 988–95; 13 Southwestern Reporter (1890), 619–33; and McKitrick, *Public Land System of Texas*, 135–38.

23. *1875 Convention Journal*, 612–13; McKay, *Debates*, 399–400.

24. McKitrick, *Public Land System of Texas*, 119; Gates, *Public Land Law Development*, 804.

25. *LT*, 8:148–51.

26. For asylum appropriations, see *LT*, 6:296, 1006, 7:610–11, 666, 668, 8:228–29, 384–85, 463–64, 531, 558, 1050, 1084–86, 1318–19, 1362–63, 1456, 9:76–77.

27. *GDN*, Feb. 15, Mar. 29, Apr. 7, 23, May 6, Nov. 11, 13, 1874.

28. *1875 Convention Journal*, 534; *Governors' Messages*, 253, 310, 394, 746–48.

29. *Texas Constitution of 1869*, art. 12, sec. 25; *LT*, 6:292–93, 1008; E. J. Davis to F. L. Hatch, June 19, 1873, Letterpress, Davis Records.

30. Winkler, *Platforms*, 162; *GDN*, Apr. 17, May 3, 14, 24, 1873.

31. *LT*, 8:116–20; *House Journal, 13th Leg.*, 1375–79; *GDN*, June 3, 1873, Mar. 8, Apr. 17, 1874.

32. *GDN*, Jan. 30, 1875; *LT*, 8:484, 897–99, 1086, 1478; E. T. Miller, *Financial History of Texas*, 200–201, 231, 238; Darden, *Annual Report of the Comptroller . . . 1876[–]1878*, 4, 29.

33. *LT*, 8:1334–35, 1475–77, 9:127–28, 214.

34. William Pitt Ballinger Diary, Sept. 10, 1875, Ballinger Papers.

35. *1875 Convention Journal*, 136–39, 142–43, 318–19, 340–42, 518–19; McKay, *Debates*, 215–18, 222–23, 332–40, 359–67.

36. McKay, *Debates*, 214–15, 220–22, 226–33, 340–41, 355, 357, 396–97; *1875 Convention Journal*, 190–91, 329–33, 519, 610–11.

37. *1875 Convention Journal*, 245–47, 397–401; McKay, *Debates*, 100–113 [first quotation, 110; second quotation, 111], 195–96 [third quotation, 196], 219, 222, 225, 355–57.

38. McKay, *Debates*, 219–20, 224, 226, 350–54.

39. Ibid., 342 [quotation], 396

40. Ibid., 196–98, 201, 213, 233–34.

41. *ADDS*, July 21, 1875; McKay, *Debates*, 332; *1875 Convention Journal*, 511–12.

42. For Democratic criticisms of the education provisions, see Ashbel Smith to Horace Cone, Nov. 15, 1875, Smith Papers; Hollingsworth, *Fifth Annual Report of the Superintendent of Public Instruction*, 28; and McKay, *Making the Texas Constitution*, 105–6.

43. *1875 Convention Journal*, 243–47, 336–37, 395–401, 511–14, 516–21, 523–24, 609–11, 615–16.

44. Ibid., 519–20, 538.

45. Hollingsworth, *Fifth Annual Report of the Superintendent of Public Instruction*, 12–14; *Constitution of the State of Texas* [1876], art. 7, sec. 6.

46. *1875 Convention Journal*, 790–91; *Constitution of the State of Texas* [1876], art. 11, sec. 10.

47. *Constitution of the State of Texas* [1876], art. 7, secs. 1–8.

48. *LT*, 8:1035–46.

49. Ibid., 863–64, 1034; *First Biennial Report of the Board of Education . . . 1877[–]1878*, 60–64; *Second Biennial Report of the State Board of Education . . . 1879[–]1880*, 4. On the identification of dog ownership with the poor and particularly the black poor, and for consequent Republican opposition to dog taxes, see *GDN*, Nov. 30, 1873, Apr. 28, July 8, 1874; and *House Journal, 13th Leg.*, 588–89, 591.

50. *Statutes at Large of the United States of America* 16 (1870), 81; S. B. Maxey to [Marilda Maxey], May 30, 1876, Maxey Papers.

51. L. Rice, *Negro in Texas*, 218–20.

52. *Second Biennial Report of the State Board of Education . . . 1879[–]1880*, 14.

53. *First Biennial Report of the Board of Education . . . 1877[–]1878*, 28–32; *Second Biennial Report of the State Board of Education . . . 1879[–]1880*, 3–5; *Third Biennial Report of the State Board of Education . . . 1881[–]1882*, 11, 260, 262, 264; U.S. House, *Report of the Commissioner of Education* (1880–81), 311–12; U.S. House, *Report of the Commissioner of Education* (1881–82), 246–48; U.S. House, *Report of the Commissioner of Education* (1882–83), 249–50; *LT*, 8:1248–49, 9:25, 81–82.

54. Such characterizations appear even in the most trenchant analyses of Texas constitution making, such as Mauer, "State Constitutions in a Time of Crisis."

55. The late Robert Calvert of Texas A&M University kindly provided county-by-county figures for the number of Grange lodges in Texas in 1876.

56. W. P. Ballinger to O. M. Roberts, Aug. 19, 1878, Roberts Papers.

57. South Texan Stockdale, for instance, had interested himself in shipping beef by rail in refrigerated cars. R. Tyler et al., *New Handbook of Texas*, 6:107. Reagan hailed from the East Texas town of Palestine and Throckmorton from Collin County in North Texas.

58. *1875 Convention Journal*, 402–3, 609–11, 624.

59. C. S. West to Ashbel Smith, Sept. 14, 1875, Smith Papers.

60. See, for example, Anderson, *Education of Blacks in the South*, 20–27.

61. McKay, *Debates*, 452.

62. See *SADH* [citing *Waco Examiner*], Oct. 30, Nov. 5, 1875; *ADDS*, Aug. 13, 1875 [quotation]; S. D. Smith, "Schools and Schoolmen," 54–57, 60–61, 65–66, 89–95, 120–21.

63. *Navasota Weekly Tablet*, Nov. 23, 1877.

64. *ADDS*, July 21, 1875; *GDN*, June 24, 1875; McKay, *Debates*, 225, 355–57; *Governors' Messages*, 717–18.
65. *GDN*, Mar. 4, Oct. 19, 1875.
66. *1875 Convention Journal*, 332, 624; *GDN*, Aug. 7, 1875.
67. I tabulated fourteen roll-call votes, including one on a poll-tax restriction on the franchise, one banning grants of public land to railroads, two on educational taxation, one on establishing a state-funded immigration bureau, one involving judicial gerrymandering in the interest of black-belt Democrats, two on official salaries, two on limiting the state debt, one establishing a two-year rather than four-year gubernatorial term, one on usury laws, and two on taxation. Ten Grangers voted for the putative Grange position in ten or more of these votes. Eight more voted thusly on nine of fourteen votes, but four of these broke with the others to support the poll tax, the issue often taken to most distinguish Grange from non-Grange Democrats. *1875 Convention Journal*, 225–27, 286–87, 297, 308–9, 325, 330–33, 402–3, 465–67, 624, 642, 653–54, 687, 726.
68. McKay, *Debates*, 459.
69. Going, "South and the Blair Education Bill," 267–90; Barr, *Reconstruction to Reform*, 74; S. D. Smith, "Schools and Schoolmen," 114–18; *Congressional Record*, 48th Cong., 1st sess. (1883–84), 2207–8, 2245–47, 2460–66, 2724; 49th Cong., 1st sess. (1885–86), 2105, 2882; 50th Cong., 1st sess. (1887–88), 1223; 51st Cong., 1st sess. (1889–90), 2436; Winkler, *Platforms*, 219–20, 238; Upchurch, *Legislating Racism*, 48, 57–59.
70. Coke to S. B. Maxey, Sept. 7, 1874, Letterpress, Coke Records.
71. Census Office, Tenth Census, *Report on Valuation, Taxation, and Public Indebtedness*, 19; U.S. House, *Report of the Commissioner of Education* (1881–82), 326–27; Hair, *Bourbonism and Agrarian Protest*, 119–27.
72. U.S. House, *Report of the Commissioner of Education* (1880–81), 310; U.S. House, *Report of the Commissioner of Education* (1881–82), 320, 322, 326–27.
73. Hollingsworth, *Fourth Annual Report of the Superintendent of Public Instruction*, 91–92; Hollingsworth, *Fifth Annual Report of the Superintendent of Public Instruction*, 24; *First Biennial Report of the Board of Education . . . 1877[–]1878*, 56–64, 82; *Second Biennial Report of the State Board of Education . . . 1879[–]1880*, 29–68; Lang, *Financial History of the Public Lands*, 215.
74. U.S. House, *Report of the Commissioner of Education* (1880–81), 308–9; *LT*, 8:1086.

6. CRISIS OF REDEEMER GOVERNMENT

1. Smith to Edward Atkinson, May 24, 1879, Smith Papers; C. L. Cleveland to Oran Roberts, Oct. 23, 1879, Roberts Papers.
2. E. T. Miller, *Financial History of Texas*, 191–94, 196–97, 229–39; *GDN*, Feb. 11, 13, 1874, Jan. 13, 1875; *ADDS*, Feb. 28, Mar. 4, 1874; *LT*, 7:603–5, 8:18–20, 876–79; Darden, *Annual Report of the Comptroller . . . 1874*, 80–81; Darden, *Annual Report of the Comptroller . . . 1875*, 72–73; Darden, *Annual Report of the Comptroller . . . 1876*, 39; Darden, *Annual Report of the Comptroller . . . 1876[–]1878*, 29.
3. Coke to W. L. Moody, Dec. 17, 1874, Letterpress, Coke Records; E. T. Miller, *Financial History of Texas*, 213.
4. See the legislatures' general appropriation laws in *LT*, 8:226–33, 528–32, 554–58,

1048–50, 1082–88, 1478–80. But considerable sums were also appropriated by individual statute.

5. *Governors' Messages*, 258–59, 719–24; Day and Winfrey, *Texas Indian Papers*, 392–99; Raines, *Analytical Index to the Laws of Texas*, 285.

6. *GDN*, Jan. 28, Feb. 3, 13, 1874; *LT*, 8:61–64, 1089, 1333; Pool, *History of Bosque County*, 60–61; Hyman, *Anti-Redeemers*, 64–74; *Navasota Weekly Tablet*, Nov. 9, 1877.

7. E. T. Miller, *Financial History of Texas*, 208–11, 213, 405.

8. Thornton, "Fiscal Policy and the Failure of Radical Reconstruction," 386–87.

9. E. T. Miller, *Financial History of Texas*, 412.

10. Darden, *Annual Report of the Comptroller . . . 1876*, 67; G. Tyler, *History of Bell County*, 304–5; Campbell, *Southern Community in Crisis*, 356–57.

11. W. W. Lang to O. M. Roberts, Mar. 16, 1879, Roberts Papers.

12. Winkler, *Platforms*, 180–81, 187–90, 198–201.

13. Barr, *Reconstruction to Reform*, 38–62; McMath, "Sandy Land and Hogs," 212–13, 226n23; Martin, "Greenback Party in Texas," 161–77; R. Tyler et al., *New Handbook of Texas*, 1:695–96, 2:29, 469, 3:434; Dohoney, *Average American*, 232–41; A. M. Smith, "William Harrison Hamman."

14. Kingston, Attlesey, and Crawford, *Texas Almanac's Political History of Texas*, 58–65, 72–75. For the Greenback appeal to African Americans, see H. F. Gillette to Ashbel Smith, Aug. 1, 1878, Smith Papers; A. W. Terrell to Oran Roberts, July 31, 1878, Roberts Papers; D. B. Culberson to John H. Reagan, Sept. 25, 1879, Reagan Papers; *Navasota Weekly Tablet*, Apr. 5, June 21, 1878; and L. Rice, *Negro in Texas*, 55–60.

15. Winkler, *Platforms*, 191–93.

16. *Navasota Weekly Tablet*, Feb. 22, Mar. 15, May 10, 24, 1878; Richard Coke to Oran Roberts, Aug. 15, 1878, Roberts Papers; Democratic Executive Committee of Lamar County, *Response to Greenbackism*; A. M. Smith, "William Harrison Hamman," 147–48.

17. Winkler, *Platforms*, 183, 185.

18. Roberts to W. P. Ballinger, Dec. 28, 1879, Roberts Papers.

19. Barr, *Reconstruction to Reform*, 39–42; Brockman, "Railroads, Radicals, and Democrats," 223–25; Elliott, *Leathercoat*, 253–76; Roberts, "Political, Legislative, and Judicial History," 225–28; W. W. Lang to O. M. Roberts, Mar. 16, 1879, Roberts Papers; J. W. Throckmorton to O. M. Roberts, Aug. 6, 1878, Correspondence, Roberts Records.

20. *Governors' Messages*, 335.

21. Ibid., 267–70; *LT*, 8:1420–25; E. T. Miller, *Financial History of Texas*, 235–36.

22. *Governors' Messages*, 242; *LT*, 8:1334–35, 1475–77.

23. *Governors' Messages*, 290, 305–8 [quotation, 307].

24. *Second Biennial Report of the State Board of Education . . . 1879[–]1880*, 4, 29–68; *Governors' Messages*, 285–91; *LT*, 9:36–37, 76; Eby, *Development of Education in Texas*, 174–76; U.S. House, *Report of the Commissioner of Education* (1880–81), 309; U.S. House, *Report of the Commissioner of Education* (1881–82), 246; Roberts, "Political, Legislative, and Judicial History," 236–38; Barr, *Reconstruction to Reform*, 77–79. Federal and state sources differ as to the final amount of the budget cut, but the figures generally range from slightly under $190,000 to somewhat over $200,000. The federal commissioner of education in the next year's report revised

downward estimates for spending in the school year preceding the cut, leaving an absolute decline in educational expenditure of $84,567. Even at the lowest estimates, the schools sustained at least a 10 percent budget cut.

25. *Governors' Messages,* 285–91 [quotation, 291]; *LT,* 9:35–36.

26. See, for instance, George Mason to Roberts, Apr. 24, 1879, James Masterson to Roberts, Apr. 26, 1879, M. D. K. Taylor to Roberts, Apr. 28, 1879, Edwin Hobby to Roberts, May 2, 1879, A. M. Hobby to Roberts, May 5, 1879, Ashbel Smith to Roberts, May 12, 1879, Gustave Cooke to Roberts, May 28, 1879, E. M. Daggett to Roberts, May 30, 1879, and Rufus Burleson to Roberts, June 7, 1879, Roberts Papers; and *GDN,* Apr. 24–25, 29, 1879.

27. *GDN,* Apr. 25, 29–30, May 1–2, 1879; Winkler, *Platforms,* 196, 200, 204; Barr, *Reconstruction to Reform,* 58–59; Lewis, "History of the State School System," 140–41, 143.

28. Roberts to W. P. Ballinger, Dec. 28, 1879, Roberts Papers.

29. *Governors' Messages,* 218–20 [quotation, 218], 241; *LT,* 8:1443–50; E. T. Miller, *Financial History of Texas,* 111–13, 215–17, 294–300.

30. *LT,* 9:64–65, 71–72; E. T. Miller, *Financial History of Texas,* 170–71, 214, 217–18.

31. *LT,* 8:1371–76; *Governors' Messages,* 219. These liquor taxes accounted for slightly over 50 percent of total occupation taxes assessed in 1880. The new taxes on corporations, however, amounted to only 4.3 percent. E. T. Miller, *Financial History of Texas,* 218.

32. H. S. Hastings to O. M. Roberts, Nov. 21, 1879 [quotation], Roberts Papers; Winkler, *Platforms,* 196, 200, 204; Roberts, "Political, Legislative, and Judicial History," 240.

33. Quoted in *GDN,* May 1, 1879.

34. E. T. Miller, *Financial History of Texas,* 203.

35. See, for instance, Darden, *Annual Report of the Comptroller . . . 1876[–]1878,* 55.

36. Roberts, "Political, Legislative, and Judicial History," 212, 216; Roberts, *Our Federal Relations,* 158 [first and second quotations]; Roberts, *Description of Texas,* i [third quotation], 38, 129.

37. Barr, *Reconstruction to Reform,* 59.

38. Harper, "Farming Someone Else's Land," 175, 199–200; Sanders, *Farm Ownership and Tenancy,* 4–5.

39. *Governors' Messages,* 221–24, 295; Roberts, "Political, Legislative, and Judicial History," 247–48; *LT,* 9:55–59, 80–81.

40. *GDN,* May 24, Aug 15, 1873; *ADDS,* Mar. 11, Apr. 28, 1874.

41. *Constitution of the State of Texas* [1876], art. 14, sec. 6.

42. Wallace, *Charles DeMorse,* 202–7, 210–11 [quotation, 211]; J. B. Robertson to Roberts, Feb. 17, 1879, Correspondence, Roberts Records.

43. [Walsh], "Memories of a Texas Land Commissioner," 487 [second quotation], 495 [first quotation]; Walsh, *Special Report of the Commissioner of the General Land Office,* 3–4, 6–10; Walsh, *Biennial Report of the Commissioner of the General Land Office . . . 1880[–]1882,* 4–8 [third quotation, 4; fourth and fifth quotations, 7; sixth quotation, 8].

44. *Governors' Messages,* 222–23; Roberts, "Political, Legislative, and Judicial History," 247–48; Dolman, "Public Lands of Western Texas," 252.

45. Hollingsworth, *Fourth Annual Report of the Superintendent of Public Instruction,* 91–92; Census Office, Tenth Census, *Report on the Productions of Agriculture,* 134, 205–6, 242; Barr, *Reconstruction to Reform,* 80–81.

46. Roberts won 63 percent of the vote, Davis 24 percent, and Hamman 13 percent. Barr, *Reconstruction to Reform,* 56–60, 79; Winkler, *Platforms,* 200, 203–5 [quotation, 205].

47. *LT,* 9:107, 161–63, 176–86, 283–88.

48. R. Tyler et al., *New Handbook of Texas,* 6:742–43.

49. Walker, *Penology for Profit,* 65, 75.

50. *LT,* 9:145–51, 278–83; E. T. Miller, *Financial History of Texas,* 409, 412.

51. *LT,* 9:183; *Third Biennial Report of the State Board of Education . . . 1881[–]1882,* 31–268; Barr, *Reconstruction to Reform,* 79.

52. *LT,* 9:211–14, 296; Walsh, *Special Report of the Commissioner of the General Land Office,* 7–8.

53. *LT,* 8:1309–11, 1475–77, 9:127–28, 214.

54. *Governors' Messages,* 724–25; Walsh, *Report of the Commissioner of the General Land Office . . . , 1880,* 15–16; Walsh, *Special Report of the Commissioner of the General Land Office,* 4–5; Walsh, *Biennial Report of the Commissioner of the General Land Office . . . 1880[–]1882,* 10–11; Dolman, "Public Lands of Western Texas," 106–7, 253; T. L. Miller, *Public Lands of Texas,* 52–53; Williams, "Development of a Market Economy in Texas," 440–45.

55. *Governors' Messages,* 413; *LT,* 9:263.

56. McKitrick, *Public Land System of Texas,* 70; Reed, *Texas Railroads,* 155–56, 164–75; Lang, *Financial History of the Public Lands,* 110; Williams, "Development of a Market Economy in Texas," 439–50.

57. E. T. Miller, *Financial History of Texas,* 244–48; Walker, *Penology for Profit,* 92, 161; Buenger, *Path to a Modern South,* 46, 105–8; Foley, *White Scourge,* 49–50; Campbell, *Gone to Texas,* 363.

58. *LT,* 9:319, 804.

59. *Governors' Messages,* 431; E. T. Miller, *Financial History of Texas,* 405; Lang, *Financial History of the Public Lands,* 234.

60. Winkler, *Platforms,* 207 [first quotation], 213 [second quotation]; Barr, *Reconstruction to Reform,* 50–51, 54, 63–69; R. Tyler et al., *New Handbook of Texas,* 3:982–83; L. Rice, *Negro in Texas,* 64–65.

61. *LT,* 9:211–14, 296.

62. Winkler, *Platforms,* 210 [quotations]; Barr, *Reconstruction to Reform,* 65–66; *Governors' Messages,* 472–73.

63. Barr, *Reconstruction to Reform,* 69.

64. *LT,* 9:308–9, 321–22, 377.

65. E. T. Miller, *Financial History of Texas,* 355–60, 395–96, 428; Lang, *Financial History of the Public Lands,* 59; *LT,* 9:859–60.

66. *LT,* 9:391–95; Walsh, *Biennial Report of the Commissioner of the General Land Office . . . 1880[–]1882,* 7–8.

67. [Walsh], "Memories of a Texas Land Commissioner," 486–87; Dolman, "Public Lands of Western Texas," 257–64; Lang, *Financial History of the Public Lands,* 190–93; E. T. Miller, *Financial History of Texas,* 332–36; Barr, *Reconstruction to Reform,* 82–84.

68. *LT,* 9:342–44; E. T. Miller, *Financial History of Texas,* 250–51; Walker, *Penology for Profit,* 69–83.

69. *GDN,* Apr. 29, 1879.

70. *First Biennial Report of the Board of Education . . . 1877[–]1878,* 21; *Second Biennial Report of the State Board of Education . . . 1879[–]1880,* 9–19; *Third Biennial Report of the State Board of Education . . . 1881[–]1882,* 39, 56, 74, 91, 107, 115, 122, 169, 185, 225, 246, 250; *LT,* 8:1469, 9:440, 570–88.

71. *First Biennial Report of the Board of Education . . . 1877[–]1878,* 22–23 [quotations, 23]; *Second Biennial Report of the State Board of Education . . . 1879[–]1880,* 6–7.

72. *Third Biennial Report of the State Board of Education . . . 1881[–]1882,* 36, 39, 46, 56, 62, 122, 142, 146, 149, 217 [quotation], 231.

73. *LT,* 9:440, 570, 599–600; Winkler, *Platforms,* 210; *Congressional Record,* 48th Cong., 1st sess. (1883–84), 2246; Lewis, "History of the State School System," 184–89. During the 1880s, occupation taxes contributed approximately one-fifth to one-fourth of total tax revenue. E. T. Miller, *Financial History of Texas,* 409.

74. *Governors' Messages,* 305, 455–57, 479; *LT,* 9:155–56, 206–7, 440; *Third Biennial Report of the State Board of Education . . . 1881[–]1882,* 62, 133, 169, 210, 225, 229, 250.

75. *LT,* 9:584–85, 648–49.

76. Eby, *Development of Education in Texas,* 197–98, 216–17, 222; L. Rice, *Negro in Texas,* 218.

77. E. T. Miller, *Financial History of Texas,* 244, 367, 395–96.

78. Moore, "Origins of the Solid South," 297–98; Thornton, "Fiscal Policy and the Failure of Radical Reconstruction," 387–88; Wallenstein, *Slave South to New South,* 210–13; Going, *Bourbon Democracy in Alabama,* 152, 205–6.

79. Joseph Sayers, Roberts's lieutenant governor, did serve as governor between 1899 and 1903, but he had begun his public career later than Redeemer governors Coke, Hubbard, Roberts, Ireland, and Ross.

80. Buenger, *Path to a Modern South,* 3–9 [quotation, 8]; Barr, *Reconstruction to Reform,* 88–92; Ivy, *No Saloon in the Valley,* 65–66, 97–99.

81. McMath, *American Populism,* 66–82; McMath, *Populist Vanguard,* 22–26; Goodwyn, *Populist Moment,* 25–124; Barr, *Reconstruction to Reform,* 93–110.

82. Roberts, "Political, Legislative, and Judicial History," 296.

83. Winkler, *Platforms,* 315–16, 318–20, 332–34, 339–42, 380–83; Key, *Southern Politics,* 255 [quotation].

CONCLUSION: REDEMPTION'S FINAL ACT

1. James Throckmorton to Ashbel Smith, Dec. 22, 1878, Smith Papers; *Governors' Messages,* 274–76, 414–15, 441–42, 481, 509–10, 591–95, 643–45; Benner, *Sul Ross,* 175–76, 191–95.

2. Potts, *Railroad Transportation in Texas,* 56, 74–82, 116–23; Barr, *Reconstruction to Reform,* 111–42; Reed, *Texas Railroads,* 543–58, 573–80; Cotner, *James Stephen Hogg,* 117–319.

3. Prindle, *Petroleum Politics and the Texas Railroad Commission;* Barr, *Reconstruction to Reform,* 122; Nash, "Chapter from an Active Life," 109–10.

4. *General Laws of the . . . Twenty-Seventh Legislature,* 322–23.

5. Kousser, *Shaping of Southern Politics*, 206–7.

6. *General Laws of the . . . Twenty-Eighth Legislature*, 133–58; Anders, *Boss Rule*, 91–92; Hine, *Black Victory*, 25–53.

7. Platt, *City Building in the New South*, 201; R. Miller, "Fort Worth and the Progressive Era," 100; F. Turner, *Women, Culture, and Community*, 236; Ayers, *Promise of the New South*, 410.

8. Heard and Strong, *Southern Primaries and Elections*, 189–91.

9. Martin, *People's Party in Texas*, esp. 30–34, 63–65, 135–39, 210–29.

10. Kingston, Attlesey, and Crawford, *Texas Almanac's Political History of Texas*, 58–69.

11. In 1890, 41.9 percent of the farms in Texas were operated by tenants; in 1900, 49.7 percent; in 1910, 52.6 percent; in 1920, 53.3 percent. Goldenweiser and Truesdell, *Farm Tenancy in the United States*, 149.

12. J. Green, "Tenant Farmer Discontent and Socialist Protest in Texas," 133–54; Foley, *White Scourge*, 92–117; Buenger, *Path to a Modern South*, 118–23; Gould, *Progressives and Prohibitionists*, 127–44, 237.

13. L. Rice, *Negro in Texas*, 58–59, 61, 68–85.

14. Cantrell and Barton, "Texas Populists," 690–92; Miller, "Building a Progressive Coalition in Texas," 172–75; Perman, *Struggle for Mastery*, 275–80; Buenger, *Path to a Modern South*, 84–91; Gould, *Alexander Watkins Terrell*, 103–11, 114–18, 123.

15. Cantrell, "'Dark Tactics,'" 85–93; Ivy, *No Saloon in the Valley*, 59–62, 92–97.

16. Buenger, *Path to a Modern South*, 87–89; Campbell, *Gone to Texas*, 337–38, 346; Cantrell, *Kenneth and John B. Rayner*.

17. Montejano, *Anglos and Mexicans*, 110–16, 129–51; Anders, *Boss Rule*, 63, 102–4, 168–70, 250, 283; *General and Special Laws . . . by the Fourth Called Session of the Thirty-Fifth Legislature*, 54, 137; Keyssar, *Right to Vote*, 136–38.

18. Buenger, *Path to the Modern South*, 91–100; Perman, *Struggle for Mastery*, 276.

19. Kousser, *Shaping of Southern Politics*, 71, 208–9; Key, *Southern Politics*, 533–35; Kingston, *1992–1993 Texas Almanac*, 135, 440–41.

20. Foley, *White Scourge*, 28–63; Buenger, *Path to a Modern South*, 64.

21. Montejano, *Anglos and Mexicans*, 159–69, 191–95, 235–54, 279–81, 292–97; Anders, *Boss Rule*, 176; Foley, *White Scourge*, 40–42; G. Green, *Establishment in Texas Politics*, 80–81; Campbell, *Gone to Texas*, 420, 428.

22. *Hogue v. Baker*, 45 Southwestern Reporter (1898), 1004–7.

23. T. L. Miller, *Public Lands of Texas*, 169; Buenger, *Path to a Modern South*, xvi–xvii, 162; Campbell, *Gone to Texas*, 361–63, 378, 407–8. Of the other former Confederate states, only Louisiana became a nationally important petroleum producer, but it did not remotely approach Texas' yields until after 1960. U.S. Bureau of Mines, *Minerals Yearbook, 1937*, 1008–9; Bureau of Mines, *Minerals Yearbook, 1951*, 947; Bureau of Mines, *Minerals Yearbook, 1976, Volume One*, 964.

24. Key, *Southern Politics*, 254–76; G. Green, *Establishment in Texas Politics*, 190; Campbell, *Gone to Texas*, 425–27, 432.

25. Lipari, "Income Texas," 4; Campbell, *Gone to Texas*, 432, 467; E. T. Miller, "Development of the Texas State Tax System."

26. Bureau of the Census, *Statistical Abstract of the United States: 1981*, 143, 144, 191; Bureau of the Census, *Statistical Abstract of the United States: 1982–83*, 427, 443.

27. Bureau of the Census, *Statistical Abstract of the United States: 1980*, 447; U.S.

Department of Education, *Digest of Education Statistics, 1993,* 162; Campbell, *Gone to Texas,* 415, 452.

28. *Edgewood Independent School District v. William Kirby,* 777 Southwestern Reporter, 2nd ser. (1989), 391–99.
29. Ibid., 395.
30. Campbell, *Gone to Texas,* 454–60, 464–66; Bureau of the Census, *Statistical Abstract of the United States: 2004–2005,* 103, 143, 434, 454, http://www.census.gov/prod/2004pubs/04statab.

Bibliography

ARCHIVAL SOURCES

Center for American History, University of Texas at Austin. William Pitt Ballinger Papers. Guy M. Bryan Papers. Edward Burleson Jr. Papers. Richard Coke Scrapbook. Benjamin Epperson Papers. John S. Ford Papers. James P. Newcomb (Sr.) Papers. Oran Roberts Papers. Ashbel Smith Papers (microfilm copy, Butler Library, Columbia University). James B. Wells Papers.

Archives Division, Texas State Library, Austin. Broadside Collection. Gov. Richard Coke Records (RG 301). Gov. Edmund J. Davis Records (RG 301). Samuel Bell Maxey Papers. John H. Reagan Papers (microfilm copy, Butler Library, Columbia University). Records of the Legislature (RG 100). Gov. Oran M. Roberts Records (RG 301). Secretary of State Records (RG 307).

NEWSPAPERS

Austin Daily Democratic Statesman, 1874–76.
Galveston Daily News, 1872–79.
Navasota Weekly Tablet, 1877–79.
North Texas Enterprise (Bonham), 1872–75.
San Antonio Daily Herald, 1874–76.

STATE AND FEDERAL DOCUMENTS

Alexander, William. *Report of the Attorney General of the State of Texas, for the Year 1872.* Austin: James P. Newcomb, 1873.
The Constitution of the State of Arkansas, Framed and Adopted by the Convention which Assembled at Little Rock, July 14th, 1874, and Ratified by the People of the State, at the Election Held Oct. 13, 1874. Little Rock: P. A. Ladue, 1876.
The Constitution of the State of Texas Adopted by the Constitutional Convention Begun and Held at the City of Austin on the Sixth Day of September, 1875. Austin: Institution for the Deaf and Dumb, 1877.
Darden, Stephen. *Annual Report of the Comptroller of Public Accounts of the State of Texas, for Fiscal Year Ending the 31st August, A.D. 1874.* Houston: A. C. Gray, State Printer, 1874.

———. *Annual Report of the Comptroller of Public Accounts of the State of Texas, for the Fiscal Year Ending the 31st August, A.D. 1875, and Supplemental Report to February 1, 1876.* Houston: A. C. Gray, State Printer, 1876.

———. *Annual Report of the Comptroller of Public Accounts of the State of Texas, for the Fiscal Year Ending Aug. 31, 1876.* Galveston: Shaw & Blaylock, State Printers, 1877.

———. *Annual Report of the Comptroller of Public Accounts of the State of Texas for the Two Fiscal Years Commencing Sept. 1, 1876, and Ending August 31, 1878.* Galveston: *Galveston News,* 1878.

Evidence Taken before the Joint Committee of the Thirteenth Legislature, Investigating Charges against Judge T. C. Barden, of the Sixteenth Judicial District. Austin: John Cardwell, State Printer, 1873.

First Biennial Report of the Board of Education for the Scholastic Years Ending Aug. 31, 1877 and 1878. Galveston: *Galveston News,* 1878.

General and Special Laws of the State of Texas Passed by the Fourth Called Session of the Thirty-Fifth Legislature Convened at the City of Austin, February 26, 1918, and Adjourned March 27, 1918. Austin: A. C. Baldwin & Sons, [1918].

General Laws of the State of Texas Passed at the Regular Session of the Twenty-Eighth Legislature Convened at the City of Austin, January 13, 1903, and Adjourned April 1, 1903. Austin: Von Boeckmann-Jones, State Printer, 1903.

General Laws of the State of Texas Passed at the Regular Session of the Twenty-Seventh Legislature Convened at the City of Austin, January 8, 1901, and Adjourned April 9, 1901. Austin: Von Boeckmann, Schutze, State Printer, 1901.

Goldenweiser, E. A., and Leon E. Truesdell. *Farm Tenancy in the United States.* Census Monograph, vol. 4. Washington, D.C.: Government Printing Office, 1924.

Hollingsworth, O. N. *Fifth Annual Report of the Superintendent of Public Instruction of the State of Texas, for the Scholastic Year Ending August 31, 1875.* Houston: A. C. Gray, State Printer, 1876.

———. *Fourth Annual Report of the Superintendent of Public Instruction of the State of Texas, for the Scholastic Year Ending August 31, 1874.* Houston: A. C. Gray, State Printer, 1874.

In the Matter of Charges against Hon. J. B. Williamson, Judge Sixth District. N.p., 1874.

In the Matter of Charges against Judge M. Priest. N.p., 1874.

In the Matter of the Address against Judge Henry Maney. N.p., 1874.

Journal of the Constitutional Convention of the State of Texas Begun and Held at the City of Austin, September 6, 1875. Galveston: News Office, 1875.

Journal of the House of Representatives of Texas; Being the Second Session of the Fourteenth Legislature, Begun and Held at the City of Austin, January 12, 1875. Houston: A. C. Gray, State Printer, 1875.

Journal of the House of Representatives of the State of Texas; Being the Session of the Fourteenth Legislature Begun and Held at the City of Austin, January 13, 1874. Austin: Cardwell & Walker, 1874.

Journal of the House of Representatives of the State of Texas; Being the Session of the Thirteenth Legislature Begun and Held at the City of Austin, January 14, 1873. Austin: John Cardwell, State Printer, 1873.

Journal of the Senate of Texas; Being the Second Session of the Fourteenth Legislature, Begun and Held at the City of Austin, January 12, 1875. Houston: A. C. Gray, State Printer, 1875.

Bibliography

Journal of the Senate of the State of Texas; Being the Session of the Fourteenth Legislature Begun and Held at the City of Austin, January 13, 1874. Austin: Cardwell & Walker, 1874.

Journal of the Senate of Texas; Being the Session of the Thirteenth Legislature Begun and Held at the City of Austin, January 14, 1873. Austin: John Cardwell, State Printer, 1873.

Official Returns of a General Election Held in the State of Texas . . . November 5th, 6th, 7th, and 8th, 1872. Austin: James P. Newcomb, 1873.

Report of the Adjutant General of the State of Texas, for the Year 1874. Houston: A. C. Gray, State Printer, 1874.

Report of the Special Joint Committee of the Thirteenth Legislature, for Investigation into the Official Conduct and Accounts of the Superintendent of Public Instruction and of His Subordinates. Austin: John Cardwell, State Printer, 1873.

Sanders, J. T. *Farm Ownership and Tenancy in the Black Prairie of Texas.* U.S. Department of Agriculture Bulletin 1068. Washington, D.C.: Government Printing Office, 1922.

Second Biennial Report of the State Board of Education for the Scholastic Years Ending August 31, 1879 and 1880. Galveston: Galveston News, 1881.

The State of Texas against Hon. James R. Burnett, Judge Thirtieth Judicial District. Evidence Taken before the Joint Committee of the Fourteenth Legislature, Appointed to Investigate Charges Preferred by an Address for Removal from Office. Austin: J. D. Elliott, State Printer, 1874.

The State of Texas against Hon. L. W. Cooper, Judge Third Judicial District. Austin: Cardwell & Walker, 1874.

The State of Texas against Hon. S. B. Newcomb, Judge Twenty-Fifth Judicial District. Evidence Taken before the Joint Committee of the Fourteenth Legislature, Appointed to Investigate Charges Preferred by an Address for Removal from Office. Austin: J. D. Elliott, State Printer, 1874.

The State of Texas against Judge John G. Scott, of the Tenth Judicial District, Impeached for High Crimes and Misdemeanors in Office. Austin: John Cardwell, State Printer, 1873.

The State of Texas against William Chambers, Judge First Judicial District, before the Senate of the Fourteenth Legislature, Sitting as a High Court of Impeachment. Austin: Cardwell & Walker, 1874.

Third Biennial Report of the State Board of Education for the Scholastic Years Ending August 31, 1881 and 1882. Austin: E. W. Swindells, State Printer, 1883.

U.S. Bureau of Mines. *Minerals Yearbook, 1937.* Washington, D.C.: Government Printing Office, 1937.

———. *Minerals Yearbook, 1951.* Washington, D.C.: Government Printing Office, 1954.

———. *Minerals Yearbook, 1976, Volume One: Metals, Minerals, and Fuels.* Washington, D.C.: Government Printing Office, 1978.

U.S. Bureau of the Census. *Negro Population, 1790–1915.* Washington, D.C.: Government Printing Office, 1918.

———. *Statistical Abstract of the United States: 1980.* Washington, D.C.: Government Printing Office, 1980.

———. *Statistical Abstract of the United States: 1981.* Washington, D.C.: Government Printing Office, 1981.

———. *Statistical Abstract of the United States: 1982–83.* Washington, D.C.: Government Printing Office, 1982.

U.S. Census Office, Eighth Census. *Manufactures of the United States in 1860*. Washington, D.C.: Government Printing Office, 1865.

U.S. Census Office, Ninth Census. *A Compendium of the Ninth Census (June 1, 1870)*. Compiled by Francis A. Walker. Washington, D.C.: Government Printing Office, 1872.

———. *The Statistics of the Population of the United States*. Washington, D.C.: Government Printing Office, 1872.

———. *The Statistics of the Wealth and Industry of the United States*. Washington, D.C.: Government Printing Office, 1872.

U.S. Census Office, Tenth Census. *Compendium of the Tenth Census (June 1, 1880)*. 2 parts. Washington, D.C.: Government Printing Office, 1883.

———. *Report of the Cotton Production of the State of Texas, with a Discussion of the General Agricultural Features of the State*. By R. H. Loughridge. Washington, D.C.: Government Printing Office, 1884.

———. *Report on the Productions of Agriculture as Returned at the Tenth Census (June 1, 1880)*. Washington, D.C.: Government Printing Office, 1883.

———. *Report on Valuation, Taxation, and Public Indebtedness in the United States, as Returned at the Tenth Census (June 1, 1880)*. Washington, D.C.: Government Printing Office, 1884.

U.S. Census Office, Eleventh Census. *Compendium of the Eleventh Census: 1890, Part 1*. Washington, D.C.: Government Printing Office, 1892.

———. *Compendium of the Eleventh Census: 1890, Part 3*. Washington, D.C.: Government Printing Office, 1897.

———. *Report on Farms and Homes: Proprietorship and Indebtedness in the United States at the Eleventh Census: 1890*. Washington, D.C.: Government Printing Office, 1896.

———. *Report on the Population of the United States at the Eleventh Census: 1890; Part 1*. Washington, D.C.: Government Printing Office, 1895.

U.S. Census Office, Twelfth Census. *Abstract of the Twelfth Census of the United States 1900*. Washington, D.C.: Government Printing Office, 1902.

———. *Wealth, Debt, and Taxation*. Washington, D.C.: Government Printing Office, 1907.

U. S. Congress. House. *Report of the Commissioner of Education*. H. Exec. Doc. 1, 42nd Cong., 2nd sess., 1871.

———. *Report of the Commissioner of Education for the Year 1873*. H. Exec. Doc. 1, pt. 5, 43rd Cong., 1st sess., 1873.

———. *Report of the Commissioner of Education*. H. Exec. Doc. 1, 46th Cong., 3d sess., 1880–81.

———. *Report of the Commissioner of Education*. H. Exec. Doc. 1, 47th Cong., 1st sess., 1881–82.

———. *Report of the Commissioner of Education*. H. Exec. Doc. 1, 47th Cong., 2nd sess., 1882–83.

———. *The Texas and Pacific Railroad. . . . Views of the Minority*. H. Rpt. 619, pt. 2, 45th Cong., 2nd sess., 1877–78.

———. *Use of the Army in Certain of the Southern States*. H. Exec. Doc. 30, 44th Cong., 2d sess., 1876–77.

U.S. Congress. Senate. *Testimony on the Alleged Election Outrages in Texas*. S. Misc. Doc. 62, 50th Cong, 2nd sess., 1889.

U.S. Department of Education. *Digest of Education Statistics, 1993.* Washington, D.C.: Government Printing Office, 1993.

Walsh, W. C. *Biennial Report of the Commissioner of the General Land Office of the State of Texas, from August 31, 1880, to August 31, 1882.* Austin: E. W. Swindells, State Printer, 1883.

———. *Report of the Commissioner of the General Land Office of the State of Texas, for the Fiscal Year Ending August 31, 1880.* Galveston: *Galveston News,* 1880.

———. *Special Report of the Commissioner of the General Land Office of the State of Texas, from August 31, 1881, to March 1, 1882.* Galveston: A. H. Belo, 1882.

BOOKS AND ARTICLES

Anders, Evan. *Boss Rule in South Texas: The Progressive Era.* Austin: University of Texas Press, 1982.

Anderson, James D. *The Education of Blacks in the South, 1860–1935.* Chapel Hill: University of North Carolina Press, 1988.

Ayers, Edward L. *The Promise of the New South: Life after Reconstruction.* New York: Oxford University Press, 1992.

Baenziger, Ann Patton. "The Texas State Police during Reconstruction: A Reexamination." *Southwestern Historical Quarterly* 72 (April 1969): 470–91.

Baggett, James A. *The Scalawags: Southern Dissenters in the Civil War and Reconstruction.* Baton Rouge: Louisiana State University Press, 2003.

Barker, W. J. *Directory of the Members of the Thirteenth Legislature of the State of Texas.* Austin: State Journal, 1873.

Barr, Alwyn. *Black Texans: A History of Negroes in Texas, 1528–1971.* Austin: Jenkins, 1973.

———. "The Impact of Race in Shaping Judicial Districts, 1876–1907." *Southwestern Historical Quarterly* 108 (April 2005): 423–39.

———. *Reconstruction to Reform: Texas Politics, 1876–1906.* Austin: University of Texas Press, 1971.

Baum, Dale. *The Shattering of Texas Unionism: Politics in the Lone Star State during the Civil War Era.* Baton Rouge: Louisiana State University Press, 1998.

Baum, Dale, and Robert Calvert. "Texas Patrons of Husbandry: Geography, Social Contexts, and Voting Behavior." *Agricultural History* 63 (Fall 1989): 36–55.

Baum, Dale, and Worth Robert Miller. "Ethnic Conflict and Machine Politics in San Antonio, 1892–1899." *Journal of Urban History* 19 (August 1993): 63–84.

Beckert, Sven. "Democracy and Its Discontents: Contesting Suffrage Rights in Gilded Age New York." *Past & Present* 174 (February 2002): 116–57.

Benner, Judith Ann. *Sul Ross: Soldier, Statesman, Educator.* College Station: Texas A&M University Press, 1983.

Bentley, H. L., and Thomas Pilgrim. *The Texas Legal Directory for 1876–77.* Austin: Democratic Statesman Office, 1877.

Brammer, William. *The Gay Place.* Boston: Houghton Mifflin, 1961.

Buenger, Walter. *The Path to a Modern South: Northeast Texas between Reconstruction and the Great Depression.* Austin: University of Texas Press, 2001.

Butterfield, F. E., and C. M. Rundlett. *Directory of the City of Dallas . . . for the Year 1875.* St. Louis: *St. Louis Democrat,* n.d.

Calvert, Robert, Arnoldo De León, and Gregg Cantrell. *The History of Texas*. 3d. ed. Wheeling, Ill.: Harlan Davidson, 2002.

Campbell, Randolph. "The District Judges of Texas in 1866–1867: An Episode in the Failure of Presidential Reconstruction." *Southwestern Historical Quarterly* 93 (January 1990): 357–77.

———. *Gone to Texas: A History of the Lone Star State*. New York: Oxford University Press, 2003.

———. *Grass-Roots Reconstruction in Texas, 1865–1880*. Baton Rouge: Louisiana State University Press, 1997.

———. "Population Persistence and Social Change in Nineteenth-Century Texas: Harrison County, 1850–1880." *Journal of Southern History* 48 (May 1982): 185–204.

———. "Scalawag District Judges: The E. J. Davis Appointees, 1870–1873." *Houston Review* 14, no. 2 (1992): 75–88.

———. *A Southern Community in Crisis: Harrison County, Texas, 1850–1880*. Austin: Texas State Historical Association, 1983.

Cantrell, Gregg. "'Dark Tactics': Black Politics in the 1887 Texas Prohibition Campaign." *Journal of American Studies* 25 (April 1991): 85–93.

———. *Kenneth and John B. Rayner and the Limits of Southern Dissent*. Urbana: University of Illinois Press, 1993.

———. "Racial Violence and Reconstruction Politics in Texas, 1867–1868." *Southwestern Historical Quarterly* 93 (January 1990): 333–55.

Cantrell, Gregg, and D. Scott Barton. "Texas Populists and the Failure of Biracial Politics." *Journal of Southern History* 55 (November 1989): 659–92.

Cardwell, John. *Sketches of Legislators and State Officers, 1876–1878*. Austin: Democratic Statesman Office, 1876.

Carrigan, William D. *The Making of a Lynching Culture: Violence and Vigilantism in Central Texas, 1836–1916*. Urbana: University of Illinois Press, 2004.

Casdorph, Paul. *History of the Republican Party in Texas, 1865–1965*. Austin: Pemberton, 1965.

Cashion, Ty. *A Texas Frontier: The Clear Fork Country and Fort Griffin, 1849–1887*. Norman: University of Oklahoma Press, 1996.

Cockrell, Fred. "The Making of the Constitution of 1875." *West Texas Historical Association Year Book* 5 (1929): 116–24.

Cooper, Lance. "'A Slobbering Lame Thing'? The Semicolon Case Reconsidered." *Southwestern Historical Quarterly* 101 (January 1998): 321–39.

Cotner, Robert. *James Stephen Hogg: A Biography*. Austin: University of Texas Press, 1959.

Crouch, Barry. "A Spirit of Lawlessness: White Violence, Texas Blacks, 1865–1868." *Journal of Social History* 18 (Winter1984): 217–32.

Crouch, Barry, and Donaly Brice. *Cullen Montgomery Baker, Reconstruction Desperado*. Baton Rouge: Louisiana State University Press, 1997.

Day, James M., and Dorman Winfrey, eds. *Texas Indian Papers, 1860–1916*. Austin: Texas State Library, 1961.

De León, Arnoldo. *The Tejano Community, 1836–1900*. Albuquerque: University of New Mexico Press, 1982.

———. *They Called Them Greasers: Anglo Attitudes toward Mexicans in Texas, 1821–1900*. Austin: University of Texas Press, 1983.

De León, Arnoldo, and Kenneth Stewart. *Tejanos and the Numbers Game: A Socio-Historical Interpretation from the Federal Censuses, 1850–1900.* Albuquerque: University of New Mexico Press, 1989.

Democratic Executive Committee of Lamar County, Texas. *A Response to Greenbackism. The Record of the Democracy.* Paris, Tex.: Banner, 1880.

Dobbs, Ricky Floyd. "Defying Davis: The Walker County Rebellion, 1871." *East Texas Historical Journal* 32, no. 2 (1993): 34–47.

Dohoney, E. L. *An Average American.* Paris, Tex.: Dohoney, 1907.

Doyle, Don. *New Men, New Cities, New South: Atlanta, Nashville, Charleston, Mobile, 1860–1910.* Chapel Hill: University of North Carolina Press, 1990.

Eby, Frederick. *The Development of Education in Texas.* New York: Macmillan, 1925.

Elliott, Claude. *Leathercoat: The Life History of a Texas Patriot.* San Antonio: Standard Printing, 1938.

Fayman, W. A., and T. W. Reilly. *Fayman & Reilly's Galveston City Directory for 1875–6.* Galveston: Strickland & Clarke, 1875.

Foley, Neil. *The White Scourge: Mexicans, Blacks, and Poor Whites in Texas Cotton Culture.* Berkeley: University of California Press, 1997.

Foner, Eric. *Nothing but Freedom: Emancipation and Its Legacy.* Baton Rouge: Louisiana University Press, 1983.

———. *Reconstruction: America's Unfinished Revolution, 1863–1877.* New York: Harper & Row, 1988.

Ford, John S. *Rip Ford's Texas.* Edited by Stephen Oates. Austin: University of Texas Press, 1963.

Francaviglia, Richard. *The Cast Iron Forest: A Natural and Cultural History of the North American Cross Timbers.* Austin: University of Texas Press, 2000.

Gammel, H. P. N. *The Laws of Texas, 1822–1897.* Austin: Gammel Book, 1898.

García, Mario. *Desert Immigrants: The Mexicans of El Paso, 1880–1920.* New Haven, Conn.: Yale University Press, 1981.

Gard, Wayne. "The Fence-Cutters." *Southwestern Historical Quarterly* 51 (July 1947): 1–15.

Gates, Paul W. *History of Public Land Law Development.* Washington, D.C.: Government Printing Office, 1968.

Gibson, A. M. *The Life and Death of Colonel Albert Jennings Fountain.* Norman: University of Oklahoma Press, 1965.

Going, Allen J. *Bourbon Democracy in Alabama, 1874–1890.* University: University of Alabama Press, 1951.

———. "The South and the Blair Education Bill." *Mississippi Valley Historical Review* 44 (September 1957): 267–90.

Goldman, Robert. *"A Free Ballot and a Fair Count": The Department of Justice and the Enforcement of Voting Rights in the South, 1877–1893.* 2d. ed. New York: Fordham University Press, 2001.

Goodrich, Carter. *Government Promotion of American Canals and Railroads, 1800–1890.* New York: Columbia University Press, 1960.

Goodwyn, Lawrence. "Populist Dreams and Negro Rights: East Texas as a Case Study." *American Historical Review* 76 (December 1971): 1435–56.

———. *The Populist Moment: A Short History of the Agrarian Revolt in America.* New York: Oxford University Press, 1978.

Gould, Lewis. *Alexander Watkins Terrell: Civil War Soldier, Texas Lawmaker, American Diplomat.* Austin: University of Texas Press, 2004.

———. *Progressives and Prohibitionists: Texas Democrats in the Wilson Era.* Austin: University of Texas Press, 1973.

Governors' Messages, Coke to Ross, 1874–1891. Austin: Archives and History Department of the Texas State Library, 1916.

Graves, John. "Negro Disfranchisement in Arkansas." *Arkansas Historical Quarterly* 26 (Autumn 1967): 199–225.

Green, George. *The Establishment in Texas Politics: The Primitive Years, 1938–1957.* Westport, Conn.: Greenwood, 1979.

Green, James. "Tenant Farmer Discontent and Socialist Protest in Texas, 1901–1917." *Southwestern Historical Quarterly* 81 (October 1977): 133–54.

Gunn, L. Ray. *The Decline of Authority: Public Economic Policy and Political Development in New York, 1800–1860.* Ithaca, N.Y.: Cornell University Press, 1988.

Hahn, Steven. *A Nation under Our Feet: Black Political Struggles in the Rural South from Slavery to the Great Migration.* Cambridge, Mass.: Harvard University Press, 2003.

———. "Hunting, Fishing, and Foraging: Common Rights and Class Relations in the Postbellum South." *Radical History Review* 26 (1982): 37–64.

Hair, William Ivy. *Bourbonism and Agrarian Protest: Louisiana Politics 1877–1900.* Baton Rouge: Louisiana State University Press, 1969.

Hales, Douglas. *A Southern Family in Black and White: The Cuneys of Texas.* College Station: Texas A&M University Press, 2003.

Haley, James L. *The Buffalo War: The History of the Red River Indian Uprising of 1874.* Garden City, N.J.: Doubleday, 1976.

Hardin, John Wesley. *The Life of John Wesley Hardin as Written by Himself.* Seguin, Tex.: Smith & Moore, 1896; reprint, Norman: University of Oklahoma Press, 1961.

Heard, Alexander, and Donald Strong. *Southern Primaries and Elections, 1920–1949.* University: University of Alabama Press, 1950.

Heller, John H., ed. *Heller's Galveston City Directory, 1876–7.* Galveston: n.p., [1876].

Henderson, Nat Q. *Directory of the Members and Officers of the Fourteenth Legislature of the State of Texas and also the State Officers of the State of Texas.* Austin: Cardwell & Walker, 1874.

Hibbard, Benjamin H. *A History of the Public Land Policies.* New York: Macmillan, 1924.

Hine, Darlene Clark. *Black Victory: The Rise and Fall of the White Primary in Texas.* Millwood, N.Y.: KTO Press, 1979.

Holt, R. D. "The Introduction of Barbed Wire into Texas and the Fence Cutting War." *West Texas Historical Association Year Book* 6 (1930): 72–88.

Horton, Louise. *Samuel Bell Maxey: A Biography.* Austin: University of Texas Press, 1974.

Hyman, Michael. *The Anti-Redeemers: Hill-Country Political Dissenters in the Lower South from Redemption to Populism.* Baton Rouge: Louisiana State University Press, 1990.

Ivy, James. *No Saloon in the Valley: The Southern Strategy of Texas Prohibitionists in the 1880s.* Waco: Baylor University Press, 2003.

Johnson, David. "Frugal and Sparing: Interest Groups, Politics, and City Building in San Antonio, 1870–85." In *Urban Texas: Politics and Development,* edited by Char Miller and Heywood Sanders, 33–57. College Station: Texas A&M University Press, 1990.

Jordan, Terry. *German Seed in Texas Soil: Immigrant Farmers in Nineteenth-Century Texas.* Austin: University of Texas Press, 1966.

———. "The Imprint of the Upper and Lower South on Mid-Nineteenth-Century Texas." *Annals of the Association of American Geographers* 57 (December 1967): 667–90.

Katz, Philip. *From Appomattox to Montmartre: Americans and the Paris Commune.* Cambridge, Mass.: Harvard University Press, 1998.

Kearney, Milo, and Anthony Knopp. *Boom and Bust: The Historical Cycles of Matamoros and Brownsville.* Austin: Eakin, 1991.

Keller, Morton. *Affairs of State: Public Life in Late Nineteenth Century America.* Cambridge, Mass.: Harvard University Press, 1977.

Kerr, Homer. "Migration into Texas, 1860–1880." *Southwestern Historical Quarterly* 70 (October 1966): 184–216.

Key, V. O. *Southern Politics in State and Nation.* New York: Knopf, 1949.

Keyssar, Alexander. *The Right to Vote: The Contested History of Democracy in the United States.* New York: Basic Books, 2000.

King, Edward. *The Great South: A Record of Journeys in Louisiana, Texas, the Indian Territory, Missouri, Arkansas, Mississippi, Alabama, Georgia, Florida, South Carolina, North Carolina, Kentucky, Tennessee, Virginia, West Virginia, and Maryland.* Hartford, Conn.: American Publishing, 1875.

Kingston, Mike, ed. *1992–1993 Texas Almanac and State Industrial Guide.* Dallas: *Dallas Morning News,* 1991.

Kingston, Mike, Sam Attlesey, and Mary Crawford. *The Texas Almanac's Political History of Texas.* Austin: Eakin, 1992.

Kinsey, Winston Lee. "The Immigrant in Texas Agriculture during Reconstruction." *Agricultural History* 53 (January 1979): 125–41.

Kittrell, Norman G. *Governors Who Have Been, and Other Public Men of Texas.* Houston: Dealy-Adey-Elgin, 1921.

Kousser, J. Morgan. "Progressivism—For Middle-Class Whites Only: North Carolina Education, 1880–1910." *Journal of Southern History* 46 (May 1980): 169–94.

———. *The Shaping of Southern Politics: Suffrage Restriction and the Establishment of the One-Party South, 1880–1910.* New Haven, Conn.: Yale University Press, 1974.

Lang, Aldon S. *Financial History of the Public Lands in Texas.* Waco: *Baylor University Bulletin* 35, no. 3, 1932.

Leiker, James N. *Racial Borders: Black Soldiers along the Rio Grande.* College Station: Texas A&M University Press, 2002.

Lipari, Lisbeth. "Income Texas." *Texas Observer,* July 12, 1991, 4–5, 15.

Lowe, Richard, and Randolph Campbell. *Planters and Plain Folk: Agriculture in Antebellum Texas.* Dallas: Southern Methodist University Press, 1987.

Lynch, James. *The Bench and Bar of Texas.* St. Louis: Nixon-Jones, 1885.

Marten, James. *Texas Divided: Loyalty and Dissent in the Lone Star State, 1856–1874.* Lexington: University Press of Kentucky, 1990.

Martin, Roscoe. "The Greenback Party in Texas." *Southwestern Historical Quarterly* 30 (January 1927): 161–77.

———. *The People's Party in Texas: A Study in Third Party Politics.* Austin: University of Texas Bulletin 3308, 1933.

Mauer, John W. "State Constitutions in a Time of Crisis: The Case of the Texas Constitution of 1876." *Texas Law Review* 68 (June 1990): 1615–47.

McCaslin, Richard. *Tainted Breeze: The Great Hanging at Gainesville, Texas, 1862.* Baton Rouge: Louisiana State University Press, 1994.

McGerr, Michael. *The Decline of Popular Politics: The American North, 1865–1928.* New York: Oxford University Press, 1986.

McKay, Seth S., ed. *Debates in the Texas Constitutional Convention of 1875.* Austin: University of Texas, 1930.

———. *Making the Texas Constitution of 1876.* Philadelphia: n.p., 1924.

McKitrick, Reuben. *The Public Land System of Texas, 1823–1910.* Madison: *University of Wisconsin Bulletin* 905, 1918.

McMath, Robert, Jr. *American Populism: A Social History, 1877–1898.* New York: Hill & Wang, 1993.

———. *Populist Vanguard: A History of the Southern Farmers' Alliance.* Chapel Hill: University of North Carolina Press, 1975.

———. "Sandy Land and Hogs in the Timber: (Agri)Cultural Origins of the Farmers' Alliance in Texas." In *The Countryside in the Age of Capitalist Transformation,* edited by Steven Hahn and Jonathan Prude, 205–29. Chapel Hill: University of North Carolina Press, 1985.

Members of the Texas Legislature, 1846–1962. [Austin: State of Texas, 1962].

Miller, Char, and D. R. Johnson. "The Rise of Urban Texas." In *Urban Texas: Politics and Development,* edited by Char Miller and Heywood Sanders, 3–29. College Station: Texas A&M University Press, 1990.

Miller, Edmund T. *A Financial History of Texas.* Austin: *Bulletin of the University of Texas* 37, 1916.

———. "The Historical Development of the Texas State Tax System." *Southwestern Historical Quarterly* 55 (July 1951): 1–29.

Miller, Richard. "Fort Worth and the Progressive Era: The Movement for Charter Revision, 1899–1907." In *Essays on Urban America,* edited by Margaret F. Morris and Elliott West, 89–121. Austin: University of Texas Press, 1975.

Miller, Thomas L. *The Public Lands of Texas, 1519–1970.* Norman: University of Oklahoma Press, 1972.

Miller, Worth Robert. "Building a Progressive Coalition in Texas: The Populist-Reform Democrat Rapprochement, 1900–1907." *Journal of Southern History* 52 (May 1986): 163–82.

———. "Harrison County Methods: Election Fraud in Late Nineteenth-Century Texas." *Locus* 7 (Spring 1995): 111–28.

Mills, W. W. *Forty Years at El Paso, 1858–1898: Recollections of War, Politics, Adventure, Events, Narratives, Sketches, Etc.* Chicago: W. B. Conkey, 1901.

Minutes of the Democratic State Convention of the State of Texas: Held at the City of Austin, September 3d, 4th, and 5th, 1873. Austin: Statesman, 1873.

Moneyhon, Carl. *Arkansas and the New South, 1874–1929.* Fayetteville: University of Arkansas Press, 1997.

———. "Edmund J. Davis in the Coke-Davis Election Dispute of 1874: A Reassessment of Character." *Southwestern Historical Quarterly* 100 (October 1996): 131–51.

————. "Public Education and Texas Reconstruction Politics, 1871–1874." *Southwestern Historical Quarterly* 92 (January 1989): 393–416.

————. *Republicanism in Reconstruction Texas.* Austin: University of Texas Press, 1980.

————. *Texas after the Civil War: The Struggle of Reconstruction.* College Station: Texas A&M University Press, 2004.

Montejano, David. *Anglos and Mexicans in the Making of Texas, 1836–1986.* Austin: University of Texas Press, 1987.

Moore, James Tice. "Origins of the Solid South: Redeemer Democrats and the Popular Will, 1870–1900." *Southern Studies* 22 (Fall 1983): 285–301.

————. "Redeemers Reconsidered: Change and Continuity in the Democratic South, 1870–1900." *Journal of Southern History* 44 (August 1978): 357–78.

Moretta, John. *William Pitt Ballinger: Texas Lawyer, Southern Statesman, 1825–1888.* Austin: Texas State Historical Association, 2000.

Moseley, J. A. R. "The Citizens White Primary of Marion County." *Southwestern Historical Quarterly* 49 (April 1946): 524–31.

Nieman, Donald. "Black Political Power and Criminal Justice: Washington County, Texas, 1868–1884." *Journal of Southern History* 55 (August 1989): 391–420.

Nunn, W. C. *Texas under the Carpetbaggers.* Austin: University of Texas Press, 1962.

Pate, J'Nell. "Indians on Trial in a White Man's Court." *Great Plains Journal* 14 (Fall 1974): 56–71.

Perman, Michael. *The Road to Redemption: Southern Politics, 1869–1879.* Chapel Hill: University of North Carolina Press, 1984.

————. *Struggle for Mastery: Disfranchisement in the South, 1888–1908.* Chapel Hill: University of North Carolina Press, 2001.

Pitre, Merline. *Through Many Dangers, Toils, and Snares: The Black Leadership of Texas, 1868–1900.* Austin: Eakin, 1985.

Platt, Harold. *City Building in the New South: The Growth of Public Services in Houston, Texas, 1830–1910.* Philadelphia: Temple University Press, 1983.

————. "The Stillbirth of Urban Politics in the Reconstruction South: Houston, Texas, as a Test Case." *Houston Review* 4 (Summer 1982): 55–74.

Pool, William. *A History of Bosque County, Texas.* San Marcos, Tex.: *San Marcos Record*, 1954.

Poor, Henry V. *Manual of the Railroads of the United States, for 1875–1876.* New York: H. V. & H. W. Poor, 1875.

Potts, Charles. *Railroad Transportation in Texas.* Austin: University of Texas Bulletin 119, 1909.

Prindle, David. *Petroleum Politics and the Texas Railroad Commission.* Austin: University of Texas Press, 1981.

Procter, Ben. *Not without Honor: The Life of John H. Reagan.* Austin: University of Texas Press, 1962.

Raines, Cadwell. *Analytical Index to the Laws of Texas, 1823–1905.* Austin: Von Boeckmann-Jones, 1906.

Ramsdell, Charles W. *Reconstruction in Texas.* New York: Columbia University Press, 1910.

Ratchford, B. U. *American State Debts.* Durham, N.C.: Duke University Press, 1941.

Reed, S. G. *A History of the Texas Railroads and of Transportation Conditions under Spain and Mexico and the Republic and the State.* Houston: St. Clair, 1941.

Reese, James V. "The Early History of Labor Organizations in Texas, 1838–1876." *South-western Historical Quarterly* 72 (July 1968): 1–20.

Rice, Bradley. *Progressive Cities: The Commission Government Movement in America, 1901–1920.* Austin: University of Texas Press, 1977.

Rice, Lawrence. *The Negro in Texas, 1874–1900.* Baton Rouge: Louisiana State University Press, 1971.

Roberts, Oran Milo. *A Description of Texas, Its Advantages and Resources, with Some Account of their Development, Past, Present and Future.* St. Louis: Gilbert Book, 1881.

———. *Our Federal Relations, from a Southern View of Them.* Austin: Von Boeckmann, 1892.

———. "The Political, Legislative, and Judicial History of Texas for Its Fifty Years of Statehood, 1845–1895." In *A Comprehensive History of Texas 1685 to 1897,* edited by Dudley Wooten, vol. 2:7–325. Dallas: William Scarff, 1898.

Rodriquez, Alicia E. "Disfranchisement in Dallas: The Democratic Party and the Suppression of Independent Political Challenges in Dallas, Texas, 1891–1894." *Southwestern Historical Quarterly* 108 (July 2004): 43–64.

Schwartz, Michael. *Radical Protest and Social Structure: The Southern Farmers' Alliance and Cotton Tenancy, 1880–1890.* New York: Academic, 1976.

Shook, Robert. "The Texas 'Election Outrage' of 1886." *East Texas Historical Journal* 10 (Spring 1972): 20–30.

Silverthorne, Elizabeth. *Ashbel Smith of Texas, Pioneer, Patriot, Statesman, 1805–1886.* College Station: Texas A&M University Press, 1982.

Smallwood, James. *Time of Hope, Time of Despair: Black Texans during Reconstruction.* Port Washington, N.Y.: National University Publications, 1981.

Smith, Ralph. "The Grange Movement in Texas, 1873–1900." *Southwestern Historical Quarterly* 42 (April 1939): 297–315.

Sonnichsen, C. L. *Pass of the North: Four Centuries on the Rio Grande.* El Paso: Texas Western Press, 1968.

Spaw, Patsy McDonald, ed. *The Texas Senate, Vol. II: Civil War to the Eve of Reform, 1861–1889.* College Station: Texas A&M University Press, 1999.

Speer, William, and John Henry Brown, eds. *Encyclopedia of the New West.* Marshall, Tex.: United States Biographical Publishing, 1881.

Spratt, John Stricklin. *The Road to Spindletop: Economic Change in Texas, 1875–1901.* Dallas: Southern Methodist University Press, 1955.

Sproat, John. *"The Best Men": Liberal Reformers in the Gilded Age.* New York: Oxford University Press, 1968.

Summers, Mark W. *Railroads, Reconstruction, and the Gospel of Prosperity: Aid under the Radical Republicans, 1865–1877.* Princeton: Princeton University Press, 1984.

Terrell, Alexander W. *Speech of Hon. A. W. Terrell, Senator from 25th Senatorial District, Delivered in the Senate July 19, 1876.* N.p., n.d.

"The Texas Idea: City Government by a Board of Directors." *Outlook* 85 (January–April 1907): 839–43.

Thompson, Jerry D. *Juan Cortina and the Texas-Mexico Frontier, 1859–1877.* El Paso: Texas Western Press, 1994.

Thornton, J. Mills, III. "Fiscal Policy and the Failure of Radical Reconstruction in the Lower South." In *Region, Race, and Reconstruction: Essays in Honor of C. Vann Woodward,* edited by J. Morgan Kousser and James McPherson, 349–94. New York: Oxford University Press, 1982.

Turner, Elizabeth Hayes. *Women, Culture, and Community: Religion and Reform in Galveston, 1880–1920.* New York: Oxford University Press, 1997.

Turner, Martha Anne. *Richard Bennett Hubbard: An American Life.* Austin: Shoal Creek, 1979.

Tyler, George. *The History of Bell County.* Edited by Charles Ramsdell. San Antonio: Naylor, 1936.

Tyler, Ron, et al. *The New Handbook of Texas.* 6 vols. Austin: Texas State Historical Association, 1996.

Upchurch, Thomas Adams. *Legislating Racism: The Billion Dollar Congress and the Birth of Jim Crow.* Lexington: University Press of Kentucky, 2004.

Utley, Robert M. *Lone Star Justice: The First Century of the Texas Rangers.* New York: Oxford University Press, 2002.

Vernon, Edward, ed. *American Railroad Manual for the United States and the Dominion.* New York: American Railroad Manual, 1873.

———. *American Railroad Manual for the United States and the Dominion.* New York: American Railroad Manual, 1874.

Walker, Donald R. *Penology for Profit: A History of the Texas Prison System, 1867–1912.* College Station: Texas A&M University Press, 1988.

Wallace, Ernest. *Charles DeMorse: Pioneer Editor and Statesman.* Lubbock: Texas Technological College Press, 1943.

Wallenstein, Peter. *From Slave South to New South: Public Policy in Nineteenth-Century Georgia.* Chapel Hill: University of North Carolina Press, 1987.

Walsh & Pilgrim's Directory of the Officers and Members of the Constitutional Convention of the State of Texas, A.D. 1875. Austin: Democratic Statesman Office, 1875.

[Walsh, W. C.] "Memories of a Texas Land Commissioner, W. C. Walsh." *Southwestern Historical Quarterly* 44 (April 1941): 481–97.

Webb, Walter P. *The Texas Rangers: A Century of Frontier Defense.* Austin: University of Texas Press, 1965.

Webb, Walter P., and H. Bailey Carroll, eds. *The Handbook of Texas.* 2 vols. Austin: Texas State Historical Association, 1952.

Wheeler, Kenneth. *To Wear a City's Crown: The Beginnings of Urban Growth in Texas, 1836–1865.* Cambridge, Mass.: Harvard University Press, 1968.

Wheeler, T. B. "Reminiscences of Reconstruction in Texas." *The Quarterly of the Texas State Historical Association* 11 (July 1907): 56–65.

Winkler, Ernest, ed. *Journal of the Secession Convention of Texas 1861.* Austin: Texas State Library, 1912.

———. *Platforms of Political Parties in Texas.* Austin: University of Texas Bulletin 53, 1916.

Woodward, C. Vann. *Origins of the New South, 1877–1913.* Baton Rouge: Louisiana State University Press, 1951.

Zeigler, Robert. "The Houston Worker: 1865–1890." *East Texas Historical Journal* 10 (Spring 1972): 40–54.

Baggett, James Alex. "The Rise and Fall of the Texas Radicals, 1867–1883." Ph.D. dissertation, North Texas State University, 1972.

Bailey, Lelia. "The Life and Public Career of O. M. Roberts, 1815–1883." Ph.D. dissertation, University of Texas, 1932.

Brockman, John. "Railroads, Radicals, and Democrats: A Study in Texas Politics, 1865–1900." Ph.D. dissertation, University of Texas, 1975.

Carrier, John P. "A Political History of Texas during the Reconstruction, 1865–1874." Ph.D. dissertation, Vanderbilt University, 1971.

Crews, James Robert. "Reconstruction in Brownsville, Texas." M.A. thesis, Texas Tech University, 1969.

Dolman, Wilson Elbert. "The Public Lands of Western Texas, 1870–1900: The Conflict of Public and Private Interests." Ph.D. dissertation, University of Texas, 1974.

Ericson, J. E. "An Inquiry into the Sources of the Texas Constitution." Ph.D. dissertation, Texas Tech University, 1957.

Evans, Samuel Lee. "Texas Agriculture, 1880–1930." Ph.D. dissertation, University of Texas, 1960.

Gray, Ronald N. "Edmund J. Davis: Radical Republican and Reconstruction Governor of Texas." Ph.D. dissertation, Texas Tech University, 1976.

Harper, Cecil, Jr. "Farming Someone Else's Land: Farm Tenancy in the Texas Brazos River Valley, 1850–1880." Ph.D. dissertation, University of North Texas, 1988.

Kellam, George. "A Shadow of Itself: The Rise and Decline of Cooperative Radicalism in Texas, 1875–1896." M.A. thesis, University of Texas at Arlington, 1987.

Lewis, Leonard. "A History of the State School System in Texas, 1876–1884." Ph.D. dissertation, University of Texas, 1946.

Mauer, John W. "The Poll Tax, Suffrage, and the Making of the Texas Constitution of 1876." M.A. thesis, Texas Tech University, 1973.

———. "Southern State Constitutions in the 1870s: A Case Study of Texas." Ph.D. dissertation, Rice University, 1983.

Merseburger, Marion. "A Political History of Houston, Texas, during the Reconstruction Period as Recorded by the Press: 1868–1873." M.A. thesis, Rice University, 1950.

Nash, Gerald. "A Chapter from an Active Life: John H. Reagan and Railroad Regulation." M.A. thesis, Columbia University, 1952.

Peterson, Robert. "State Regulation of Railroads in Texas, 1836–1920." Ph.D. dissertation, University of Texas, 1960.

Rodriquez, Alicia E. "Urban Populism: Challenges to Democratic Party Control in Dallas, Texas, 1887–1900." Ph.D. dissertation, University of California at Santa Barbara, 1998.

Smith, Ada M. "The Life and Times of William Harrison Hamman." M.A. thesis, University of Texas, 1952.

Smith, Stewart D. "Schools and Schoolmen: Chapters in Texas Education, 1870–1900." Ph. D. dissertation, North Texas State University, 1974.

Van Zant, Lee. "State Promotion of Railroad Construction in Texas, 1836–1900." Ph.D. dissertation, University of Texas, 1967.

Williams, Harry, Jr. "The Development of a Market Economy in Texas: The Establishment of the Railway Network, 1836–1900." Ph.D. dissertation, University of Texas, 1957.

Index

Blanco County, 146
Bledsoe, A., 96
board of education, state, 21, 131, 161
Bond, Frank: quoted, 111
bonds, security, for public officials, 39, 58–59, 79
Booty, A. J., 57
Borajo, Antonio, 47
borderlands. *See* South Texas borderlands
Bosque County, 104
Brady, J. T., 146
Brammer, Bill: quoted, 3
Brazoria County, 11, 25, 59, 78, 80
Brazos County, 171
Brazos River, 2, 55
Broaddus, A. S., 49–50
Brown, John Henry, 55, 73–74
Brownsville, 24, 64
Bryan, Guy M., 52, 99–100
Bryan, Moses Austin, 90
Bureau of Immigration, Texas, 107–8
Burkhart, William, 46
Burnet County, 32
Burnett, James, 43, 45, 46, 48

Callahan County, 154
Cameron County, 132
Campbell, Randolph, 42, 80
Cantrell, Gregg, 172
Cardis, Louis, 48, 133
Catholics, in Texas: and Democrats, 30; and public schools, 21, 135
Chambers, B. J., 146
Chambers, William, 43, 44, 45, 46, 48, 77, 192n. 78
Cherokee County, 39
Cheyennes, southern, 1
cities and towns, in Texas: African Americans in, 83; at-large officeholding imposed, 83–84; city commission system in, 84; education in, 130–31, 132–33, 134, 164, 191n. 63; elite divisions in, 69; growth of, 65; officeholding qualifications in, 67, 82; and panic of 1873, 67; politics in, 64–70, 75, 81–84; poll tax's

impact in, 169; property-holding in, 82; secret ballot in, 83; taxation in, 75, 130–31; voter registration in, 82–83; voting rights in, 66–67, 70, 74–75, 190n. 24; working class in, 65–70, 81–82, 84
Citizens party (Harrison County), 57, 80, 81
Citizens ticket (Houston), 37
Citizens' White Primary (Marion), 80
civil rights movement, in Texas, 174, 176
Clark, George, 48–49, 100, 165, 168
Coke, Richard, 11, 182n. 27; and antimonopoly politics, 29, 100; and appointive judiciary, 77; on black suffrage, 62; and Blair bill, 138; and constitution of 1876, 77, 112; and education, 120, 123–24, 138; and election imbroglio (1874), 15–16, 34; and election of 1873, 15, 33; and gubernatorial nomination 1873, 28–29; and immigration aid, 108; inauguration of, 15; and International controversy, 28–29, 32, 95–96, 99–101; and Latinos, 8–9; and law enforcement, 20; and "local self-government" doctrine, 50; and prohibitionism, 165; and railroads, 29, 109; during Reconstruction, 41; and Republican judiciary, 41; and segregation, 138; and state debt, 143; and suffrage, 70, 77
Coke-Davis election imbroglio, 15–16, 33–34
Coleman County, 154
Collin County, 77
Colorado County, 30, 54, 56
Colorado River (Texas), 2, 12, 55, 98
Comanche County, 104, 170
Comanches, 1, 3, 31
Compromise of 1850, 120
comptroller, state, 143–44
constitution, Texas: revision proposed 1874, 52–53, 62
constitution, Texas, 1845, 121
constitution, Texas, 1866, 122
constitution, Texas, 1869: amendments to, 41, 103; and apportionment, 25; educa-

Democratic Party (Texas): "agrarian"
interests in, 10–11, 89–91, 109, 133,
153–54; and appointive officeholding,
50–53, 77–78, 84; and apportionment,
25–26, 55–56, 183–84n. 49, 184n. 51;
and asylums, 125–26; and at-large officeholding, 53–55, 83–84; and black-
majority counties, 37, 58–59, 79–81,
170; and Blair bill, 138; and bonding
requirements, 58–60, 79; and "centralization," 12, 21, 24, 50; and civil rights
movement, 176; and constitution of
1876, 77–78; convention 1872, 95; convention 1873, 28–29; convention 1880,
154; and convict lease, 10, 91, 157; and
corporate regulation, 108–11, 115–16,
118, 167–68; divisions within, 10–12,
26–30, 40, 63, 95–96, 133–37, 147, 165,
173; and economic development, 11,
91–108, 111, 113–18, 134, 136–37, 156–57,
176; and education, 20–23, 119–20,
122–25, 128–40, 146, 148–49, 154,
155–56, 158–64; and election contests,
57, 60; and election imbroglio (1874),
15–16, 33–34; and election laws, 24–25,
33–34, 183n. 45; and election of 1871,
17; and election of 1872, 17–18, 25; and
election of 1873, 15, 27–33, 181n. 3; and
election of 1876, 77–78; and election
of 1878, 146–47; and election of 1880,
154–55, 205n. 46; and election of 1882,
158–59; and election of 1892, 165–66,
168; and ethnic politics, 10, 21, 22,
29–30, 64–65, 108, 150; and federal
government, 9, 81, 105–6, 132, 138–39,
166, 176; and fence laws, 90–91; fiscal
argument against Reconstruction,
4, 22, 62–63, 92, 94–95, 96; and fiscal
policy, 142–45, 147–55, 158–60, 164–65;
foreign-born legislators in, 19, 22, 48;
and frontier defense, 4, 30, 32, 92, 143,
155; generational shift in, 165; and
Greenback Party, 146; gubernatorial
nomination 1873, 27–29; gubernatorial nomination 1878, 147; gubernatorial
nomination 1880, 154; and Houston,

36–37, 40, 51, 84; ideology of, 21, 29,
50–51, 55, 96–97, 120, 126, 136–37; and
immigration aid, 107–8, 114, 154; and
International Railroad controversy,
27–29, 32–33, 94–101, 196n. 47, 196n.
48; and judiciary, 23, 37–50, 52–57,
186n. 21, 186n. 29; and juror qualifications, 70–71, 75–77; and landlord-tenant laws, 10, 33, 89–90; and landowners' interests, 10, 89–91, 150–51; and
Latinos, 6–9, 64–65, 172–73, 174–75;
and law enforcement, 18–20, 143;
leadership of, 5, 179n. 15; and local
government, 37–40, 50–60, 79–84; and
"local self-government" doctrine, 21,
32, 40, 50–51, 55, 61, 63–64, 78; and the
"New Departure," 27; "New South"
element in, 10–11, 111, 114, 133; and official salaries, 112, 113, 148; and out-of-
state businesses, 105, 111, 150, 168; and
planters, 6, 11, 89–91, 107; platform
1873, 28, 29, 30, 127; platform 1876, 77;
platform 1880, 154; platforms 1892,
1894, 166; political security of, and Redemption, 5, 40, 51, 59, 73, 78, 84–85;
and politics of retrenchment, 4, 21–22,
32, 92, 107–8, 112, 114, 117–18, 120, 122,
124, 126, 127, 142, 143; and population
growth, 4–5, 35, 40, 59, 92, 143–44; and
Populists, 165–66, 170–72; and prohibitionism, 29–30, 165, 172; and public
land, 11, 101–5, 108, 114–15, 117, 124–25,
127, 138–40, 151–60, 164, 175; racist
appeals of, 7, 32, 62–63; and railroads,
27–29, 32–33, 93–106, 108–11, 113–18,
156–57, 167–68; during Reconstruction, 4, 17, 27, 92, 94–95; "Redeemer"
defined, 179n. 2; and Republican state
officials, 23; and "repudiation," 27–28,
97–98, 142–43, 148–49; sectionalism
in, 12, 98–99, 115, 147; and South Texas
borderlands, 6–9, 64–65, 172–73; and
spending, 1872–1875, 92; and spending, 1876–1878, 143–44; and spending,
1879–1882, 155; spending after 1882,
160, 164–65; and state debt, 97–98, 112,

113, 127, 142–43, 147–49, 152, 159; and
suffrage, 61–70, 71–75, 77–79, 81–85,
169–74, 191n. 56; and taxation, 4, 10,
22, 92, 112–13, 128–31, 143–45, 147,
149–51, 154, 155, 162–64, 191n. 62; and
tax exemption for industry, 106–7, 114;
and Texas & Pacific Railway, 94–95,
103–6, 115; unionists in, 12; and urban
politics, 64–70, 74–75, 81–84, 169–70;
and usury laws, 10, 90; and veterans'
pensions, 126–27, 148, 160, 164; and
violence, 62, 80–81; Whigs in, 12;
and yeoman settlement, 105, 152–54,
159–60, 175

DeMorse, Charles, 29, 75, 128, 136–37, 153

Denison, 83

Devine, Thomas J., 147

Diaz, Porfirio, 2, 143

disfranchisement, in Texas. *See* suffrage
restriction

dog tax, in Texas, 132, 201n. 49

Dohoney, E. L., 128, 129–30, 184n. 51

Dougherty, Edward, 49

Eastland County, 154

Ector, Matthew, 49

Edgewood v. Kirby, 177–78

education, public, in Texas: administration of, 21–22, 121–23, 128, 131–32,
161–62, 163; and African Americans,
122, 124, 132, 163–64; in antebellum era,
120–22; in cities and towns, 130–31,
132–33, 164, 191n. 63; Democrats and,
20–23, 119–20, 122–25, 128–40, 146,
149, 154, 155–56, 158–64; disparities in,
132–33, 163–64, 177; and ethnic politics,
21, 22, 135; federal aid to, 138–39; funding of, 21–22, 120–25, 128–32, 139–40,
144, 148–49, 155, 158, 162–64, 182n. 33,
203–4n. 24, 206n. 73; land reserved for,
105, 120–22, 124–25, 139, 152–56, 158–60,
175, 200n. 22; local funding of, 21–22,
75, 121, 130–33, 163–64, 177–78, 191n. 63;
and O. M. Roberts, 148–49, 152, 155,
161, 163; and plantation-area whites,
135; during Reconstruction, 21–22,

122; Redemption's impact on, 22–23,
131–33, 139–40; taxation for, 21–22,
121–24, 128–33, 139, 162–64; in twentieth century, 177–78

election contests, 57–58

election laws, 24–25, 33–34, 183n. 45

elections, in Texas: congressional 1871,
17; congressional 1874, 96; congressional 1878, 158, 183–84n. 49; constitutional ratification 1876, 77–78, 192n.
78; gubernatorial 1869, 17, 23–24, 31;
gubernatorial 1873, 15, 27–33, 181n. 3;
gubernatorial 1876, 77–78, 192n. 78;
gubernatorial 1878, 146–47; gubernatorial 1880, 154–55, 205n. 46; gubernatorial 1882, 158–59; gubernatorial
1892, 165, 168; gubernatorial 1896, 170;
land grant amendment 1872, 103, 104;
legislative 1872, 17–18, 25; legislative
1873, 33; legislative 1894, 170; poll tax
amendment 1902, 169, 170, 172; presidential 1872, 27; presidential 1880, 146;
prohibition referendum 1887, 165, 172

El Paso (city), 83, 84

El Paso County, 7, 24, 47, 76, 187n. 45

enabling act (1870), 24

Encyclopedia Britannica, 9th ed., 119

Epperson, Benjamin, 11, 43, 111

Erath, George, 48

Erath County, 170

Erhard, Cayton, 128

Farmers' Alliance, in Texas, 82, 165–66, 168

Fayette County, 78

fence-cutting, in Texas, 90–91, 154

fence laws, in Texas, 90–91

Ferguson, Charles, 81

Ferguson, James ("Pa"), 171

"Fifty Cents" law (1879), 152–53, 159

Flanagan, Webster, 26, 184n. 51

Fleming, J. R., 134

Florida, 4, 9, 52

Flournoy, George, 128, 134–35, 136

Foley, Neil, 7

Ford, John S. (Rip), 128

Fort Bend County, 59, 60, 80–81

Fort Worth, 82, 83, 84, 103, 169
Fountain, Albert Jennings, 47
Fredericksburg Sentinel, 118
Freestone County, 19
Freie Presse, 150
frontier defense, in Texas, 3–4, 30, 143, 155
Fulton, Roger L., 68, 81–82
"fusion" government, in black-majority counties, 79

Galveston (city): African Americans in, 84; at-large officeholding in, 83–84; Democrats in, 68–69, 190n. 35; education in, 133; Germans in, 9–10, 64; growth of, 65; juries in, 70; officeholding qualifications in, 67; politics in, 67, 68–69, 81–82; and poll tax, 169; and railroads, 110; Republicans in, 38, 68; voter registration and secret ballot in, 83; working class in, 65–69
Galveston Cotton Exchange, 110
Galveston County, 70, 76, 78
Galveston Daily News: on apportionment, 26; on black suffrage, 62; on Coke, 29; and constitution of 1876, 112; declares Texas redeemed, 17; and education, 120, 136; and election of 1873, 32; on elective judiciary, 52; and ethnic politics, 65; on fence laws, 91; on Houston, 36, 37; on judiciary, 41–42; and local politics, 68–69; and "local self-government" doctrine, 50, 64, 78; and O. M. Roberts, 149; and Palo Duro, 2; and regulation, corporate, 110; on Republicans, 4; and state police, 20; and suffrage, 120; on urban working class, 66, 68–69; and veterans' pensions, 127
Gatesville, 29
General Land Office, Texas, 143–44
Georgia, 6
German Texans: and "Bell Punch" law, 150; and education, 21; and immigration aid, 107; and politics, 9–10, 17, 18, 19, 48, 64–65; and prohibitionism, 29–30, 172
gerrymandering. *see* apportionment

Gould, Jay, 168
Gould, Robert S., 41
Grand Prairie, 3, 93
Grange, Texas: delegates at 1875 constitutional convention, 72–74, 111, 113, 115, 116, 133, 137, 191n. 55, 202n. 67; and Democratic Party, 28, 63; established, 28; membership of, 116, 133; and railroads, 106, 116; and Richard Coke, 100; and suffrage restriction, 72–73
Grant, Ulysses S., administration, 8, 16, 31, 34, 36
Grayson County, 76
Greeley, Horace, 27
Greenback Party, in Texas: and African Americans, 146, 171; agenda of, 145–46; and election of 1878, 146–47; and election of 1880, 146, 154–55; and election of 1882, 158; leadership of, 146; and public land, 145, 146, 158; and Republicans, 146, 171; and urban politics, 82
Griffin, Charles, 41
Grimes County, 55, 56, 59, 80–81, 91
Guadalupe County, 46–47, 62
Guadalupe Times, 59

Hamilton, Andrew Jackson, 17
Hamilton County, 170
Hamman, William, 146, 154
Hardeman, William P.: quoted, 16
Hardin, John Wesley, 18
Harris County, 48, 66, 76, 78
Harrison County, 11; and apportionment, 26, 56; bonding requirements in, 58; juries in, 76; redemption of, 57, 60, 80, 81; Republican domination of, 46–47; *(Harrison County, cont.)*
    Republican judges in, 39, 44, 46–47; taxation in, 144
Hart, Hardin, 49
Haynes, Joseph, 134, 136
Helm, Jack, 19
Henderson Times: quoted, 26
Herndon, William, 95
Hickok, James B. (Wild Bill), 18
hill country, of Texas, 3, 9–10

New Handbook of Texas: quoted, 112
New York Herald, 2
New York Times, 64
Nieman, Donald, 76
North Carolina, 52
North Texas Enterprise: quoted, 29
Norvell, Lipscomb, 73
Nugent, Thomas, 115, 133, 165, 168

Ogden, Wesley, 34
oil industry, in Texas, 157, 168, 175–78,
    207n. 23
Oliver, John W., 49
Osterhout, John, 43

Palestine Advocate, 19
Palestine (Texas), 94, 133
Palo Duro canyon: battle at, 1, 2
Palo Pinto County, 151, 170
panic of 1873, 36, 67, 91, 115, 145
Panola County, 26
Paris Commune, 64
Parker, Quanah, 1
Parsons, William H., 108
Patrons of Husbandry. See Grange, Texas
pensions, for veterans, 126–27, 148, 156,
    160, 164
Perman, Michael, 6, 111
plains, southern, 154. see also Llano Es-
    tacado
poll tax. See suffrage restriction; taxation
Populism, in Texas, 6, 63, 76–77, 81, 82,
    165–66, 170; and suffrage restriction,
    170–72
Powers, Stephen, 7
Prendergast, D. M., 49
Priest, Mijamin, 39, 43, 45, 46, 47–48
Prindle, David, 168
prison system, Texas, 91, 155, 160, 164
prohibitionism, in Texas: and African
    Americans, 172; and "Bell Punch" law,
    150; and Democrats, 29–30, 165; local
    option, 30, 132, 165, 172; "Ohio" law, 29;
    referendum 1887, 165, 172; and suffrage
    restriction, 172
public domain. see land, public, in Texas

Quanah, 1

railroad commission, Texas, 109, 167–68
railroads, in Texas. See also individual
    companies: construction deadlines
    for, 103, 115; and convict lease, 91, 157;
    Democrats and, 27–29, 32–33, 93–106,
    108–11, 113–18, 156–57, 167–68; and
    economic development, 93; and elec-
    tion imbroglio (1874), 34; and election
    of 1873, 27–29, 32–33; expansion of,
    65–66, 93; International controversy,
    94–101; land grants to, 101–5, 114–15,
    156–57; local support of, 95; during
    Reconstruction, 93–95; regulation
    of, 108–11, 115–16, 167–68; subsidy of,
    93–95, 105–6, 113–14, 199n. 5; taxation
    of, 149–50
Ramey, William Neal, 56
Rayner, John B., 171, 172
Reagan, John H.: and appointive judi-
    ciary, 53; and at-large officeholding,
    54; and Blair bill, 138; and Democratic
    convention 1878, 147; and economic
    development, 134, 136; and education,
    124, 129, 135; and election of 1873, 28;
    as Granger, 133; in International con-
    troversy, 28, 94–95, 147; and juries, 71;
    and prohibitionism, 165; and railroad
    regulation, 115, 168; during Recon-
    struction, 27; and suffrage, 63, 73, 172;
    and urban politics, 64, 191n. 61
Reconstruction, in Texas: education dur-
    ing, 21–22, 122, 182n. 33; election laws
    during, 24–25; end of, 16; and frontier
    defense, 3–4; law enforcement during,
    18–19; and local government, 24, 39;
    and public land, 103; and railroads,
    93–95, 103, 104; Republican agenda
    for, 3; Republicans divided during, 17;
    taxation during, 4, 62–63, 92, 112; and
    tax exemption for industry, 106; urban
    politics during, 66–67; and veterans'
    pensions, 126–27; violence during,
    18–19; and voting rights, 62, 66–67
Redeemer Democrat, defined, 179n. 2

Redemption, in Texas: in black-majority counties, 57, 59, 79–81; and judiciary, 37–50, 52–56; and local government, 37–40, 50–60; and population growth, 4–5, 40, 59; staggered nature of, 16, 35, 37–39, 78–79; Thirteenth Legislature (1873) and, 16–26

Red River, 1, 2

Reeves, Reuben, 41

regulation, corporate: business support for, 109–10, 168; Democrats and, 108–11, 115–16, 167–68; of insurance industry, 111; of railroads, 108–11, 113, 115–16, 167–68

Republican Party (Texas): and African Americans, 4–5, 17; and black-majority counties, 37, 79–81; in cities, 83; constituency, 4–5, 17, 181n. 12; and constitution of 1876, 77–78, 117, 192n. 78; divisions within, 17, 26, 31, 183n. 38; and education, 21–22, 122, 128, 182n. 33; and election imbroglio (1874), 15–16, 33–34; and election laws, 24–25; and election of 1869, 17, 23–24, 31; and election of 1871, 17; and election of 1872, 17–18; and election of 1873, 28, 32–33; and election of 1876, 77–78, 192n. 78; and election of 1878, 146–47; and election of 1880, 154–55; and election of 1882, 158; in El Paso County, 47; and frontier defense, 3–4; in Galveston, 38, 68, 81–82, 83; and Greenback Party, 146, 171; in Houston, 36–37, 83; and immigration aid, 107–8; and judiciary, 23, 37; and juror qualifications, 75, 76; and law enforcement, 18–19; in legislature (1876), 56; and local government, 24, 37–38, 50–51, 79–81; and Native Americans, 3, 31; and population growth, 4–5; and public land, 103, 158; and railroads, 94–95, 103; Reconstruction agenda of, 3–4; regional strength within state, 17–18, 54, 55; and South Texas borderlands, 6–8; "straight-out" faction (1878), 146–47

Richardson, J. P., 42

Rio Grande borderlands. *See* South Texas borderlands

Roberts, Meshack (Shack), 90

Roberts, Oran M.: "agrarian" orientation of, 151; and asylums, 126; as chief justice, 41; and education, 126, 148–49, 155, 161, 163, 203–4n. 24; and election of 1878, 147; and election of 1880, 154–55; fiscal policy of, 147–55, 158; and landowners, 151, 153–54; opposition to, among Democrats, 149, 152–54, 158–59; and Populism, 166; and prohibitionism, 165; and public land, 151–54, 157; during Reconstruction, 27; and retrenchment, 148–49; and secession, 147; and state debt, 147–49, 152, 158; and taxation, 147, 149–51, 153–54, 155, 158, 163

Robertson, E. S. C., 133, 135

Robertson County, 78, 171

Rockport Transcript, 59

Rodriguez, Joseph (José), 33

Rodriquez, Alicia, 82

Rogers, James H., 49–50

Ross, Lawrence Sullivan (Sul), 165, 167

Rugely, E. S., 53

Rusk County, 26

Russell, Jonathan, 128–29, 137

Russell, Stilwell H., 58

Russell, William H., 42, 45

Sabine County, 170

San Antonio: education in, 133; Germans in, 9–10; growth of, 65; and International controversy, 98–99; Latino politics in, 7, 8, 65; during Reconstruction, 7, 24; voter registration and secret ballot in, 83

San Antonio Daily Herald: and E. J. Davis, 32; and Latinos, quoted, 7; and lawlessness, 20; and sectionalism, 98; and suffrage, 63, 65

San Augustine County, 49, 81

San Jacinto County, 56

Sansom, Richard, 129

Satanta, 31–32

Sayers, Joseph D., 149, 154, 206n. 79
Scanlan, T. H., 36–37
Schmidt, E. F., 48
Scott, John, 23, 43, 186n. 29
Scott, Thomas, 103
secession convention, Texas, 5, 41, 49–50
segregation, racial: in education, 21,
    131–32; and Latinos, 174–75; in public
    accommodations, 174
separate coach law (1891), 174
sharecropping and tenant farming, in
    Texas, 6, 38, 89–90, 151, 165, 170–71, 174,
    207n. 11
Sheridan, Philip, 158
Short, Daniel M., 28
Smith, Ashbel, 11, 97, 142
Smith, C. R., 134
Smith County, 38
socialists, in Texas, 171
South Texas borderlands, 3; border raid-
    ing, 2, 3, 9–10, 92; politics in, 6–9, 47,
    64–65, 170, 171, 172–73, 174–75; and
    railroads, 99; social relations in, 9, 173,
    174–75; and suffrage restriction, 172–73
Soward, Charles, 49
Spindletop, 175
state guard (militia), 18–20
state police, Texas, 18–20
Stayton, John, 115
Steele, William: quoted, 20
Stockdale, Fletcher, 54, 95, 116, 128–29, 134,
    135, 136, 201n. 57
stock laws. *See* fence laws, in Texas
stockraising, in Texas, 2–3, 38, 74, 90–91,
    93, 99, 104, 154, 160
suffrage restriction, in Texas: African
    Americans as targets, 62–63, 71, 84,
    169–70, 171–72; and ballot law of 1879,
    79; and constitutional convention of
    1875, 71–75; *de facto,* in black-majority
    counties, 79–81, 170; Democrats and,
    10, 61–70, 71–75, 77–79, 81–85, 169–74,
    191n. 56; impact of, 169, 173–74; and
    Latinos, 64–65, 172–74; in municipal
    franchise, 70, 74–75, 191n. 63; and non-
    citizens, 173; poll tax as means of, 62,

65, 71–74, 77, 79, 169–74, 191n. 56; and
    prohibitionism, 172; as reform, 171–72;
    secret ballot as means of, 83, 169; and
    South Texas borderlands, 172–73; and
    urban politics, 64–70, 75, 82–83, 169–
    70, 191n. 61, 191n. 62; voter challenges
    as means of, 82; voter registration as
    means of, 82–83; white primaries as
    means of, 80, 169, 172, 173; whites as
    targets, 63–70, 83, 170–71
sugar cultivation in Texas, 91
supreme court, Texas, 15, 33–34, 37, 39, 45,
    99, 175, 177, 200n. 22; and district judi-
    ciary, 56–57; redemption of, 41

Tarrant County, 76
taxation, in Texas: and absentee landown-
    ers, 112–13, 198n. 106; ad valorem, 10,
    112–13, 144–45, 151, 155, 162–64; "Bell
    Punch" tax (1879), 150, 154, 155, 204n.
    31; corporate, 149–50, 155, 204n. 31;
    Democrats and, 4, 10, 22, 92, 112–13,
    128–31, 143–45, 147, 149–51, 154, 155,
    162–64, 191n. 62; of dogs, 132, 201n. 49;
    education, 21–22, 75, 121–24, 128–32,
    162–64; exemption for industry, 106–7,
    113–14; gasoline, 157; local, 4, 92, 112–13,
    130–32, 144–45, 163–64; under O. M.
    Roberts, 149–51, 155, 204n. 31; occupa-
    tion, 10, 149, 151, 154, 155, 162, 206n. 73;
    poll (i.e. capitation) tax, 10, 21, 72, 122,
    128, 129, 130, 145, 151, 155; receipts, 144, 155,
    158; during Reconstruction, 4, 92, 144,
    149–50; for roads and bridges, 92, 112;
    tax burden shifted by Democrats, 145,
    150–51; in the twentieth century, 176
Tax Payers' Union (Brazoria), 80
Tejanos. *See* Latinos, in Texas
Tennessee, 17
Terrell, Alexander W., 63, 76, 79, 169, 172–73
Texas: agriculture in, 2–3, 6, 74, 93, 154,
    174; borderlands of, 2, 6–9, 172–73, 174;
    demography of (postbellum), 4–5, 6,
    9, 17, 65, 174; division of, proposed,
    98–99; economic growth in twentieth
    century, 175–78; economic growth

ISBN-13: 978-1-58544-573-8
ISBN-10: 1-58544-573-8